Storr's
The Art of
Psychotherapy

Third edition

Storr's The Art of Psychotherapy

Jeremy Holmes

Completely updated, rewritten and revised

CRC Press
Taylor & Francis Group
Boca Raton London New York

CRC Press is an imprint of the
Taylor & Francis Group, an **informa** business

CRC Press
Taylor & Francis Group
6000 Broken Sound Parkway NW, Suite 300
Boca Raton, FL 33487-2742

© 2012 by Taylor & Francis Group, LLC
CRC Press is an imprint of Taylor & Francis Group, an Informa business

No claim to original U.S. Government works

ISBN-13: 9781444144109 (pbk)

This book contains information obtained from authentic and highly regarded sources. While all reasonable efforts have been made to publish reliable data and information, neither the author[s] nor the publisher can accept any legal respon-sibility or liability for any errors or omissions that may be made. The publishers wish to make clear that any views or opinions expressed in this book by individual editors, authors or contributors are personal to them and do not neces-sarily reflect the views/opinions of the publishers. The information or guidance contained in this book is intended for use by medical, scientific or health-care professionals and is provided strictly as a supplement to the medical or other professional's own judgement, their knowledge of the patient's medical history, relevant manufacturer's instructions and the appropriate best practice guidelines. Because of the rapid advances in medical science, any information or advice on dosages, procedures or diagnoses should be independently verified. The reader is strongly urged to consult the relevant national drug formulary and the drug companies' and device or material manufacturers' printed instructions, and their websites, before administering or utilizing any of the drugs, devices or materials mentioned in this book. This book does not indicate whether a particular treatment is appropriate or suitable for a particular individual. Ultimately it is the sole responsibility of the medical professional to make his or her own professional judgements, so as to advise and treat patients appropriately. The authors and publishers have also attempted to trace the copyright holders of all mate-rial reproduced in this publication and apologize to copyright holders if permission to publish in this form has not been obtained. If any copyright material has not been acknowledged please write and let us know so we may rectify in any future reprint.

Except as permitted under U.S. Copyright Law, no part of this book may be reprinted, reproduced, transmitted, or uti-lized in any form by any electronic, mechanical, or other means, now known or hereafter invented, including photocopy-ing, microfilming, and recording, or in any information storage or retrieval system, without written permission from the publishers.

For permission to photocopy or use material electronically from this work, please access www.copyright.com (http://www.copyright.com/) or contact the Copyright Clearance Center, Inc. (CCC), 222 Rosewood Drive, Danvers, MA 01923, 978-750-8400. CCC is a not-for-profit organization that provides licenses and registration for a variety of users. For organizations that have been granted a photocopy license by the CCC, a separate system of payment has been arranged.

Trademark Notice: Product or corporate names may be trademarks or registered trademarks, and are used only for identification and explanation without intent to infringe.

Visit the Taylor & Francis Web site at
http://www.taylorandfrancis.com

and the CRC Press Web site at
http://www.crcpress.com

To the memory of Anthony Storr

Contents

Acknowledgements	vii
Prologue: Anthony Storr and the Art of Psychotherapy	viii
Introduction	
Chapter 1 The setting	1
Chapter 2 The initial interview	4
Chapter 3 Getting going: overcoming initial resistance	11
Chapter 4 Making progress	16
Chapter 5 Interpretation	21
Chapter 6 Dreams, daydreams and creativity	31
Chapter 7 The nature of the therapeutic relationship: boundaried intimacy	39
Chapter 8 Transference and counter-transference	50
Chapter 9 Diagnosis and psychodynamic formulation	59
Chapter 10 Depression	64
Chapter 11 Anxiety	73
Chapter 12 Patterns of personality	81
Chapter 13 The science of psychotherapy	98
Chapter 14 The end of therapy	102
Chapter 15 The life and work of a psychotherapist	111
Epilogue: Beyond therapy	124
References	129
Index	137

Acknowledgements

I am grateful to Anthony Storr's widow, Catherine Peters, and his fellow medical psychotherapist daughter, Sophia Hartland, for helpful corrections, comments and suggestions, all of which have improved both the tone and accuracy of the text. Responsibility for defects and omissions rests of course with the authors!

Prologue

Anthony Storr and the Art of Psychotherapy

The Art of Psychotherapy (AOP) is a classic. First published in 1979, it has been continuously in print ever since. It described in a practical way how to set about offering therapy to psychologically troubled people – a surprisingly rare phenomenon despite a voluminous psychoanalytic literature. It helped demystify a subject which, at worst, is plagued by arcane theorizing and esoteric cultism. Storr brought his many personal and intellectual strengths to this delicate task. His urbane and felicitous style meant that each chapter had the feel of an elegant essay. He comfortably inhabited the wider Western cultural tradition, so that his range of reference extended well beyond the standard psychoanalytic canon. Trained as a Jungian, with a later Freudian analysis, having worked both in private practice and in the National Health Service, and a well-known author in his own right, he was free from the petty demarcations endemic to psychotherapy politics. He brought a truly eclectic and synoptic overview of the aspirations, achievements, realities and limitations of psychotherapy and psychotherapists.

Changed times

But, despite AOP's longevity, times have changed. In the 1970s, Cognitive Behaviour Therapy and Family Therapy were still in their infancy; psychotherapy *was* psychodynamic psychotherapy. No qualifiers were needed; Storr could assume that people would know what he was talking about and generally think of psychoanalysis in positive terms. Today public and professionals alike equate psychotherapy with 'Cognitive Behavioural Therapy' (CBT), while psychoanalytic voices have to fight to make themselves heard.

Storr's book made a number of other assumptions which sound strangely anachronistic to contemporary ears. It was originally directed at psychiatric trainees who wished to learn psychotherapy, and presumed that its audience would be medically qualified males. His advice that therapists should 'not display photographs of their wife and children' in their consulting rooms, despite being sound, is at best amusingly out of date. Today female doctors outnumber males, and psychiatrists form a tiny proportion of psychotherapy practitioners. Most therapists today are women, and come from a diverse range of professions in addition to medicine, including psychology, social work, nursing, teaching, academia, and counselling.

When Storr was writing, the dominant force in psychoanalytic psychotherapy was the British Psychoanalytic Society (BPS) and through it the International Psychoanalytic Association (IPA). There were one or two free spirits like Storr himself – his friend Charles Rycroft was another – but on the whole hegemony rested with the analytic hierarchy. There was no coherent public voice for psychotherapy, which consisted of a number of separate training bodies, infected with the usual rivalries and mutual contempt that bedevil psychoanalytic organizations. After much discussion and at least one schism, there are now umbrella bodies which oversee the training and ethical standards of their member organizations and try to speak with one voice on the public arena. There is a plethora of psychoanalytic psychotherapy trainings, some of which are based in universities, and one that provides an alternative route to membership to the IPA.

Psychotherapy and counselling in their widest sense today have a much more coherent political presence than in the 1970s. The public have put pressure on governments to provide better psychological therapy services, and for mental health services to rely less on drugs and incarceration. In the UK, the Improving Access to Psychological Therapies (IAPT) programme came about through the effective lobbying of CBT therapists, but the still small voice of psychodynamic therapy is also now audible (Lemma *et al* 2008; Lemma, Target and Fonagy 2012).

As psychotherapy moves into the public arena, so its sources of legitimacy have shifted. When Storr was first writing, status, experience and public recognition were sufficient to gain attention. Today, governments and the public demand evidence before they will entertain the claims of authority, however eminent. From the perspective of psychotherapy this is a mixed blessing. Psychoanalysis has always had a strong hierarchical tradition, and has found it hard to accommodate to this democratic shift. Gathering evidence for the effectiveness of psychoanalytic therapies, and showing that it provides added value over that provided by shorter cheaper treatments, is a continuing challenge (see Chapter 13). There are those who feel that the essence of psychoanalytic work cannot be adequately captured by the instrumental values and crude psychometric measures which evidence-based practice requires, and that therapy is as much a secular spiritual journey as it is a biomedical treatment for psychological illnesses. This is a view with which, as a Jungian, Storr had some sympathy, describing the process of individuation which psychotherapy aims to promote as 'a kind of Pilgrim's Progress without a creed, aiming not at heaven, but at integration and wholeness' (Storr 1997).

Nevertheless there are enduring aspects to psychotherapy practice that remain unaltered. While many of Freud's theories have been modified, developed or superseded, his papers on technique (Freud 1911–15) remain as fresh and indispensable to practitioners today as they were a century ago. Similarly, AOP embodies the fruits of a fine intelligence and sensibility combined with deep clinical experience, from which all practitioners can benefit. The skills of psychotherapy can only be acquired by *doing*, under the guidance of an experienced teacher. Therapists learn their trade like any other craft – cookery, beekeeping, playing the piano, skiing, joinery – by supervised practice. Finding an older, wiser, sympathetic mentor is essential; Storr was just such a person and his book was a summation of the knowledge and experience he wished to pass on to the next generation.

Having known Storr, first as a family friend and later colleague, I was therefore delighted and honoured when asked by the publishers and Storr's family to take on the task of updating AOP. This is the result of that work. Readers of the earlier editions will find it changed in many ways. I have used 'reversed sexism', so that therapists are all now female, their patients mostly male; I apologize to my male colleagues if they are offended by this. I have broken up the mellifluous flow of Storr's chapters with subheadings. I have cut and pared ruthlessly. I have added four new chapters, re-titled some, reorganized several, and added new material to all. Despite this, I hope to have remained true to the tone and spirit of the original. I like to think of this new edition as a fresh stem grafted onto exceptionally sound and strong root-stock.

I am an enthusiastic joint-author (Holmes and Lindley1997; Bateman and Holmes 1995; Holmes and Elder 2001; Holmes and Bateman 2002; Gabbard, Beck and Holmes 2005), but have never collaborated posthumously. I hope that AS would approve of what I have done, and not object that I have changed many instances of 'I' to 'we'. On the whole I have not found it hard to decide what to leave, what to rephrase, and what to cut. There remains but one sentence which my better judgement told me to remove, but was so heartfelt that I felt it should stay; I leave it to the diligent reader to pick it out. I am deeply grateful to AS in that he has saved me the hard graft of writing a book such as this *ab initio*, yet has provided a place where I too could transmit some of the psychotherapy lore I have assimilated over the years.

Anthony Storr (1920–2001)

Anthony Storr was one of that very select band of psychiatrists who have crossed the mysterious barrier between professional eminence to public recognition. For a while he was *the* face of psychiatry on BBC television, and he remains one of the very few psychotherapists who have appeared on the radio programme *Desert Island Discs*, an accolade far more coveted than a knighthood. Most educated people have heard of him, mainly through his best-selling books that throw psychological light on subjects of general interest including aggression (Storr 1968); gurus and their followers (Storr 1997); creativity (Storr 1972); solitude (Storr 1989); sex and sexual deviation (Storr 1968); music (Storr 1992); as well as accessible introductions to the work of Freud (Storr 1989) and Jung (Storr 1973). All illustrate Storr's enviable capacity to communicate complex ideas without oversimplification.

Anthony's parents (his father a distinguished cleric) were cousins; he was the youngest of four children by 10 years, and thus virtually an only child. His early childhood was solitary but not unhappy. Misery set in when, according to the mores of the English upper-middle classes, he was sent away to boarding school. At Winchester, he was lonely and bullied, but acquired life-long passions for both music – he was a gifted pianist and viola player – and reading. A turning point in his life was his friendship with the novelist and scientist C.P. Snow, his tutor at Cambridge. Snow encouraged and valued him, and endorsed Anthony's wish to become a psychiatrist. Snow is best known for his phrase 'the two cultures' – science and the arts – and the deep divide in intellectual life between them (Snow 1973). Storr was comfortably able to reconcile these two aspects, in both his work and writings. Having finally found his vocation and voice – and first wife – Storr did well at medical school and after qualification as a physician, trained in psychiatry at the Maudsley Hospital, then dominated by its intimidating director and guru (see Storr 1997), Sir Aubrey Lewis. Storr (Guardian 2001) commented 'I owed Lewis one thing, at least. Once you had suffered the experience of presenting a case at one of his Monday morning conferences, no other public appearance, whether on radio, TV or the lecture platform, could hold any terrors for you.'

Storr's career can be divided into three main phases. Soon after completing his psychotherapy training, and leaving the Maudsley, he set up in private practice in Harley Street as a Jungian psychoanalyst. Through his personal charisma and writings, especially the best-selling *The Integrity of the Personality* (Storr 1960), he soon became a very successful and fashionable analyst, through whose consulting rooms passed many eminent men and women, academics, artists, writers, musicians and politicians.

Phase two started in 1974 when Storr gave up his private practice, left London, having remarried, and moved to Oxford to take up a post as Consultant Psychotherapist at the Warneford Hospital, under the encouragement of Professor Michael Gelder. He found the academic atmosphere of Oxford extremely congenial, and was friends with leading local figures such as the pianist Alfred Brendel and philosopher Isaiah Berlin. Following retirement from the National Health Service, he remained highly productive in this third phase, continuing to write, and as an active member of Green College where he was a fellow. He was made an honorary fellow of the Royal College of Psychiatrists in 1993, again one of the very few psychotherapists to be so chosen. He was also a fellow of the Royal Society of Literature – again a very rare honour for a psychiatrist and one that meant a great deal to him.

Storr's life illustrates many of the principles he sets out in AOP. The origins of a person's character and conflicts are to be found in childhood. Genetic inheritance sets the scene, physically (Storr attributed his asthma to his parents' consanguinity) and mentally. Developmental pathways, both traumatic (sent to boarding school at an early age; bullying; physical illness) and resilience-enhancing (musical abilities; self-sufficiency) set up life-long dispositions. Solitude can be painful but productive. Creativity helps overcome unhappiness. Sex matters. Resentment and anger (AS's response to bullying; parents who failed to recognize his unhappiness at school) need to be acknowledged and given vent; appropriate assertiveness has a necessary aggressive edge. Finding a sympathetic, older, wiser friend or parent-figure (Snow) can make all the difference to a troubled adolescent. Stress can be strengthening as well as destructive. 'Success' carries narcissistic dangers as well as rewards. Mid-life is a moment for re-evaluation and reviving adolescent aspirations and abilities. Friendship is important to mental health, as is being part of a community. Life post-retirement can be productive and enjoyable.

Parameters

It is now time to move from these preliminaries to the main business of this book – our detailed exposition of how to do one's work as a psychotherapist. A few implicit parameters must be mentioned. As already mentioned, the female personal pronoun is used for therapists. I have expunged the labelling implications of terms like 'the depressive personality' and 'schizophrenics', using instead phrases, admittedly more clumsy, like 'depression-sufferers'. Those seeking psychotherapeutic help are generally, as in AS' terminology, described as 'patients', but occasionally, in more contemporary conventional parlance as 'clients'. The work here described is exclusively about working with adults or late adolescents. For those wishing to explore child psychotherapy Waddell (1998) and Tuber and Catflisch (2011) provide comparable jumping-off points. The nouns psychotherapy, psychoanalysis, psychodynamic psychotherapy, and psychodynamics are used throughout more or less interchangeably, and unashamedly so, since we believe the similarities between them are far greater than any differences. The focus of the book is on the actuality of what goes on in the consulting room, so theory, although a necessary background presence, is kept to a bare minimum. No specific school of psychotherapy is espoused. Our viewpoint is eclectic and integrative, and, wherever possible, evidence-based. Case material is illustrative and fictionalized but has its origins in reality. With that in mind we now invite the reader to embark with us on the fascinating, sometimes perilous, life-enhancing, life-changing journey that is psychoanalytic psychotherapy.

Introduction

Questions, questions

Most people feel pretty anxious when they take on their first psychotherapy or counselling client. How shall I address my patient – formally or informally? Likewise, what shall I call myself? How should I be dressed? How shall I arrange the chairs in the room? Or should I encourage my client to lie on a couch from the start, and if so where should I position my chair? What happens when we 'start' – shall I stay silent or 'take a history'? How much should I guide the interview, or should I just let the conversation unfold? What do I say if the client asks me about my qualifications? What about more personal questions – asking me if I am married, or have ever had a major bereavement, how do I handle that? What happens if they don't turn up – should I telephone or text them? Am I supposed to make 'interpretations'? If so, what exactly *is* an 'interpretation', and how does one 'make' one? What if I am really worried about a client and suspect they may be suicidal? How do I bring the session to an end – what if the client seems to want to go on, or has just got to something interesting, when time is up? Do I take notes during the session, or write the case up afterwards? Help!

There are other important issues depending on the context in which the client is being seen. If it is in private practice – how much should I charge? Should I tell the client how often I expect to be paid – after each session or at regular intervals? If the practitioner has a 'day job' – psychiatry, clinical psychology, or banking (!) – what do I do if my mobile/pager goes off in the middle of a session? At what time of day should I see clients? Is it alright for me to sip my morning coffee when I see them at 7.00 am?

This book is intended to provide some guidance about these sorts of questions, although in the end practitioners will work out for themselves their own way of doing things, and what suits them and their clients best. Our primary focus is always on the *practice* rather than the theory of psychotherapy, although appropriate theoretical texts will be referred to as we go along. Psychotherapy, both for the patient and for the therapist, is an individual, personal matter; any approach which seeks to convey something of what actually goes on during psychotherapy, rather than listing and discussing theories, is bound to be idiosyncratic. Indeed there are those (Bacal 2006) who hold that it is the very essence of psychotherapy to be specific, unique, ungeneralizable. No psychotherapist, and no system or theory, has the key to understanding human beings. But it is possible to assert some general principles about the practice of psychotherapy with which the majority of psychotherapists would agree, however they might argue about points of theory; and this is what we have tried to do in this book.

Definition

We define psychotherapy as follows: the art of *alleviating personal difficulties* through *conversation* in the context of a personal, professional *relationship*. This brings out the three essential components of our work: a suffering individual or patient (as in the Latin, *patiens*, to suffer), the vital importance of speech and language, and a particular kind of relationship, that is at once intimate and yet professional.

The definition of psychotherapy given above may surprise those who think of psychotherapy primarily as a means of curing mental illness. When Freud began his psychoanalytic work in Vienna toward the end of the nineteenth century, abolition of neurotic symptoms was certainly his primary aim, and his patients, though not suffering from physical disease, resembled medical patients closely enough to be labelled 'ill'. Today, psychotherapists are consulted by people whose symptoms are ill defined and many who are not unwell in any conventional, medical sense. A primary motivation in seeking psychotherapeutic help is with what Szasz (1965) has called 'problems in living'; they are seeking self-knowledge, self-acceptance, and better ways of managing their lives. Psychotherapy is as much concerned with understanding people as a whole, and with changing attitudes, as with the abolition of symptoms.

Classifying psychodynamic therapies

This brings us to the question of the many different types and modalities of psychotherapy. We shall be concerned here only with those within the psychoanalytic tradition; that is therapies whose style and theoretical basis originate with Freud and his followers. Students will soon discover that the 'narcissism of minor differences' (Freud 1929) affects the world of psychoanalysis no less than that of politics, and that disputes about what constitutes the 'pure gold' (Freud 1919) of 'real' psychoanalysis, expressive and supportive psychotherapy, high and low intensity analysis etc, are endlessly and sometimes acrimoniously debated. We tend to think that these distinctions, while important, can be over-emphasised, and represent gradations, rather than differences in kind. According to the psychoanalyst Matte-Blanco (1975), the unconscious mind tends toward 'symmetrization' (i.e. abolition of differences), while the conscious mind is drawn to distinctions and asymmetries. Creative living entails both the poetic ability to use metaphor (which is a species of symmetry), and to classify and understand difference (c.f. Dalal 2012).

The psychoanalytic set of cousins within the wider psychotherapy clan are conventionally divided according to frequency of sessions as follows:

Four or five sessions a week: psychoanalysis
Three sessions a week: psychoanalytic psychotherapy
One to two sessions per week: psychodynamic psychotherapy.

It is the last with which we shall be primarily concerned here, and we shall not be addressing other modalities of therapy – CBT, psychodrama etc – or other settings, such as marital and group psychotherapy.

The focus for this book is the kind of therapy that is carried out by psychodynamic counsellors and psychoanalytic psychotherapists, whether in private or externally funded practice, e.g. National Health Service, voluntary sector, or insurance-based mental health provision. Typical frequency of sessions is once or twice a week. We shall not be dealing with psychoanalytic therapies that entail four or five sessions per week. In practice even psychoanalysts see relatively few patients so often (unless they be fellow psychoanalysts in training); and in third-party funded or subsidized services such concentrated therapy is virtually impossible. Although there are some patients who may, for a time, need more frequent sessions, the majority can benefit from being seen only once or twice weekly. If one bases one's position on psychotherapy research findings, there is scant evidence that the results obtained by 3–5 times weekly analysis are superior to those achieved by less intensive therapy, although studies do suggest that prolonged therapy outperforms brief treatments (Shedler 2010).

Let us turn now to thinking about the setting in which psychotherapy is, or should be, conducted.

The Setting

The 'gift' of psychotherapy (Yalom 2002) can be thought of in terms of *space*: a physical space where patient and therapist can meet, protected from intrusion; a 'space in time' that is sacrosanct and set aside exclusively for the patient each week. Above all, patients are offered a space in the therapists' mind, free from extraneous concerns, where they can guarantee that all their attention and focus will be devoted to their clients. Without this psychic space no useful work can be done. Some therapists are oblivious to their surroundings – one devoted NHS analyst claimed that she was prepared to see her patients in a broom cupboard if needs be – but in this first chapter we shall look mainly at the externals and how they can influence therapy, for good or ill.

The room

A number of what commonly might be thought of as inessential details are highly important in psychotherapy. The room that the therapist uses, and the way it is arranged, are significant. In private practice, one is free to arrange and furnish one's consulting room in any way one likes. In hospitals, clinics, social service departments, schools etc where trainees often take their first steps in psychotherapy practice, students are lucky if they have any choice in either the location of the room or in its furnishing and appearance. Nevertheless, there are defined features of how the space in which one is to practice psychotherapy should be arranged; we would urge all psychotherapists to insist that these basic requirements are met by their managers, and to express dissatisfaction when they are not.

Ideally, a room in which psychotherapy is to be undertaken should be furnished as follows. First, there should be a minimum of two comfortable chairs in which both therapist and patients can relax. Psychoanalytic therapy can be described as 'symmetrical but lopsided', a point to which we shall return. The physical manifestation of this is that both client and therapist should be seated on chairs comparable in height and comfort, and indeed ideally of the same design. Some patients will be so tense at first that they will be unable to make proper use of a welcoming chair; but one hopes that as the therapy progresses they will increasingly be able to do so. Being perched on the edge of a hard chair is not conducive to personal revelation, and may put the patient at a disadvantage compared with the therapist, especially if she is more comfortably seated.

Second, there should ideally also be a couch on which the patient can lie down. This should not be an examination couch of the kind which physicians use for physical examinations, but something far more comfortable. A divan bed often proves satisfactory. If suitably covered, this does not look like a bed, to which some patients might object, and which others might welcome with misplaced enthusiasm. It should have at its foot end an extra piece of the same material in which it is covered, which can easily be removed for cleaning. This enables patients to lie down without having to take off their shoes (although most don't mind doing so), which might otherwise dirty the cover. At the other end of the couch should be a number of suitably covered cushions which patients can arrange in any way they find comfortable. The couch should be so placed that the therapist can sit at the head end, out of sight of the patient, without having to rearrange the furniture every time the couch is used.

The majority of psychotherapists, especially beginners, do not follow the psychoanalytical practice of using a couch. But it is useful with some patients, for reasons we shall discuss later; if possible, it is good to have it as an available alternative if the patient finds it easier to relax when lying down, or easier to talk if he is not face-to-face with the therapist (Holmes 2012b).

It is useful to have one or two extra chairs easily available in case it may be necessary to see relatives together with the patient. In the individual psychotherapy with which we are primarily concerned here, such interviews will be infrequent, and normally confined to the initial or second meeting with the patient; but there are exceptions, and it is therefore wise to be prepared to seat one or two more people when needed.

Where the therapists are in a position to exercise personal choice in the room's furnishings, they may well like to hang some pictures on the walls, and fill the bookshelves (if there are any) with their own books. This is entirely reasonable; but it is important that the room should not contain anything which too stridently asserts the therapists' taste or which is likely to reveal a great deal of their personal life. Suppose, to take a slightly unlikely example, that the therapist is a devout Catholic. If his or her bookshelf is full of devotional works and there is a crucifix upon the wall, this may well alienate the patient who is agnostic or a convinced Protestant; and patients become guarded in their speech for fear of offending the therapist's religious sensibilities.

Photographs

Many professional people like to bring reminders of home into their offices by displaying photographs of their spouses and children. It is inadvisable for psychotherapists to do this. A degree of neutrality is essential, and is an aspect of the restraint and partial suppression of personality entailed in working as a psychotherapist. When patients become deeply involved in the psychotherapeutic process, they are likely to experience powerful feelings of love, hate, envy, or jealousy toward the therapist. Explicit reminders of the therapist's life outside the consulting room of the kind provided by family photographs may inhibit the expression of these feelings (see Chapter 8 for further discussion of transference). Patients will certainly have thoughts about the therapist's personal life, the content of which may be important in understanding them. For example, someone may be struggling with his sexuality or gender identity and have fantasies about the therapist's sexual life. A photograph of the therapist's spouse and children may convey a message of unattainable normality or marital bliss, and thus may inhibit the patient's fantasy, or arouse envy. If the therapist is male, female patients may compare themselves, favourably or unfavourably with the woman depicted in the photograph; and, while this may prove to be a valuable piece of exploration of the patient's psyche, it introduces a disturbing element of 'reality' into the psychotherapeutic relationship, which, as we shall see, is inimical to the analytic process. Conversely if the therapist is female and the patient male, the depiction of a male partner may inhibit a burgeoning idealization of the therapist, and/or reinforce a sense of inferiority in the patient, rather than letting these two feelings remain in the realm of fantasy where they can be explored.

Sound

It is important that, if at all possible, the room should be quiet. Extraneous noise is not only disturbing in itself, but may also cause the patient to feel anxious. Attachment theory tells us that anxiety inhibits exploration, including the self-exploration that is the essence of psychotherapy (Holmes 2010). If noise from without can come into the room, it is likely that sounds from within can be heard outside it. Nothing is more inimical to frank disclosure than the belief that one may be overheard. Clinic rooms usually contain a telephone. It goes without saying that during the time of a psychotherapeutic session the therapist does not make or take telephone calls. If the student is a doctor, she should arrange psychotherapy sessions at times when she is not 'on call', or at least ensure that a colleague covers during the time during which she is practising psychotherapy.

One one occasion, when JH was working in a hospital practice as both a psychiatrist and psychotherapist, engrossed at a particularly delicate moment in a psychotherapy session with a rather inhibited client, the door flung wide open and a patient from the ward, justifiably annoyed at his compulsory detention, burst in, shouted 'Dr Holmes, you are an absolute fucking bastard!', and then disappeared. There was a moment's silence in which client and therapist looked at one another with a mixture of dismay, horror and amusement. The client, for whom difficulty in expressing anger had been a main theme, then commented 'isn't that exactly what you have been trying to get me to say to you ever since I first started!?'.

All these things are perhaps more easily arranged in private than in public service practice. But whether patients are paying for treatment directly by private fees, or indirectly by taxation, they are entitled to feel that the time spent with the therapist is *their* time; and that this will not be in any way disturbed by interruptions.

Note-taking

When one has had the opportunity of getting to know a patient really well over a period of time, taking notes may be superfluous. But for beginners, 'process recording' – i.e. writing as detailed notes as is possible recording the exact ebb and flow of the session – is essential. They form the basis of supervision, and it is in these 'minute particulars' that the really interesting and important issues emerge (Hobson 1985). Whether notes are written up immediately after the session or during it is a matter of personal preference. If done during the session it should be done as unobtrusively as possible, in order not to interrupt the patient's discourse. Where the patient is seen sitting up, as they will be in most cases at least for the first session, JH uses a clipboard perched on his knee which permits eye contact to be maintained; the offending clipboard is then discarded for ongoing therapy. When process recording is performed post-session (our preference), students should allow enough time for writing up their notes before their next patient. Even if one is not writing extensive notes, it is important to arrange the times of psychotherapeutic sessions so that there is a gap of ten minutes or more between patients. This not only enables the therapist to relax in preparation for their next patient but, when the occasion demands, to deal with telephone calls or other matters which may have arisen in the meantime.

2

The initial interview

There is a game in which the participants are invited to boil down any chosen subject into two contrasting precepts. Of soccer one might say: the two things you need to know about soccer are that all that matters is scoring goals; and scoring goals is very difficult. Or philosophy is the most important branch of knowledge with implications for every member of the human race; yet there is only a tiny handful of people capable of thinking philosophically. Of psychotherapy one might say that the two most important things are that the therapist creates an utterly reliable, secure, and dependable setting; and that she fosters conditions of maximum ambiguity and possibility.

This Janus precept is what is known as the 'analytic attitude' (Lemma 2003). But how does one set about creating that attitude in oneself and communicating it to the patient, especially when one is caught up in a myriad of practical issues? As we have already outlined, the beginner therapist will inevitably feel somewhat apprehensive at having a new patient referred to him for treatment. Will she be able to do anything to help? Understand what the patient is talking about? Will the patient divine her inexperience? What will the patient think of her?

These worries are to a certain extent justified. The therapist is likely to be confronted with a wide variety of people with whose style of life and mode of expression she is not necessarily familiar. Many of the patients will be older than herself, some will be more intelligent. All this matters less than the inexperienced therapist commonly supposes. Provided she is genuinely interested in the patient as a person, she is likely to be able to overcome any initial difficulties which unfamiliarity with the patient's type of social background may pose. Indeed enlisting the patient's help in understanding, say, what it is like to be a child of first-generation immigrants, the mores of an English public school, the social milieu of a modern council estate, or the problems of growing up in a bilingual household, may in itself be beneficial, fostering the collaborative atmosphere which characterizes successful therapy. Occasionally, if the patient comes from an entirely different culture, the basic social assumptions of the therapist and patient may be so widely discrepant that communication becomes impossible, but this is rare. Let us for the moment assume that the therapist has been referred a patient who does not present any such problem. How does one set about conducting the first interview?

Increasingly, people seeking help with their personal problems present themselves directly to a psychotherapist. But in public service psychotherapy and training organizations the patient will be likely to have arrived via a referral pathway, the end result of which is arrival in the psychotherapist's consulting room. This means that the therapist will have a letter about the patient, and possibly other notes. The therapist ought to familiarize herself with these well before the first appointment with the patient. Many patients are alarmed at the prospect of meeting members of the psycho-professions: psychotherapists, psychoanalysts, psychologists, psychiatrists. Confiding in strangers is not easy; and the patient who has been sitting apprehensively in a waiting-room for longer than he needs, is less likely to be at ease when the therapist finally sees him.

Greeting one's patient; touch

Now we come to names. Christian or surnames? Professional titles (Dr, Professor, etc) or no monikers? There are no hard and fast rules. The important thing is a) to choose a mode of address (and dress) with which you feel comfortable and b) consistency. The patient is now to be collected from the waiting area. It is courteous to greet him by his name. 'Mr Robinson? Good morning/hello. I'm Dr Y/Ms X/Joan Bloggs'. This both establishes that the therapist actually knows the patient's name, and also indicates that he is to be treated as a person, not merely as a numbered case.

Ella Sharpe's (1930) summary of the way the analyst should deal with these parameters was to 'treat the patient as you would an informal guest in your office'. This raises the question of touch, its benefits and dangers (Casement 1985; Dimen 2011). JH's routine practice is to shake a new patient's hand at the first session but generally not thereafter. People vary in how 'tactile' they are. Some patients proffer a handshake at the end of every session. Very occasionally, after a very emotional session, one might lightly touch a patient on the back as they leave. On the whole bodies are rather rigidly kept at bay in consulting rooms, and when they intrude – the patient is cold and needs a blanket, or wet and requires a towel, needs to go to the toilet in the middle of the session, asks for a hug – it is always noteworthy and always needs to be thought about carefully afterwards.

A salutary example occurred for JH when he was conducting a 'master class' for therapists in a South American country. The presented patient was a teenage girl with an eating disorder; the therapist, a kindly and clever middle-aged married woman, reported that at the end of a particular session she had hugged her patient. JH questioned this, not, he hoped, in a critical way, but merely to explore its possible meaning – why hug in this session with this particular patient? What might it have been like for the patient had the therapist been male and hugged her? Would it matter if the patient had worries about homosexuality? The audience laughingly accused JH of being a typical uptight Anglo-Saxon male. It emerged that routine practice in that country involves kissing the patient on the cheek at the beginning and end of each session, it being normal to greet 'informal guests' with a kiss in that country. Since the therapist is always alert to departures from the expected, here the point to be noted would be the patient who shrank from such contact.

As with most phenomena in psychotherapy the important thing is a) to be on the look out for anomalies (which might be nothing more than: 'you looked a little stressed as you came in today. I wonder if something has upset you'); b) to try to understand their meaning; and c) to find a way to bring up a) or b), or both, with the patient.

Preliminaries

Having invited the patient to sit down in a chair appropriately placed in the way already described, what does the therapist do next? In general it is a good idea to start with what might be called 'preliminaries'. This entails checking that you have the patient's correct full name, contact details, age, and the names of any other professionals with whom the patient may have seen. It is also an opportunity to set out the terms of this initial session. One might say something like 'this is very much a first meeting. After we have talked, let's decide at the end whether we feel regular therapy might be helpful, and if so, how often, when, and for how long'. Or: 'I think it was your GP/psychiatrist/husband who set up this appointment. What do *you* think about the idea of coming into therapy?'.

With the therapist thus taking the initiative, this gives the patient's anxiety levels a chance to lessen slightly. As always, the therapist has to tread a fine line between helping to lower the patient's anxiety so that exploration can begin, while remaining non-seductively reticent and neutral, so that the patient feels the therapeutic space is theirs to make use of however they choose, rather than conforming to the therapists' dictates. It also conveys, right from the start, that psychotherapy is a joint enterprise rather than a series of interviews in which the patient is given instructions or advice, as happens in ordinary medical consultations. Some therapists however like to impose as little structure on the session as possible from the outset, and to allow, as it were, the patient's unconscious to guide proceedings. For them, the opening move might be no more than an encouraging grunt, or a gesture indicating to the patient that the floor is theirs. They assume that the issues and possible conflicts implicit in the above remarks will emerge spontaneously in the course of the session or subsequent ones.

History-taking

Indeed the therapist is already faced with a dilemma. Should she, or should she not, 'take a history'? The patient will probably already have given his story at length to the referring professionals. He may assume that the nature of his complaint and the details of his personal and family history are known and is justified in the assumption that the therapist will have read his notes. Many patients resent giving their history yet again, and often say so. But psychotherapy is a living experience, not a series of dead facts. One wants the details of the patient's problems and its antecedents to come to life in the session. Taking the history from a patient gives one an unrivalled opportunity of assessing what a particular symptom *means* to the patient; something which is difficult to convey in notes or letters. When a person talks to one about his family and his past experience, his tone of voice, the phraseology he uses, whether he looks at one or hangs his head, may be revealing in a way that medical notes are not. Only the greatest novelists can make people come alive for us in writing; and it is too much to hope that referring colleagues can achieve this.

Psychoanalysts used not to take histories. Instead, their practice was, even at a first interview, to instruct the patient to lie upon the couch and then to proceed to say whatever occurred to him. This may work for patients who are familiar with the psychoanalytic setup, and who therefore know what is expected of them, but is not suitable for those who are less sophisticated. Moreover, the therapist who adopts this procedure runs the risk of missing important information. AS recalls that he once treated a patient who suffered from depression who had seen so many doctors before she came to him that he did not bother to take a formal history. It emerged long into therapy that far from being the virginal person he had supposed, she had had several affairs about which she was extremely reticent.

We are therefore in favour of the therapist starting from the beginning. One might say: 'I've read your notes/doctor's letter and I have some idea of your background and symptoms, but I'd really like to hear the story in your own words. What is the main thing that is troubling you? (Or 'what, from your point of view is the main issue that you need help with?'). How is it affecting your life? How did it start? What's the sequence of events that has led you to be sitting in this room, having this conversation with me?'

This kind of approach usually dispels any feeling of resentment which the patient may have at being asked to repeat himself.

However, the therapist, especially if medically qualified, needs to learn to adopt a different history-taking style from that with which she is accustomed. Doctors are trained to obtain essentials, to ask a great many questions, and to follow formal schemes of enquiry which ensure that they do not omit anything which may be vital. Present complaint; previous illnesses; family history; personal history; use of drugs, tobacco, and alcohol, risk assessment including suicidal thoughts or plans, and so on. But asking too many questions interrupts the flow of the patient's discourse, constantly attempting to pin him down, when what *he* wants to talk about may be something entirely different.

Nevertheless as therapy proceeds, it is important to have an outline picture of the patient's family background and current circumstances, and indeed some sense of the rhythms and minutiae of their day-to-day life, especially as it is affected by their symptoms or illness. Sketching out a 'genogram' or family tree is a good way to achieve this. We need to know whether or not the patient is married; whether his parents are alive or dead; how many siblings he has and what the age gaps are between them; whether he has any children, and to have an outline of his childhood development and any previous illnesses. But there should be no sense of rush. As Winnicott (1965) said, 'psychoanalysis is an extended form of history-taking'. Details will emerge in their own time, so long as the therapist is sensitive to areas which are conspicuous by their omission (as we have said, one of the skills of a therapist is to notice anomalies – the dogs that didn't bark in the night), as in AS's case above, when it may be necessary to say something like 'you haven't said much about your father/schooldays/early boyfriends/sexual life/the extent to which you feel life is/isn't worth living' etc.

In general the patient should feel free to wander; to expand upon topics which he did not have time to deal with in previous interviews. Suppose, for example, that the patient described his father as 'strict', and that this bare description has been dutifully recorded in the notes. The psychotherapist, when the patient's relationship with his parents is being discussed, may say: 'I see you describe your father as having been strict. Can you tell me more about this? In what way was he strict? Shall we think about some examples.'

Examples; anecdotes; specifics

When a novelist wants to make his characters come alive, he will usually depict them in action. Creative writing courses encourage would-be authors to 'show, don't tell'. Merely informing the reader that so and so was mean or courageous or cruel will not bring the character to life so vividly as will incident. We remember Mr Murdstone's vicious flogging of David Copperfield with greater clarity than we remember his appearance or speech. In the same way, we and the patient himself will remember incidents from the patient's past which illustrate his behaviour and relations with others more vividly than mere adjectival descriptions. The devil is in the detail. Suppose, for example, that the patient with a strict father tells us that the latter was very particular about what time he came in at night. 'Once, I came in five minutes after the time I was supposed to be in by. There was my father, watch in hand, waiting up for me. I shall never forget how frightened I was. I expected him to hit me; but what he did was to dock my pocket money; so much for every minute I was late.' Such an anecdote is far more revealing of the character of the patient's father, and of the patient's relation with him, than is the label 'strict'.

Time and timing

How long should the initial interview last? Some therapists set aside an hour and a half for an initial interview, so as to cover what may be a wide range of history and current difficulties, and leave time for negotiating a therapeutic contract at the end. While this gives the therapist a better opportunity of getting to know his new patient quickly, it may also carry the disadvantage of raising false expectations. He may think that all subsequent interviews are to be as long as the first; or, if he feels he needs more time at any particular session, that the therapist will easily be able to give it to him. As in all such matters of style, there are no absolute precepts. Whatever is practicable and feels comfortable should be the rule, so long as they are made explicit and mutually understood.

Generally, the initial interview, like those which follow, should last 45 to 50 minutes. This period of time may seem arbitrary, but this is not so. Shorter interviews are apt to be frustrating, both for the therapist and patient, in that not enough time is allowed for topics to be pursued in depth. Longer interviews, though both patient and therapist may sometimes want them, are apt to be tiring for both. Psychotherapy, properly carried out, requires concentration and alertness; and most of us know, from experience of lectures, that attention is difficult to sustain without a break beyond a time-span of 45 to 50 minutes. The 50-minute hour, now hallowed by tradition, allows the therapist to make appointments on the hour, and gives her ten minutes between each patient to collect her thoughts, deal with telephone messages, or have a cup of coffee; all of which may be essential in a day in which she is seeing a series of patients.

The contract

The psychotherapist should try to bring the initial interview with a patient to an end a few minutes before the appointed time of ending. This gives therapist and patient time to reflect together on the experience. 'How have you found today's session? Would you like to meet on a regular basis? I am happy to proceed if you are. I have a regular slot at such-and-such a time, would you like to take that up, or do you want to go home and think about it, and perhaps discuss it with your husband and then let me know?' The message to be conveyed is that it is the patient's choice, and he or she is being encouraged to take responsibility for deciding to embark on therapy, rather than it being something that is prescribed or imposed.

It would be convenient both for the psychotherapist and patient if, at this point, the number of sessions could be decided. 'How long shall I need to go on coming?' is a reasonable question for the patient to ask, but it is not one which can be answered immediately. A useful device is to say something like: 'at this early stage it's hard to tell, but shall we meet on six occasions and then review the situation?' Although, by the sixth session, it may still not be possible to give an accurate prediction of the length of therapy needed, this probationary period is usually long enough for the therapist and the patient to decide whether or not they are likely to be able to work fruitfully together. Sometimes of course the length is determined not by patient need but by arbitrary factors such as the therapist's training requirements and if so this should be mentioned at the outset. The patient's unconscious responses to this will, as therapy proceeds, often be useful grist to the therapeutic mill.

It is also helpful, at this initial interview, to remind the patient what the length of each session will be. Fifty minutes is our preferred period, for the reasons given above.

Frequency of sessions is a question which, unfortunately, is often decided by expediency. Some would argue that ideally patients should be seen three times per week. As we have said, good results can often be achieved if the patient is seen once or twice per week. An absolute minimum would be fortnightly. Anything less means that the therapy is almost entirely supportive and the expressive/dynamic processes with which we are concerned in this book cannot manifest themselves. Infrequent sessions mean that it is difficult to get to know the patient intimately, to remember what he says from one session to the next, or to maintain a sense of continuity in the therapeutic process. At the end of an assessment interview the therapist suggested that the patient would need to come for at least 6 months at a minimum of once a week sessions. 'Oh dear' said the patient, 'does that mean my case is really bad?' The therapist responded 'no, it's nothing to do with how "bad" you are, whatever that may mean (we must find time to explore that feeling), it's just that's how psychotherapy works. When our GP prescribes antibiotics three times a day it doesn't mean that our infection is particularly bad - but simply that's the most effective frequency of dosage'

Location: ideally, the patient should come to the same room, at the same time, on the same day of the week, for each appointment. This is part of the analytic frame, and induces that sense of security already mentioned which is the precondition of self-exploration. It also means that any variations – such as the patient coming on the wrong day or at the wrong time – can be seen and discussed as manifestations of the patient's unconscious, rather than the therapist's vagaries. If a patient misses an appointment, it may be because of his reluctance to face some of his problems, or for other psychological reasons. When patients want to alter appointments for what seem to be good reasons, the psychotherapist should seek to accommodate them, if she can do so without too much inconvenience. On the other hand, the wish to alter appointments can be a testing-out by the patient of how compliant the therapist will be. In most instances, it is easy enough to see when an ulterior motive of this kind is operating. The therapist need not punish herself by being too accommodating. On the other hand, she need not punish the patient by being rigidly inflexible. The important thing is to look *post-hoc*, together with the patient (and usually with the help of a supervisor), at the possible meanings behind a piece of minor 'acting out' of this sort.

When arrangements for future appointments have been made, some patients, particularly those who are uninformed about psychotherapy, may ask what the point of such future meetings may be. Expecting medicines or some dramatic intervention, they may say: 'But what is going to happen, doctor? Is it going to be just talk?' In answer to this very natural question one might reply: 'You have had these problems for some time. If we are going to understand them together, it is necessary for us to go into them in a lot of detail. This is why we must meet on a number of occasions.' This kind of statement is usually adequate to reassure the puzzled patient for the moment. If subsequent meetings go well, he will probably never ask such a question again, as 'just talk' will have acquired a new significance for him.

Confidentiality

Another question which often arises in a first interview is that of confidentiality. Patients in psychotherapy reveal aspects of themselves which they may never have confided to any other person. It is natural that they should be anxious about who may have access to this intimate material. For the inexperienced therapist two separate questions arise. First, given that her treatment of patients is being supervised, should she reveal to the patient that what she says is being discussed with a supervisor and, if the therapist is part of a group, with other therapists? On the whole we think she should. We require that patients should be honest with us. Should we not lay upon ourselves an equal obligation? However it is surprising how commonly the patient appears to accept the therapist and not to question her credentials, seniority, or supervision arrangements.

Most patients will accept the notion that their case is being discussed from time to time with a more experienced, senior therapist or with other colleagues. But what is the therapist to say if they object? We have not encountered this problem in reality, but if it does occur, the therapist might suggest that the patient has an interview with the senior therapist or leader of the group with whom his problems are to be discussed. This should serve to allay their anxiety.

Much more troublesome is the question of case-notes, whether electronic or manual, especially for those working in a public setting such as hospitals or psychology departments. In the UK under the Freedom of Information Act the patient has a right, except under very special circumstances, to see their notes should they desire to do so. Equally, in hospitals many different people have access to a patient's information. It is important that a patient's notes are easily available to a number of people other than the psychotherapist; perhaps the patient may need to be admitted to hospital; or perhaps someone is carrying out research into the problem from which the patient is suffering. But the patient may feel, with ample justification, that he does not want the details of his sexual life or other intimate matters to be easily available to so many different people, however firmly the necessity of confidentiality has been impressed upon them. This is especially so in small communities in which the patient may be known to members of the hospital staff in a different context.

Psychotherapy notes should therefore be kept as a separate file to which only the therapist has access. In the ordinary notes, she should record the fact of the patient's attendance, and should also briefly describe his mental state, especially if there appears to have been any significant change, or if the patient appears to be severely depressed. This is simply to provide information in case the patient needs to be admitted to hospital. The psychotherapist need not record intimate details of the patient's personal life in the ordinary case-notes. Nevertheless therapists need to be aware that psychotherapy notes cannot be entirely sequestered, and should the patient ask to see them, or a Court subpoena them, they must be surrendered.

There is also the issue of confidentiality in relation to the patient's general practitioner and other doctors. Many patients in psychotherapy express anxiety about what will be written to their family doctor. Sometimes this is because they have found him or her imperceptive or unsympathetic toward their emotional problems. Sometimes it is because they fear that letters reaching them will be read by others, or might compromise insurance or employment prospects. Sometimes it is because they know the general practitioner socially, and would be embarrassed to meet them if they felt that they knew their most intimate secrets. In one or two instances, it may emerge that the patient is emotionally involved with the doctor.

In general it is important that the family doctor knows that the patient is in therapy, and intermittent letters about progress (say every three months), without going into details which breach confidentiality are a good idea. If the patient insists that the general practitioner shall not be told certain details, that wish must be respected. It is good practice to give the patient a copy of any letter to the general practitioner, and to ask for any alterations they would like before sending it. If the patient prefers this, the doctor can be telephoned rather than put anything in writing. It is important that a summary of what has been achieved is sent when the therapy has come to an end, and here too the patient will have the right to see what one has said. Indeed some therapies (Ryle 1990) incorporate the writing and sharing of letters ('epistolotherapy') into routine practice, and see this as therapeutic in itself.

While we have been mainly concerned in this and the previous chapter with the externals of therapy – time and place, confidentiality, letters – all of this will have an impact at a dynamic level and will stimulate unconscious reactions on the part of the patient. It is important to be sensitive to this, so that, for example, if the patient is particularly concerned about confidentiality this may indicate a general level of mistrust, with important developmental implications. Thus worry about confidentiality might be an 'oedipal' issue, in which the patient is preoccupied with the implications of his parents intimacy and his own consequent feelings of exclusion. Or if a patient has in the past been betrayed in some way by those whose job it is to look after him – through abuse or abandonment as a child, or an affair as an adult – then concern about how precious personal information will be handled will be particularly salient, and evoke strong transference reactions. To repeat our 'grist-to-the-mill' leitmotiv, the important thing is for these concerns to be brought out into the open and discussed in all their ramifications.

Getting Going: Overcoming Initial Resistance

The patient has been seen for the first time, the history has been taken, a series of appointments set up. What happens next? The therapist's initial task is to create conditions in which the patient feels able to talk as freely as possible, while she herself stays in the background. This is not as easy as it sounds. Patients who have consulted mental health professionals in the past usually expect them to take the lead, issue instructions, give advice, or ask more questions. Doctors taking their first steps in psychotherapy often find it difficult to abandon their traditional medical, problem-solving role. The fact that the patient is expected to take the lead in psychotherapeutic interviews has important psychological consequences.

Free association

Of Freud's many contributions to the art of psychotherapy perhaps the most significant was his replacement of hypnosis by free association. He took time to reach this. Ernest Jones (1953) records that Freud did not entirely abandon hypnosis until 1896. In the nineteenth century, hypnosis was fashionable. When Freud and Breuer made their original discovery that hysterical symptoms could often be abolished if the patient could be persuaded to recollect and re-experience the painful emotions connected with the onset of the symptoms, they used hypnosis to facilitate recall.

As originally used, hypnosis entailed giving patients positive suggestion. Success depended upon the doctor's authority and the patient's compliance. Freud came to dislike a technique which depended upon his authority rather than upon understanding, and which was often unpredictable in its results. In Freud's view, 'free association', when honestly undertaken, would lead to the recovery of the memories which the patient appeared to have forgotten. From this perspective the purpose of dynamic psychotherapy is to help the patient to help himself through insight, and thus to increase his autonomy (Holmes and Lindley 1997).

At the second interview, therefore, by adopting an 'analytic attitude', the psychotherapist begins to establish a culture in the session in which the patient takes the lead. Some patients have so much to say that no explanation of what is expected is necessary. But a significant group do not find this easy and need to be guided if they are to make use of the sessions. As one patient replied when invited to free associate – i.e. 'say anything that comes into your head, however embarrassing, irrelevant or counter-productive that might appear to be' – 'if I could do that I would not need to be here in the first place'. Ogden (1996) discourages such direct injunctions, and emphasizes that it is important for the analyst to be able to tolerate not just the patient's silence but also the inviolable privacy of their inner world. He conceives the therapy session as creating an 'analytic third' – i.e. a shared quasi-dream space to which the reveries of analyst and patient contribute equally, albeit asymmetrically, 'involving the unconscious interplay of states of reverie of analyst and analysand ... It is through the shared but asymmetrical experiencing of the 'analytic third' that analyst and analysand acquire a sense of, and generate symbols for, formerly unspoken and unthought aspects of the internal object world of the analysand' (Ogden 1996).

Role responsiveness

The first few sessions are directed toward engaging the patients in the therapy, emotionally, intellectually and socially. Until engagement is achieved no useful work can be done. Psychotherapy research consistently shows that a positive 'therapeutic alliance' is the best predictor of good outcomes in therapy (Shedler 2010). Sandler and Sandler (1984) describe this in terms of 'role responsiveness'. At this initial stage, the therapist assumes, to an extent, the role proffered to her by the patient, and engagement then proceeds on that basis. What makes this different from collusion or perpetuation of pre-existing patterns, is that the therapist is also observing herself doing so, and trying to understand the relational constellation in terms of transference.

Mallinckrodt and co-workers (Mallinckrodt *et al* 2008) illustrate how skilful therapists accommodate to and gradually modify the presenting stance of the client. They suggest that successful therapy requires initial 'concordance' (Racker 1968) on the part of the therapist. This means partial acceptance by the therapist of the role allocated by the patient's unconscious expectations and procedures. This might mean allowing for a degree of intellectualizing with some clients, waiting patiently for the client to begin to allow feelings to surface, for example in relation to breaks – ' I used to take gaps in my stride, just telling myself that you were a hard working professional and were entitled to holidays; now I really resent your going away, and wonder who you are going away with'. With more dependent clients a degree of boundary flexibility and gratification might be allowable, accepting inter-session letters and text-messages, and occasionally offering extra sessions. Later the therapist will move to a 'complementary' (as opposed to 'concordant'), challenging, role, thereby disconfirming maladaptive client expectations, and opening the way for psychological reorganization. The therapist first pulls towards the client's pre-existing patterns, and then pulls away from them. Evidence suggests (Dozier *et al* 2008) that secure therapists redress their client's attachment insecurities in this way, while insecure ones are more likely to reinforce them.

Thus the therapeutic relationship can be seen as the resultant of two opposing sets of forces. On the one hand the analyst attempts within the limited framework of therapy to provide a secure attachment experience – to identify and assuage attachment needs and to facilitate exploration; on the other, the patient approaches the relationship with prior expectations of sub-optimal caregiving, and, unconsciously assuming an unloving and/or untrustworthy caregiver, aims mainly for a measure of security. As therapy proceeds the soothing presence of the analyst enables the client to expose themselves to, tolerate, and learn from increasing levels of anxiety.

Shaping the session

Some people may plunge into therapy with a monologue where the psychotherapist finds it hard to interrupt. Here the therapist needs to learn to say: 'hang on a moment, you are going too fast for me here', or 'can we just go over that again, I'm not sure that I've quite followed what you are saying', or even 'my goodness, you are in such a rush – I wonder if it is almost too painful to stop for a moment and think about the really difficult feelings you are describing'.

Others find great difficulty in releasing any kind of spontaneity. This may be because they are so used to treating doctors and therapists as authorities that they invariably wait for the oracle to speak first; because, consciously or unconsciously, they resent the situation; or because they are so anxious that their mind goes blank. They may be frightened that the psychotherapist will uncover things of which they are ashamed; or that she has some magical technique that will give her power over their minds.

If, at a second interview, the patient does not start talking spontaneously, there are a number of ways of getting the ball rolling. One can simply ask: 'any thoughts about our session last week?' Or: 'last time, I asked you a number of questions about your problems and background. From now on, it's a good idea for you to take the lead rather than me asking more questions. After all, you are the expert on what is going on in your mind. I wonder, what do *you* feel that you need to talk about?' If this fails to produce a response one might say: 'I wonder what was going through your mind on your way to this appointment'. To this, some patients – those who are frightened, resentful, or psychologically naive for example – might answer 'well really nothing'.

Here one might reply 'that's interesting. I wonder what sort of a nothing that is, and what it feels like'. Or: 'It's quite difficult to think of nothing. There are usually stray thoughts going through one's mind. Perhaps you were having some thoughts about coming to see me again today. Perhaps you had some sort of anticipation about what this second interview was going to be like?'

Patient: *'I thought you'd ask me some more questions.'*

Therapist: *'What kind of questions did you imagine we might explore?'*

If the patient denies having imagined anything about the forthcoming interview, and particularly if his manner and tone of voice suggest resentment, it is worth trying a different tack: 'perhaps you're not feeling like talking today. Do you by any chance feel that you've been pushed into coming? Is there someone else who has said that you *ought* to?' Note that these 'questions' are framed in the form of statements: 'I wonder...'. This tends to be less threatening than direct questions (Hobson 1985) which may merely make the patient feel that his back is against the wall and that psychotherapy is a form of 'third degree'.

Whose therapy is it anyway?

Patients who are reluctant to talk may have been over-persuaded by another person to seek psychotherapy; and it may be that their reluctance does not show itself until they are required to do something other than answer direct questions. Most patients, even if they are quite uninformed about psychotherapy, very quickly latch on to the idea that what the therapist wants to know is, first, what has been preoccupying them since their last visit, and, second, what is going on in their minds in the here-and-now of the immediate present. If they fail to grasp this, it is reasonable to assume that they are either frightened, or hostile, or both; and one possible reason for hostility is that the patient feels bullied into coming.

This is especially so in the case of the young, though not confined to them. For example, parents often push their adolescents into seeking psychiatric help. As disturbed adolescents are often in rebellion against their parents in any case, they regard being made to undergo 'treatment' as another instance of parental lack of understanding, and consequently reluctant to talk. Also, adolescents often find the whole business of exploring what is going on in their mind intensely threatening: they worry that they may be 'mad' or 'gay', and that their friends will laugh at them if they discover they are seeing a therapist or counsellor. Therapists who work in student health services often face the problem that the student with difficulties in his work, or other signs of disturbance, may have been urged to come by his tutor. Even if his relationship with his tutor is a good one, he may still feel his referral to be another manifestation of authoritarian interference. Another not uncommon scenario is that of the husband whose wife insists that he seeks 'help', and may be threatening to leave if he does not. She may well be right that his withdrawal, or infidelity or financial profligacy or drinking or gambling are problematic. But until he himself can own that these are his problems and that he is coming for his own sake rather than just to mollify his wife, it is unlikely that progress will be made.

Very often, such a patient will respond to the psychotherapist's appreciation of the possibility that he has been cajoled into coming by someone else, by revealing that it is indeed the case. It is important to convey the message that psychotherapy only works with the willing co-operation of the patient, and that if he does not want to discuss his problems further, there is absolutely no compunction to do so. Sometimes this way of handling things so disposes of the patient's hostility that he becomes immediately co-operative. Occasionally the patient gratefully accepts this escape route. In such cases, it is important to leave the door open, or to offer an appointment for the following week, in case he changes his mind. Patients may need time to reflect upon whether they really want to seek help of their own volition. It is important to acknowledge that there are valid and good reasons for *not* coming into therapy as well as championing the benefits it can bring.

Can't talk/won't talk

Patients who are frightened are sometimes so extremely tense and anxious that they are unable to talk easily. It is sometimes helpful to comment on their posture and suggest that they will find it easier to talk if they sit back in the chair and try to relax. Obviously, it is important to try to discover what is making them frightened. Some patients are generally greatly reassured when the therapist tells them that it is entirely up to them what they want to talk about; that they do not have to tell her anything which they do not wish to reveal; and that she understands that talking to a strange person about one's personal problems can be both difficult and alarming.

Some patients are reluctant to talk simply because using words to define and clarify problems is unfamiliar to them. This may be because of lack of education; a difficulty which is usually surmountable if the psychotherapist is flexible enough to adapt her use of language to the patient's range. Other patients have been brought up in such a way that they habitually have recourse to action when faced with difficulties, and do not consider 'putting things into words' as action. If one has habitually been used to dispelling anger by digging the garden, alleviating anxiety by taking alcohol, avoiding confrontation with authority by changing one's job, to 'doing something', however futile or inappropriate, it takes time to learn that clarification through words can be of use.

Some people also believe that any form of self-examination is to be deplored; that introspection is unhealthy, and talking about one's problems self-indulgent. One may respond to this by saying 'that's interesting … I wonder where that idea comes from'. It might be that as a child such a person had a sibling who was ill or psychologically disturbed which occupied a lot of parental care and worry. The patient then may have come to believe that his 'little' problems were insignificant and trivial in comparison, and to feel guilty about demanding attention.

Occasionally, the psychotherapist may have been referred a patient who turns out to be psychotic. Such patients may exhibit obvious anxiety, but are more likely to be withdrawn and unapproachable. People suffering from paranoid psychosis may fear in a delusional way that the therapist can actually read or control their minds, rather than these being metaphorical, 'as if' anxieties. Even the most experienced diagnostician may fail to detect psychosis in a single consultation. Although some psychotic patients need, and to some extent respond to, psychotherapy, they are best not taken on by beginners.

As stated at the beginning of this chapter, the psychotherapist's primary task is to help the patient to talk as freely as possible while herself remaining in the background. We have discussed some of the difficulties which may impede this. Fortunately, the majority of patients referred for psychotherapy are eager to talk about their problems, and therapy usually gets under way without too much difficulty.

4

Making progress

Let's assume that any initial difficulties in communication have been overcome; that the patient has embarked upon a series of regular visits to the psychotherapist; and that he is able to talk about himself and his problems fairly freely, without having to be urged or persuaded to do so.

Although the process of psychotherapy involves some pain, in that most people find it unpleasant to confront their less admirable aspects, the majority of patients seem to look forward to their sessions, and discover that putting their difficulties into words is in itself beneficial, even if the therapist says practically nothing.

Why words?

In ordinary social life, there is no equivalent to the psychotherapeutic situation. When lay people discuss psychotherapy, they often conceive of the process as boring for the therapist, since their experience of people who talk endlessly about themselves is one of tedium. This is partly because, in social life, conversation entails exchange, and the person who gives no opportunity for interchange may become irritating. Also, many people who talk about themselves a great deal in social settings *are* boring because their talk is superficial. They may give accounts of their activities, or tell stories about their experiences without revealing anything at all of their inner lives. Indeed, compulsive talkers who tell one 'everything' in minute detail are generally using talk as a method of concealment. If the other person cannot get a word in edgeways, there is no danger of genuine interchange. The torrent of talk acts as a kind of smokescreen that prevents the talker from being known. Occasionally such people enter psychotherapy, and, as described in the previous chapter, the therapist has to find a way to interrupt the flow and to point out how the patient is using words to conceal and avoid rather than to articulate feeling. But when people are talking genuinely and sincerely, they are seldom boring. Social life does not usually give an opportunity for people who need to do so to talk about themselves at length; sympathetic friends are usually so anxious to intervene, give advice, or 'do something' that it prevents the subject from finding out much about himself.

Are therapists necessary? It is possible, though difficult, to analyse oneself; indeed, one aim of therapy is to equip the patient with the self-reflective skills needed to negotiate the milieu in which we all live. Freud, we are told, began his self-analysis in the eighteen-nineties, and continued to set aside the last half-hour of his day for that purpose throughout his life. But few of us are as determined or as honest as Freud – or as obsessional! Most people lack the self-discipline needed for regular self-scrutiny. Some require a therapist because they too easily give themselves up to despair: others because they can understand neither themselves nor their fellow men and women. Even in those cases in which the minimum of interpretation on the part of the therapist is required, her presence acts as a spur to honesty, an implicit hope of improvement, and a guarantee that the process of self-exploration is worthwhile. Many of the patients in whom psychotherapy produces valuable results are people who have not thought themselves to be worth bothering with. The therapist's continuing presence and interest is a living proof that there is a sane and sensible person who thinks otherwise. Moreover, although insight can to some extent be achieved by a determined effort to record one's own thoughts and feelings with scrupulous honesty, self-analysis lacks one vital ingredient in psychotherapy. This is the relationship with the therapist itself, and the gradual evolution of that relationship, which takes place in every successful psychotherapeutic encounter of any prolonged kind.

Indeed the development of this relationship and the act of putting feelings into words are inseparable. Psychotherapy is in its essence a *con*versation – that is communication with another. Arriving at the truth entails an interchange of feelings and thoughts with another person, actual or symbolic, through the medium of words and gesture. Donnel Stern (2010) uses the phrase 'fusion of horizons' to capture the way in which in the course of a conversation two people, starting from different points, come to feel that they have together discovered something fresh and new. Conversation is inseparable from being human. The conversational process starts from the moment of birth, and even before if one thinks about the internal conversations mothers have with their as yet unborn babies. The proto-conversations (Trevarthen 2005) in which infants and mothers mirror one another, take turns, and play together, form the basis for all subsequent social interactions. The conversations that one has with oneself, as in self-analysis, can be seen as internalized versions of conversation with another, transposed into the inner world.

From inner to outer

But putting things into words is less simple than it might appear. There are thoughts, feelings, wishes, problems which are present in some way in one's mind but which have never been clearly formulated – because they have not been shared with another. A good deal of what the patient says in therapy is about things which he knows, but which he has never clearly spelled out; things which he may describe as being 'at the back of my mind'. In psychotherapy, much of what the patient discovers about himself are things which he has known all along but never clearly recognized. Bollas (1987) calls this the 'unthought known'; Stern's (2010) phrase is 'unformulated experience'. Such insights, especially when unflattering, may have occurred to him before, but in so fleeting a fashion that they have not been fully registered. Being with an accepting and validating other enables one to begin to look at difficult aspects of oneself. Putting things into words clarifies both what one knows and what one does not know.

This process has the effect of giving reality to unformulated mental contents. Thoughts, feelings, fantasies and daydreams which are not deliberately expressed remain insubstantial. When communicated to another person, they begin to achieve a solid existence. Putting things into words captures the ephemeral. All of us have thoughts, daydreams, and feelings which are fleeting, and which, like butterflies, disappear if not immediately netted. This is true even of new ideas for which one is searching; so that it is not surprising that it is especially the case with ideas which are unwelcome; discoveries which demonstrate that the subject is less admirable than he had previously supposed.

Many people, when not actively engaged in an external task, seem preoccupied with an internal stream of thoughts not unlike Molly Bloom's monologue at the end of *Ulysses*. Such a monologue reveals their emotional preoccupations, but is exceedingly difficult to capture, as anyone who has tried to copy Joyce's extraordinary achievement will find. Nevertheless, the patient in psychotherapy, if both relaxed and honest, will find that he becomes aware of many thoughts and feelings which influence his behaviour and attitudes to other people, but which he has never looked at closely. For example, it is not uncommon among men that their first thought on meeting another man is to wonder about the other's bank balance, or how successful he is with women. Such a patient may be very reluctant to admit that either money or competitiveness plays such a large part in his life until he finds himself examining these fleeting, quickly suppressed, thoughts. Many heterosexual men have sexual fantasies about every woman they encounter, but may be quite unaware of this until the psychotherapeutic situation encourages them to spell out their inner thoughts. The person who said: 'How do I know what I think until I hear what I say?' was posing a question which is relevant to most of us.

Putting things into words has another function. It means we can to an extent detach ourselves both from the world about us and from the inner world of our own emotions and thoughts. We can objectify, stand back from our experience and reflect upon it. Talking about oneself creates a psychical distance from the self, without which neither understanding nor control, nor willed deliberate change, is possible. It is true that when one embarks upon self-observation, one enters upon an infinite regress. I may observe myself, but I cannot observe the 'I' which is the observer; or, if I succeed in doing that, am precluded from observing the 'I' which observes the 'I' which observes ... and so on *ad infinitum*. But the fact that we can never observe the whole of ourselves need not prevent us from scrutinizing what we can with accuracy. I may not be able to see my own back; but I can get a good idea of it with the help of a mirror, or by comparison with someone like myself. One of the functions of the therapist is to provide that mirror, and to model the possibility of that empathic comparison.

The act of verbalization makes possible critical appraisal. If one can talk about an emotion, one is, at least at that moment, no longer possessed by it. To say '*that* is what I am feeling' is to be separated, however slightly, from that painful feeling. Instead of being at the mercy of an emotion, one begins to achieve some power over it. This does not mean that, by putting an emotion into words, one rids oneself of it; nor would one necessarily want to do so. But the act of talking *about* something that one is feeling, rather than simply feeling, is the first step toward control. A central aim of therapy is to foster this self-scrutinizing, monitoring, regulating part of the self, and to begin to see that one's feelings are just that – feelings – and do not necessarily represent the only possible truth or exclusive way of looking at things. The clumsy terms 'mentalising' and 'mentalisation' (Allen and Fonagy 2006; Holmes 2010) attempt to capture this aspect of the mind. Neurobiology suggests that in depression this 'cortical' regulatory process is in abeyance, which means that primitive emotions arising in the 'lower' centres – pain, panic rage – rule the mind. As normality is restored in the course of therapy, so the neo-cortex regains control (Holmes 2012d)

Unwanted aspects of the self

That is why it is helpful to put into words even unwanted or repudiated aspects of the self. Recognition of 'that is how I really am' creates a new order in the mind in which reality takes the place of fantasy. Suppose, for example, a man who has hitherto thought himself to be particularly kind and peace-loving discovers that he has an aggressive side to his character which he has never previously admitted, i.e. is using the defence mechanism of 'reaction formation' (A. Freud 1936). The discovery may not banish his aggression; but it will tend to modify his expression of it because becoming conscious of a tendency brings it more within the range of control. People who are unconscious of how aggressive they are may be over-critical 'without meaning to be'; they are too severe with their children; with friends they make hurtful asides, or denigratory jokes. When they become fully aware of the aggressive side, such unintended manifestations tend to diminish. Similarly, a woman who prides herself on her independence may through therapy discover that there is a part of herself that longs to be looked after and loved; by acquainting herself with that dependent aspect she can perhaps be less afraid of it, and allow herself to enter into relationships without feeling so threatened by the feelings they arouse in her.

Those who are both articulate and honest may therefore gain a good deal from talking about themselves and their problems at length, even if the psychotherapist makes only minimal interventions. This must be a comforting reflection for the inexperienced psychotherapist, who may feel that she does not know enough to make confident interpretations. She may rest assured that she is doing something valuable by simply being there and providing a situation in which such talk is possible.

The rule is: the therapist should always be in control – in the sense that she manages the boundaries of time and place – but is never *controlling*. We have emphasized the importance of encouraging the patient to take the lead. Most therapists will say nothing or nothing specific, at the start of a session. To ask 'how was your week?' or 'you were talking about your father last week, do you want to go on with that?' or 'you are looking a lot less depressed today', however well-meant, may pre-empt whatever the patient might be thinking and feeling, which might well be none of those things. What is going on just beneath the surface of the patient's mind right now is always the most important theme to pursue.

As discussed in the previous chapter, there are some patients who do find it very difficult to get going, and for whom the therapist's silence is oppressive or persecutory. Such people may need a little encouragement, ranging from a mere 'Hmmm…' to 'maybe you are wondering where to start today' or 'I get the feeling you might be longing for me to say something, or to ask you a question…'.

The hazards of giving advice

Most psychotherapists come to therapy via other professions. Many of us are used to sorting out problems, giving advice, trying to find solutions, and may feel an internal pressure (which may derive from our own needs or reflect those unconsciously 'put into' us by the patient) to do so. But the best policy is not to do something, but just sit there!

It is important that the therapist refrain from giving advice, although she may not be able to avoid doing this entirely. There are several reasons for this. First, it usually doesn't work! Jung once said: 'Good advice is often a doubtful remedy, but generally not dangerous since it has so little effect'. Second, patients seeking psychotherapy usually have problems to which there are no definite answers. If you go to a doctor with a pain and she says, 'You have appendicitis; this is what you should do', that is perfectly reasonable. But if you go to a psychotherapist and you are in doubt as to whether or not to get married, or want to know how to bring up a child, whether to take a particular job, or how to treat your aged mother, you are asking questions to which there are no hard and fast answers, and which may involve moral considerations about which there might be considerable disagreement. The psychotherapist's job is to help the patient to make up his own mind through discovering what he himself thinks and feels. This entails looking at the underlying developmental issues which may be expressing themselves in a current dilemma. To give a simple example, someone who is uncertain about accepting a job might be frightened of a) their competitiveness, b) 'fear of success', or c) the envy that such success might arose in others, all of which may be residues of sibling rivalry from childhood.

Another reason for not giving advice is that giving it is disempowering. Of course we all need help in fields in which we are not expert. We are generally content to accept expert advice in technical matters of which we know little or nothing. But even here, solving one's own problems is always more satisfying that relying on someone else:

> One of JH's most helpful 'experts' was a cycle-shop owner, who, when approached, say, with a faulty deraileur gear, instead of doing the job and collecting the fee, would give a five-minute seminar on what needed to be done, supply the necessary part, and tell his customer to come back for help if things didn't work out. This was rarely necessary, and gave even the mechanically incompetent JH a feeling of achievement!

Giving advice in matters which are not merely technical may seem patronizing, and tends to reinforce the patient's sense of low self-esteem and ineffectualness. The root cause of difficulty in making up one's mind is often low self-esteem. People who feel OK about themselves know that whatever course of action they take things will probably turn out alright. Their happiness does not pivot on making the 'right' decision, whereas those with low self-worth erroneously believe that only one course of action will lead to success. They therefore agonize over each and every choice. Therapy needs to home in on the problem of self-esteem. The purpose of therapy is to help people's self-understanding, and to feel better about themselves. Once that is achieved they are more likely to make good, or at least not self-defeating choices in life.

The problems that a patient brings to a psychotherapist are problems to do with living which we all have to face and which cannot be studied and mastered in the way in which electrical circuits or accountancy or law can. The psychotherapist is no more an expert at living than anyone else. Her expertise lies in making relationships with troubled people, in understanding them, and in facilitating development so that they become more confident in dealing with their own problems in living. The reluctance to give advice is intrinsically therapeutic, in that it carries the implication that, once problems are more clearly understood, the patient will be fully capable of making his own decisions.

Interpretation

Our aim in this book is to describe as best we can what it is that psychotherapists actually *do*. This is no easy task, because most psychotherapy goes on behind closed doors, and however honest one tries to be, it is impossible to give a completely accurate account of what goes on verbally, non-verbally, emotionally, and intellectually, in a psychotherapy session. Some pioneering therapists and their patients have audio and video-taped their work (Malan and Della Selva 2006), but even these accounts do not necessarily represent everyday reality, since the presence of the camera means that therapists are on their best behaviour, and patients who are prepared to expose themselves in this way are likely to be atypical.

What do therapists do?

What would the proverbial fly-on-the-wall see and hear were they to observe therapists as they go about their daily tasks? Would they be able to differentiate psychoanalysts from counsellors, Lacanians from Jungians, beginners from senior therapists, effective therapists from those who are less successful? These are important research questions, mostly beyond the scope of this book (Lambert 2004). Nevertheless two general points can be made. First, therapists engage in a number of disparate tasks: engagement, making a contract, putting patients at their ease, encouraging them to talk, helping to overcome initial resistances, and, above all, attentively and empathically listening. Second, if we look in detail at the content of therapeutic conversations (Goldfried *et al* 1998), we find there is a range of different actions and 'interventions' made by therapists. These include: asking questions, eliciting clarifications, offering encouragement and validation, praising, telling jokes, challenging, making summarizing remarks, giving advice (but see previous chapter), and above all, from the point of view of the dynamic therapist, making interpretations.

What exactly does it mean to 'make an interpretation'? The dictionary definition of interpretation (OED) mentions three aspects, all of which are relevant to psychotherapy: finding meaning; translating; and explaining. Freud considered *The Interpretation of Dreams*, published in 1900, his most important work. In it he sets out the method he devised to 'interpret' them, i.e. to *find meaning* in their seemingly bizarre and arbitrary content. Similarly he saw the task with patients suffering from 'hysteria' (which we now see in terms of somatization disorders, 'hyperactivation, or BPD see Chapter 12) as *translating* the language of the body – pain, weakness, disability etc – into the language of the mind – anxiety, anger, desire. Third, the therapist may offer an *explanation* to the patient for some troubling life-pattern or symptom. For example, suggesting that the reason someone finds it difficult to become involved in intimate relationships links to a childhood in which his parents separated, which means that he habitually holds back from full commitment in order to avoid the anticipated pain of yet another loss.

The idea of making interpretations may seem daunting to beginners, who feel that until they have become fluent in the language of psychoanalytic theory they will be ill-equipped to make the translations needed to help the patient. In fact we are always making 'interpretations' in the sense of finding meaning in, and building a coherent story out of, everyday occurrences.

Why did so-and-so ring out of the blue like that? Perhaps she was not feeling too good, or wanted to remind us that her birthday was coming up. Why did I forget to take my purse to the supermarket? Perhaps I was so distracted by the dog needing to go to the vet that I forgot. Or perhaps I was worried about my overdraft and was trying to remind myself to go easy on purchases. Why was my sister a bit 'off' when I spoke to her? Perhaps I was going on too much about my daughter's brilliant exam results, etc.

In her work the therapist naturally draws on this folk-knowledge of how human beings behave. An 'interpretation' can be something very simple and empathic.

'Active passivity'

AS tells the story of one of his teachers who once saw a patient over a period of about a year. The man came three times a week, took his place on the analytic couch, and, at every session, plunged straight into 'free association'. At the end of the year, the patient pronounced himself cured and offered his deepest thanks to the analyst. The latter asserted that, during the whole of this period, he himself said nothing whatever.

Although it is possible that the analyst may have slightly underestimated his own verbal participation, this story is not as incredible as it might appear, and reminds us interpretation emerges against a background of reticence on the therapist's part. It is as important to be able to hold back from intervening, as it is to make a 'correct' interpretation.

The inexperienced psychotherapist is not only anxious about what she should say to a patient, but may find it hard to remain in a state of 'active listening'. It is also true that too much silence on the part of the therapist may be experienced as persecutory. In ordinary social interchange, we seldom tolerate silence for long and, if we cannot think of anything interesting to say, take refuge in banalities about the weather. A patient's silence may indicate that there is something which he is reluctant to talk about, or is finding it difficult to put thoughts and feelings into words.

When a patient who has previously been talking freely becomes 'stuck', a useful device is the 'Rogerian' (Carl Rogers 1951) tactic of taking up and repeating the end of the patient's last sentence. This is done with an interrogatory tone which suggests that she knows that there is more to come and is anxious to hear what that might be.

Patient: *'And then I changed schools . . . . .' (pause).*

Therapist: *'You changed schools?'*

Patient: *'Yes . . . I changed schools . . . . .' (long pause).*

Therapist: *(after appropriate long wait) 'It sounds as if you may be remembering something about that change which is important, but perhaps difficult to talk about?'*

Patient: *'That's true. I don't know why, but I found myself thinking about a particular boy . . . He used to make models in Plasticine. One day he made a little figure of a man, and stuck on it a penis. It made the other boys laugh, but I was very embarrassed.'*

Therapist: *'Perhaps that embarrassment is still there somehow, and that's why you paused for so long.'*

This last sentence of the therapist might be called an interpretation, though that is to give a big name to the everyday therapeutic task of helping a patient to make sense of his difficulty in talking.

Interpretation

Making interpretations is only a component of the therapist's task; some would say his most important task; but the phrase has acquired a grandiose ring which is sometimes taken to imply that only those who have been initiated into the esoteric mysteries of the unconscious are entitled to embark upon it. Psychoanalytic interpretations may, in some instances, be based on assumptions about psychopathology which are familiar to the experienced psychotherapist but which may be obscure to the uninitiated. For example, Kleinian interpretations about 'internal objects', or Jungian interpretations about 'animus' and 'anima' might be fairly incomprehensible to someone who is just embarking upon her first psychotherapeutic case, and who has not yet had time or inclination to read much analytic literature. Let her take comfort from the fact that such interpretations will also be incomprehensible to most patients, and, even if accurate, would have to be rephrased into everyday language. One of the skills of the successful therapist is always to adjust their vocabulary and style of discourse to that of the patient.

Therapists who know each other, especially if they belong to the same 'school', tend to use jargon as shorthand in talking between themselves, just as do specialists in any field, from insurance to nuclear physics. This can be unnerving to the beginner, and has the effect (not entirely unintended) of making her feel an outsider and inferior. (On JH's first day at medical school a patient was presented whose report read 'MSU NAD'. 'What is MSU NAD?' JH shyly enquired. 'Oh what *bliss* not to know what those detestable acronyms mean', replied the consultant. (MSU = midstream urine; NAD = nothing abnormal detected)).

If teachers of psychotherapy start using incomprehensible jargon, the latter should be encouraged to challenge them to say exactly what they mean in straightforward language. Jargon may be convenient shorthand, but is often misused to lend an air of spurious profundity to quite ordinary observations.

Meaning making

The kinds of interpretations which can be made after only a short period of training can be divided into three main varieties. First, part of the therapist's job is to make the incomprehensible comprehensible. Most patients seeking psychotherapy suffer from symptoms which do not make sense to them, and which therefore seem more menacing than they need. To be afflicted with agoraphobia, or obsessional thoughts of violence, or an unacceptably 'perverse' sexual preoccupation, may make a person fear that he may be 'mad'; or that, if not actually mad, he is grossly different from the rest of humanity. To find that such symptoms are familiar to the psychotherapist, and cause him no particular alarm, is itself a relief. Further relief follows if the therapist is able to provide some seemingly reasonable explanation of their origin. Thus, in the course of only a few interviews, the therapist might be able to make 'interpretations' about a patient's agoraphobia.

> 'It sounds, from what you say, as if when you were a small child, your mother was so anxious about your going out alone that she made the world seem a frightening place. Most children gain more confidence as they get older, and can venture further and further independently. The interesting thing about your fear is that it has persisted, and that is something we need to try to understand.'

There are, of course, other contributory factors to agoraphobia, and other explanations of its origin; but even so simple and obvious an explanation as the one given not only relieves some of the patient's fear of the incomprehensible, but goes some way towards an explanation: it appears that, as a small child, he was over-protected. In this type of interpretation the therapist brings a developmental context to bear on the presenting symptoms, which begins to make sense when seen in terms of the persistence of childhood thoughts and feelings into the present.

Another young woman living with her parents suffered from the obsessional fear that if she mentioned certain words like 'cancer' or 'death', members of her family might contract a fatal illness. An inhibited and compliant child, it emerged as her history unfolded that she had felt her mother to be overbearing and controlling and that her older sister always grabbed the limelight. She had never been able to express any resentment or protest; for instance when her sister had been allocated a much, in her eyes, bigger and better room in the family house. Her symptoms had started when she began a new job with a very bossy superior. Suggesting that her obsessional worries might represent 'split-off' aggression that she had habitually suppressed, and that there might be a residue of anger towards her mother, sister and now her boss, struck a chord. Her worries persisted to some extent, but it helped her to feel less 'odd'.

Here the developmental story is linked to the idea that the mind is not a unitary phenomenon but a series of 'compartments' – or 'modules' (Panksepp 2004) – and that psychic health entails increasing one's awareness of these disparate aspects and working towards a more coherent self.

Making the incomprehensible comprehensible seldom abolishes symptoms, but relieves the patient's anxieties about his sanity; and helps to convert them from a shadowy, unknown adversary into a more clearly identified problem which can be worked on. Thus, someone with agoraphobic symptoms begins to tackle the whole area of dependency; while the obsessional sufferer sees that if she could begin to stand up for herself more – better able to say boo to a goose – she might be less plagued with compulsive thoughts of violence.

Interpretation is essentially about pattern-recognition. Training in psychotherapy familiarizes the student with the regular patterns formed by the varieties of psychological illness, and also of normal and sub-optimal developmental pathways. The more familiar one is with these, the easier it is to trace connections between events, symptoms, and personality characteristics. Different schools of psychotherapy differ in their theoretical superstructures, but most agree that for both genetic and environmental reasons, the child is father to the man.

Pattern detection

It is important to acknowledge that interpretations are necessarily and inevitably incomplete. As the literary critic Eagleton (see Holmes 2010) puts it, 'language is what there is always more of', and the same applies to interpretations. When one embarks upon understanding a symptom, one never knows how far this may lead. Why was the obsessional patient so submissive? Had she had parents of whom she was frightened; or had she been brought up in a Christian household in which turning the other cheek was the only legitimate response? Had she latched onto a chance occurrence, such as the death of a pet when she had neglected to clean its cage, and built her fears around that? A single symptom is like a stone causing ripples in the pond of the personality, of which the 'cause' may have long since sunk beneath the surface, but which leaves traces which spread out indefinitely.

Many behaviour patterns which were adopted in childhood may have been appropriate at the time, or indeed the only possible forms of adaptation. Some persist inappropriately into adult life, and it is helpful to think of the personality as comprising layers in which earlier phases are not so much obliterated as overlaid as development proceeds. Earlier reactions can be triggered, especially by traumatic events. We can all revert to the state of a frightened child when faced with a major unexpected threat. Interpretation reveals the way in which the past persists in the present, and can help the patient to begin to experiment with other ways of behaving.

Patients who have been 'strictly' brought up, over-dominated by parents, may remain obedient followers in situations in which leadership is demanded of them. Moreover, they may rationalize their lack of initiative in terms of consideration for other people's feelings, when the truth is that they are still behaving like frightened children. Being able to stand apart and see oneself from the outside is one of the key skills or 'gifts' that psychotherapy can bring to a person's armamentarium for successful living. But for psychological change to occur, 'experiments' (a term used by CBT therapists, but applicable equally to psychodynamic therapy), or new ways of behaving, need to be tried out in everyday life, starting in relation to the therapist.

> One patient was in a dilemma about taking antidepressants. She found it very difficult to make decisions for herself, and tried to push the therapist – who was medically qualified – into deciding for her, which she initially resisted. At the end of one session, exasperated by the patient's indecisiveness, the therapist found herself insisting that she stop vacillating, and give them a try.
>
> The patient returned the following week, admitting that she still hadn't been able to bring herself to start them. Her demeanour seemed shamefaced and guilty. The therapist pointed this out. 'Oh I thought you'd be really cross with me' she replied. The therapist then interpreted a possible parallel between the feeling that she had to please the therapist, that she would be annoyed if she didn't take her pills, and the way she and her mother related.
>
> The patient expanded: mother was her best friend, but yes, she could be demanding and difficult at times, and if crossed she would sulk. Then the patient would feel utterly wretched and abandoned, and would feel compelled to break the ice and say she was sorry. The patient's unexpressed resentment about this had played itself out in her relationship with her therapist. She didn't want to take pills; felt she was being pressurized to do so; and felt annoyed and undermined about this. For her to benefit from therapy (antidepressants aside) she would need to be able to express disagreement and resentment without feeling it would lead to rejection.

We see here how the therapist is alert to patterns of interpersonal relating, including with herself. Submissiveness, unexpressed resentment, and fear of upsetting others characterized the patient's relationship with her mother and now the therapist. 'Malan's triangles', (Malan and Della Selva 2006), describe how these three-way patterns can be observed and interpreted, making links between the present (the antidepressant dilemma), the therapist, and the past relationship with parents.

Unexpressed feelings

In addition to making the incomprehensible comprehensible, and finding developmental patterns, a third type of interpretation focuses on unexpressed feelings. The therapist points out discrepancies between what a patient says he feels, and what his behaviour – as described, or manifest in the session – indicates that he actually does feel. A patient might say that he is very fond of his wife, but his account of his marriage suggests that he habitually neglects her wishes, forgets what she tells him, or disparages her in front of others. There is an obvious mismatch between what the patient says that he feels toward her and what his behaviour indicates.

Not all interpretations of such discrepancies are negative, in the sense of revealing harsh truths about himself which the patient is avoiding. Many patients entering psychotherapy undervalue themselves, and are much nicer or more intelligent than they perceive themselves to be. A timid patient may be bolder than he gives himself credit for; or a patient concerned about hostile feelings be kinder than he realizes. If one reads Freud, one is apt to come away with the idea that all interpretation is bound to be of the kind which reveals unpleasant aspects of character which the patient has failed to recognize in himself. But although we are all apt to deceive ourselves, we do so in both directions; in overestimation not just of our virtues but also our supposed bad qualities.

How to 'give' an interpretation

Interpretations should not be dogmatically phrased or delivered in an authoritarian tone. There is no point in making interpretations which do not win the patient's assent or make sense to him; they are best seen as 'hypotheses' offered for the patient's consideration, partial acceptance, elaboration or rejection. The patient is ultimately the expert on him- or herself, the therapist always an adjunct, facilitator or midwife to the patient's self-understanding, never a font or oracle (although the patient may, for transferential reasons, wish to push the therapist into that role, and therapy will involve a gradual dismantling of that fantasy). Most therapists offer their interpretations with some tentative beginning as: 'It sounds rather as if...', or 'Perhaps...', 'Maybe...', 'It occurs to me that...'. If the patient finds the suggested interpretation illuminating, the fact that it has been phrased undogmatically will not diminish its effect: while, if he does not agree, lack of dogmatism makes it easier for him to say so. Freud (1911–15) states that interpretations should be aimed at a point just beyond where the patient's self-understanding has taken them; if either too far ahead, or adding nothing to what the patient already knows, they are unlikely to be of much value.

The term 'interpretation' can sound rather threatening. It carries with it the implication of a special expertize in puncturing patients' self-deceptions. In the lay mind, therapists are conceived of as being able to penetrate beyond appearances, people who never take things at face value, who read hidden significance into the most trivial utterance or event – which can lead to social embarrassment when therapists disclose their profession! Of course there is a sense in which this is true, in that prolonged practice in observation of others does mean one can make connections between overt utterance and underlying preoccupations which are not obvious to those who are unused or unwilling to think this way. But this is not to say that interpretation must always penetrate the mysterious depths of the psyche. The truth is often simple and obvious; our blind spots mean that we often fail to notice it, especially if doing so brings mental pain.

Inappropriate and absurd interpretations

Psychoanalysts sometimes carry interpretation-making to absurd lengths. For an egregious example of psychobabble, as well as transgression of the rule that should apply in all therapists' families: 'no interpretations except in the consulting room', take R. D. Laing's book about his children (1977), *Conversations with Adam and Natasha*. He discusses an occasion in which seven-year-old Natasha asks the question 'Can God kill himself?' One of Laing's friends who is called Monty, and who is also presumably an analyst, is told of this question of Natasha's. His comment is as follows. 'There is an incredibly close relationship between sex and death. I will tell you what the question is saying. She is asking "Does God masturbate?" ' Laing responds; 'And that is "Does daddy masturbate?" ' Monty goes on: 'Precisely. She wishes to know whether she can do it with you instead of mummy'. Does Natasha really wish to know any such thing? It seems unlikely. Laing records that his children were brought up to believe in God and to say their prayers. Monty's assumption that Natasha's question refers to her father when she speaks of God underestimates both her intelligence and the circumstances of her upbringing. While there may be a tenuous psychological connection between the experience of orgasm (the 'little death') and the idea of death, there is no reason to suppose that Natasha was confusing the two when she raises what, if she believes in God, and has a father who is a psychiatrist and therefore deals with suicidal people, is actually an interesting problem, namely 'did Jesus invite his own death?'

Psychoanalytic literature abounds with interpretations which are no less absurd. In his book on Leonardo, for example, K. R. Eissler (1962) confidently asserts that Leonardo's interest in drawing and shifting patterns made by water originated from his having been a bed-wetter in early childhood. There is no evidence that Leonardo was in fact enuretic; nor do we know what was the contemporary attitude to bed-wetting in fifteenth-century Italy.

Such interpretations derive from the assumption that anything which deeply engages human interest must derive from primitive bodily sources. This can be thought of in two distinct ways. The first, traditional, psychoanalytic approaches assume that primitive bodily satisfactions, especially if sexual or quasi-sexual, are so unacceptable that they are invariably concealed by various mental manoeuvres such as sublimation. Take Ernest Jones' (1957) statement about the arts: 'when one considers the material used in the five arts – paint, clay, stone, words, and sounds – any psychologist must conclude that the passionate interest in bringing an orderliness out of the chaos must signify at the same time an extraordinary sublimation of the most primitive infantile enjoyments and the most extreme denial of them'.

This 'classical' view has been superseded for two reasons. First, it is not so much that primitive drives are unacceptable and must be repressed, but, rather, that some feelings or affects are so painful that, rather than being felt directly, they need the help of an intimate other – such as a therapist – in order to bear them. Sometimes the act of artistic creation may fulfil the function of a surrogate other and therefore be a way of exploring feelings 'alone in the presence of one's medium', to paraphrase Winnicott (1971) (Holmes 2012b). Second, the antithesis between primitive bodily drives and sublimated refined adult creation is a false one. Our complex sophisticated 'adult' activity grows out of bodily experience, and great art is able to resonate at many levels within the psyche. Many of the metaphors used both by artists and patients in therapy derive from the body. A simple example is that of equating depression with being 'down' or 'blue' (a 'cold' colour), and happiness with feeling 'up' or 'elevated' (Lakoff and Johnson 1980). It does not follow that every utterance, every interest, or every piece of behaviour is not what it seems, or is a concealment. As we shall see, this is not even true of dreams, as Freud supposed. Although dreams may certainly require interpretation if we are to understand them, this is because they are couched in symbolic and pictorial 'language' rather than in words, not because they have been deliberately scrambled by the forces of repression.

It should be remembered that, at the time Freud was writing, concealment was much more in evidence than it is today. Indeed, it is largely on account of Freud's work that we are much more prepared than were the inhabitants of *fin-de-siècle* Vienna to accept that beneath the veneer of civilization we all have aggressive and sexual impulses. It should also be recalled that many of Freud's early patients were women, suffering from rather gross forms of both amnesic and conversion hysteria of a kind which today are seldom encountered. These are the kind of patients who, more than any other, tend to conceal their true nature from themselves, which is why they sometimes seem false in their interaction with others. Freud's discovery that piercing the veil of concealment could often abolish hysterical symptoms led him to over-generalize from this defensive style to other types of disorder, and to the assumption that interpretation must always aim at undoing such self-alienation.

The therapist's implicit ideology

Making sense of the patient's symptoms and discourse depends upon the therapist's assumptions about life and the nature of what it is to be human. No one can escape from the influence of her time and culture; no doubt future generations, better informed than we are about psychology and biology, will scoff at some of our formulations. Moreover, the theoretical tenets of the various analytical schools undoubtedly influence the type of explanatory interpretation offered. A Kleinian therapist, whose understanding of human beings rests upon the assumed vicissitudes of the infant at the breast, will trace the origin of symptoms to that phase of the infant's development (Waddell 1998). The Jungian analyst will be alert to compensatory patterns and archetypal phenomena (Storr 1973); a Winnicottian will be alert to failures of maternal mirroring (Winicott 1971); an attachment-oriented one to patterns of insecure attachment and how they manifest themselves in the relationship with the therapist (Holmes 2010); and so on.

This does not matter nearly so much as one might suppose. Many of the difficulties which arise in communications are semantic rather than real. For example, there are analogies to be found between Jung's notion of archetypes and Melanie Klein's 'internal objects'. Wallerstein (1990) argues that whatever the theoretical differences, at a clinical level there is much 'common ground' between different schools. Most psychotherapists would agree, for example, that people suffering from profound psychological disturbance such as that seen in Borderline Personality Disorder (see Chapter 12), experience the dilemma that if they allow themselves to get close to people, this is somehow dangerous; while if they remain remote, they experience intolerable isolation. The origin of this dilemma might be in dispute. Some would maintain that the patient was more frightened of the harm he might do to other people (a 'Kleinian' view) than of the damage that they might inflict on him (a more Attachment model). But all would agree that both types of fear enter into the patient's search for a relationship that is both safe and intimate.

Summarizing our discussion so far: although there is much more to therapy than interpretation, it remains a cornerstone of the dynamic psychotherapist's work. Interpretations have three main functions: making the incomprehensible comprehensible, which is inherently anxiety-relieving; pointing out recurrent self-defeating patterns in the patient's life, a first step towards changing them; and helping sufferers to get in touch with painful feelings hitherto avoided or defended against, which strengthens and deepens a person's emotional integrity and coherence.

Interpretation dos and don'ts

We are still left with the problem of *what* to say, *when*, and *how*, as we sit with real live patients. We end the chapter with a non-systematic list of some practical aspects of interpretation-making.

- Interpretations need not necessarily be complex, and are best delivered in a brief pithy way. As one colleague put it 'interpretations should be tabloid headlines, not broadsheet editorials!' Often a single word or phrase is all that the patient takes away from an interpretation:
    One patient presented with recurrent relationship difficulties in which, whenever emotional closeness threatened, he tended to walk away. His mother had been

seriously ill during his second and third year of life when he had been farmed out to various aunts. In one session he announced that he had decided that dynamic therapy was no use to him and that he was thinking of trying another approach. The therapist interpreted: 'Ah, now it is therapy that you are dumping. It seems that you dump everyone and everything you love, just as you yourself felt dumped as a small child'.

This could be seen as a 'complete interpretation' (Strachey 1934) in that it brought together the present (girlfriends), the relationship with the therapist (transference), and past, all in one concept: dumping. Later the patient revealed that the word 'dump' had really struck home, and stayed with him.

- Interpretations are best seen as hypotheses for the patient to consider, rather than *ex cathedra* truths to which only the therapist is privy.
- Interpretations should be used sparingly; 'when in doubt, don't'. Reticence, holding back, tolerating silence, or simple non-interpretive reflection and empathy are the essential preconditions for making effective interpretations.
- The therapist must be guided by her feelings. If there is a strong image or thought or response emerging in her own internal free associations in the course of a particular session, it is important for her to find some way to put it into words and communicate it to the patient.
- Interpretations should be made in everyday non-jargonistic language.
- Wherever possible the analyst should pick up on the images and metaphors of the patient and expand on them. A patient might say at the start of session: 'I really hate this dark dreary damp Devon weather'. An interpretation might be: 'I wonder if that muddy murky feeling is a bit how it was as a child when your mother suffered from one of her depressive bouts'.
- Interpretations are best confined to the middle third of a session. The first 15 minutes or so should be confined to listening and helping the patient to clarify and expand on whatever they choose to talk about. Throwing in an interpretation near the end of a session is tempting, especially if one feels that not much has been achieved that day, but it may leave the patient feeling nonplussed, and is best postponed until the next meeting.
- Since making interpretations depends on picking up on patterns and/or below-the-surface possibilities, the therapist needs not to get too bogged down in the minutiae of what the patient is saying. This is Freud's 'evenly suspended attention' (Freud 1911–1915) or 'listening with the third ear' (Reik 1948). Casement (1985) advises responding to the overall tone and tenor of what the patient is saying rather than the specific content: 'I seem to be hearing a story about ... how you feel no one has ever really listened to you, myself included', or '... I hear a story about someone who is making a huge effort and feeling they're getting nowhere' etc.
- The therapist should be alert to puns, double meanings, and innuendos. Freud (1911–1915) called these 'switch words', entrees from the conscious surface of discourse to a parallel unconscious one. A Shakespeare-aware patient, who has being trying to find a boyfriend through a lonely-hearts agency, might for example say 'today's date is the Ides of March'; the interpretation might be 'Hmmm ... I wonder how this week's 'date' turned out'.
- It is not necessary to have extensive knowledge of psychoanalytic theory in order to make interpretations. Sometimes an interpretation is no more than a simple observation: 'you looked a bit sad when you were talking about that programme on TV last night. I wonder what that stirred up for you... '.
- Some interpretations are pretty challenging. The therapist may want to help the sufferer to see that, rather than blaming those round him, he himself is responsible for some of

the misery he experiences. That is going to be difficult and painful. One way round that is to use the 'interpretation sandwich'. This means wrapping up an unpalatable truth in something that will defuse the inevitable defences that spring up when one feels judged or criticized. An example might be: 'given that you are so intelligent and such a devoted mother, it is strange that you seem to be so bad at looking after yourself, and tend to choose the most unsuitable men to go to bed with ... I wonder if we can try to work out why that might be...'.

- Finally, as Strachey noted (1934), giving interpretations is far from easy, and the therapist often feels a certain resistance or reluctance to disrupt the patient's fragile equilibrium. But, as Freud (1905) remarked, one cannot make an omelette without breaking eggs. Therapists need not be afraid of their own 'aggression', and to see, if harnessed in the service of cure, a certain freedom and assertiveness is vital and necessary. That means overcoming resistances in oneself, which in turn is one of the many reasons why personal therapy for therapists is so important (see Chapter 14).

Dreams, Daydreams and Creativity

Dreams, as Freud (1900) famously formulated, are the 'royal road' to the unconscious. The great value of dreams is that they are uncontaminated by the normal processes of shaping and manipulation by which conscious thoughts and utterances are tailored so as not to disrupt ourselves and those around us. Dreams are 'innocent' (Rycroft 1979) in ways that are impossible for the conscious mind.

Freud dissected the dream into two main ingredients: a) the 'day's residue' – some psychologically meaningful event in the preceding 24 hours – and b) a fundamental psychological preoccupation, activated by (a). The dream is thus a probe into the unconscious, and if patient and therapist together can put it under the analytic microscope there is invariably much to be learnt. It will point to the fundamental constellations of the patient's psyche, as well as often unnoticed or unconscious reactions to what is currently happening.

Patients generally know that therapists are interested in dreams. It is therefore unsurprising that in the course of her work, the psychotherapist is likely to be 'offered' a dream by the patient, for consideration and comment. Interpreting dreams is sometimes seen as an esoteric skill possessed only by those with long experience and training, so beginners often shy away from dreams as being beyond their competence. This is a pity; although not all dreams are revealing or helpful, many are both. If the therapist is prepared to tackle them, she and the patient will find within them truths that are immensely illuminating.

The first dream

Should the patient be explicitly asked for dreams? Some therapists, who adhere closely to the rule that the patient should always take the lead without prompting, say that one should never interfere with the patient's spontaneity by such an enquiry. Others (in whose camp we find ourselves) think that it is legitimate to ask whether the patient has dreams he would like to discuss, provided that the question is not interrupting the patient's flow of talk, or distracting him from some urgent emotional problem with which he is wrestling.

Indeed it is a good idea to establish in the first few sessions whether the patient remembers his dreams or attaches any significance to them. One way of approaching this is to ask: 'what do you think about while you are asleep?', which has the advantage of suggesting that dreaming is not some outlandish activity, but a continuation of normal thought, albeit in a different mode. The anxiety which accompanies going to see a therapist for the first time may provoke dreams which are remembered, and it is always worth asking a new patient whether he has any dreams which he remembers, and/or whether he had a dream on the night before the first session. For example, the patient might have dreamed that he was:

> Setting out on a journey, became anxious because he thought he was going to miss a train, and finally arrived at his destination only to find that a stationmaster or policeman was waiting for him with an impatient frown.

His attitude to authority in the shape of the therapist will be immediately obvious, and will provide a valuable and instantly revealing topic for discussion.

During the initial taking of a history, one can enquire whether the patient had nightmares or recurrent dreams during childhood. Recurrent dreams seem often to be statements about unsolved problems; and may epitomize a whole series of difficulties. For example, one man recalled that, as a small boy, he had had a recurrent, extremely unpleasant, dream in which

> he was striving, unsuccessfully, to unravel a complicated network in which pieces of string or wool formed an irregular interlacing pattern in which the threads were inextricably tangled.

The dream induced a feeling of impotent helplessness, in which the dreamer felt that no effort on his part could ever be effective in unravelling the knots. Such a dream can be understood in many different ways, and would no doubt be given different meanings by analysts of different schools. But at one level it needs no interpretation at all. It can be taken as a valuable point of departure for enquiring into the patient's childhood. Did he often feel helpless in the way that the dream depicts? If so, why had he become so discouraged? Did this feeling of helplessness apply to life in general, or only to particular aspects of his childhood strivings? Does he ever feel like this today? Such a recurrent dream usually leaves behind a vivid affective memory, and its emotional tone, often reproduced as the patient recounts it, opens a window into the inner world of the patient's feelings.

Some people claim not to remember their dreams. This should not be taken in any way as a sign of pathology and the therapist will need to find other means of access to the patient's unconscious. It is sometimes an indication of an imagination which has yet to be developed, and some will, as therapy proceeds, suddenly arrive with a vivid dream, or, as in one case, find themselves, as their chronic depression lifted, dreaming in 'technicolour' rather than black-and-white as previously. With the 'non-rememberers', confident that in fact everyone dreams (in the sense that they have REM periods in their sleep) and that the issue is one of recall, it can sometimes be helpful to nudge them: 'if you were to dream what might it be about … ?', or 'do you tend to dream about things or people … '? This may produce the unexpected response 'Ah, now you come to mention it, I *did* have an odd dream only last week…'.

The latter being an example of the 'how often do you beat your wife' interview style (apologies for sexist implications). If you ask a man 'do you beat your wife?' they will probably say 'no, of course not'; but when asked 'how often do you beat your wife?' the answer may be 'well, only twice a week'!

It is also valuable to ask for dreams when a patient who is in regular treatment comes to a session and announces that he has 'nothing to say'. Very often a dream recalled in such circumstances contains some indication of the problem which is blocking the flow of the patient's thoughts and discourse. Perhaps it is some intimate fact about himself that he has been too ashamed to reveal. Perhaps it is something which he has felt toward the therapist but which he has not realized or been able to admit. Dreams are often a useful way of indirectly circumventing an impasse.

Freud v Jung on dreams

There is still no generally accepted theory about the meaning of dreams (Solms and Turnbull 2002; Hobson 2011); but this need not deter us from making practical use of them. Freud was responsible for reviving the idea that dreams were worth taking seriously; and although his original views on dreams have not been confirmed, we owe him a debt for having re-established their importance. Freud believed that dreams represented unfulfilled, and often unacceptable, wishes, most of which referred to instinctual impulses originating in the dreamer's early childhood.

> '. . .we are justified in saying that almost every civilised man retains the infantile forms of sexual life in some respect or other. We can thus understand how it is that repressed infantile sexual wishes provide the most frequent and strongest motive-forces for the construction of dreams.' (Freud 1901).

Such wishes, he believed, did not appear directly in dreams, but are disguised in various ways in order to make them acceptable to the dreamer. Hence the dream required 'interpretation'. What the dreamer himself recalled was only the 'manifest content'; the 'latent content', the true meaning of the dream, could only be discerned after a lengthy process in which the dreamer's associations to all the images in the dream had been subjected to trained analytical scrutiny.

Although most dreams have a bizarre quality of unreality, there is no strong evidence that such 'oddness' is in the service of concealing unacceptable wishes. Freud himself recognized this when considering the dreams of people who have been subjected to some traumatic incident, and who have recurrent dreams in which the incident occurs undisguised. He postulated that this phenomenon might indicate that the dream was an attempt at mastering a disturbing stimulus; a way of looking at dreams which is perhaps more fruitful than his original theory.

Jung took a very different view of dreams. First, he did not consider that dreams were concealments, but rather that they were in essence, a natural form of human expression, using symbol and metaphor. Poetry, for example, is another kind of human utterance in which metaphor and symbol play a predominant role; but we do not think of most poetry as wilfully obscure on that account. Second, Jung believed that many kinds of things could be found in dreams.

> 'There are, it is true, dreams which manifestly represent wishes or fears; but what about all the other things? Dreams may contain ineluctable truths, philosophical pronouncements, illusions, wild phantasies, memories, plans, anticipations, irrational experiences, even telepathic visions, and heaven knows what besides.' (Jung 1954)

Third, Jung supposed that the psyche was self-regulating in the same way as the body is a homeostatic system – i.e. tending towards a state of equilibrium or balance. In this systemic view of the mind he was ahead of his time. The conscious and unconscious parts of the mind are conceived as being in reciprocal relation with one another. It follows from this that dreams, considered as emanating from the unconscious, can be considered as compensating for some conscious attitude of mind which is one-sided or extreme. One patient dreamed as a girl of her mother as a hostile and destructive figure, although, in conscious life she had nothing but good to say of her. Jung quotes instances in which men who consciously overestimate their own powers often have dreams indicating that their limit has actually been reached.

Dreams as 'polysemic' communications

Like other metaphoric communications, including poetry, dreams are 'polysemic' – that is they have many meanings, can be responded to at many different levels, and can be interpreted in many different ways. Some dreams certainly can represent wishes, very often of a sexual or ambitious kind, just as do daydreams. Dreams may serve as an outlet for impulses which have been impossible to express, or which are partially unrecognized by the dreamer. Aggressive impulses toward the therapist or toward employers, parents and other authorities are frequent contents of dreams. So are sexual impulses toward people whom the dreamer desires but who, for social or other reasons, are inaccessible. Homosexual dreams may occur in those who are predominantly heterosexual; heterosexual dreams occur in homosexuals. As Jung suggests, dreams do often have a compensatory aspect. Consciousness strives toward making life simple and clear-cut; but there is nearly always another side to any conscious attitude we may profess. Thus, dreams frequently bring out some feeling of liking towards people we had thought we wholly disliked, or *vice versa*. The atheist may discover a religious side to himself; or the scientist that he is not as rational as he had supposed.

Dreams often relate to problems with which the dreamer is struggling, but which he has not yet resolved. If we are faced with a social situation of which we are nervous, we commonly rehearse our behaviour; imagine what the occasion will be like; think of what we might say or how we might appear, and, in general, try to reduce our anxiety by being forearmed for any eventuality. Dreams often seem to bring up problems of which the patient may be only half aware, but to which he is applying anticipatory processing of this kind. This problem-solving aspect of dreaming is illustrated by those dreams of scientists and other creative people in which solutions are found. Hence the oft-quoted example of the chemist Kekule who dreamed of snakes biting their tails and woke with the solution to the problem of the structure of the benzene ring: they are circular molecules. When wrestling with a dilemma, a decision taken in a semi-dream state often seems to be the 'right' one (presumably because addressing both conscious and unconscious aspects), although answers to problems are more often encountered in states of reverie, half-way between sleep and waking; that is, in daydreams rather than in night dreams.

Dream interpretation

Psychotherapists in training may feel alarmed if their patient produces a dream, since they think that the patient will expect them to give an exact, complete interpretation of it. In practice, this seldom, if ever, happens. Patients soon realize that dreams do not have a single unequivocal meaning, but that they are often valuable indicators pointing toward emotional preoccupations to which, perhaps, the patient had not attached sufficient value.

When patients report dreams, the meaning of the dream may at once be obvious to either therapist or patient, or to both. On the other hand, it may be entirely obscure. Either way, it is advisable for the therapist, as always, to hold back. What really matters are the patient's thoughts and feelings about the dream, not the therapist's. So after a dream is reported it is a good idea to leave a 'beat' – a space of silent time. One might then ask, 'what do you make of that … ?', or 'does anything occur to you about any of that … ?' Another useful tactic is to suggest the patient recounts the dream again. Often new images or aspects emerge. Another procedure is to home in on a particular word or image from the dream, saying something like 'I thought that bit where you were underwater and couldn't breathe might be especially important … what do you make of that …?' 'Switch' words are important for the therapist to notice when working on dreams. Thus a trans-sexual man was contemplating having surgery. He dreamed '*I was abroad in a strange country. But somehow I could understand the language*'. The dream is self-explanatory; but picking up on 'abroad' = a broad = a woman (US slang) enabled him to start talking about his fears and hopes about becoming female.

Occasionally dreams provide both patient and therapist with experiences of unforgettable depth. These are the 'collective' dreams beloved by Jung and his followers that seem to come from a remote source, beyond anything which the dreamer himself could have consciously imagined. It is often possible to detect mythological themes in such dreams of the kind encountered in fairy stories and folklore. Jung believed that there is a mythological substratum to human experience of which we are not normally aware. When we become caught up in a world of heroic adventure, in which battles are fought between good and evil forces, great deeds accomplished, kingdoms won and lost, sacrifices demanded, high courage manifested, our lives take on a significance not to be found in the common round of getting and spending. Both therapist and patient may find themselves impressed and enthralled by such dreams. There are many examples of this kind of dream to be found in the works of Jung and his followers.

Here is an example, which, quite apart from its possible 'mythological' aspect, illustrates the fact that study of a single dream can raise a great number of important questions about the dreamer's life.

> A man dreamed that he was looking into the window of a shop. Inside was a statuette of a beautiful woman standing upon a square base. Since both the statuette and its base were made of some translucent material, the dreamer could see that there were letters carved upon the underside of the base. He knew that what was written there was the secret of life. But, because the letters were, from his viewpoint, upside down and the wrong way round, he could not read them.

The dream raises many questions. What is the dreamer's relation with women, and what with art? Perhaps women are to him more like works of art than warm human beings; or perhaps he idealizes them and his own feeling toward them? What manner of man is it that seeks 'the secret of life'? Is he one of those people, not infrequent amongst therapists as well as patients, who cherish the idea that there is one system of thought which will provide a complete answer to all of life's problems. Is the dream revealing another, more sceptical aspect of the dreamer's personality which is accepting that the secret of life cannot be wholly grasped or comprehended? Perhaps his whole life has been a futile striving after the impossible, and the dream reflects his despair.

All of this might have been explored during the course of this patient's therapy, even if he had not had this dream. But because it is a spontaneous product of the patient's mind which he has not willed, it leads straight into problems which might not have come to the surface for many weeks. This is an example of a dream that seems to epitomize the dreamer's attitudes and difficulties within a small compass. But we are still far from knowing all there is to know about dreams; so that dogmatic interpretation of them is always inappropriate. At one level, like works of art, dreams must often be allowed to speak for themselves.

Daydreams

Psychotherapists should also take account of daydreams. These are more easily understood since, although largely emotionally determined, consciousness imposes a certain coherence upon them which is lacking in night dreams. Everyone has daydreams, although it is sometimes hard to get people to reveal them. Indeed, it has been stated that all of us have something like a 'B-movie' going on all the time just below the level of our directed awareness; a movie in which we play the leading part or parts. Many people seem to have daydreams of love and/or success and sexual fulfilment; of what it would be like to be very rich, or very beautiful; or Prime Minister; or a great writer or painter; or of how nice it would be to go to bed with the pretty girl or good-looking boy opposite one on the train. In *Childhood, Boyhood, Youth*, Tolstoy (1964) writes:

> 'Let me not be reproached if the daydreams of my adolescence were as puerile as those of my childhood and boyhood. I am convinced that if I am destined to live to extreme old age, and my narrative continues with the years, as an old man

of seventy I shall be found dreaming dreams just as impossible and childish as now. I shall be dreaming of some charming Marya who will fall in love with me, a toothless old man, as she fell in love with Mazeppa, and of how my feeble-minded son suddenly becomes a minister of state, or that all of a sudden I shall find myself possessed of millions. I am convinced that there is no human being and no age devoid of this benign comforting capacity to dream.'

Daydreams, like so many mental productions, are Janus-faced. That is, they may be escapist fantasies; a way of avoiding the tasks and difficulties of real life. Or, on the other hand, they may be rehearsals for future actions, or valuable attempts at finding solutions to problems, a way of discovering where one's real inclinations lie.

Some highly avoidant people can become lost in daydreams, to the detriment of their engagement with the external world. When patients of this kind fail in their studies or work, it is sometimes because the inner world of daydream has become so seductive that they cannot tear themselves away from it to become involved with mundane tasks. Some may have alarming daydreams which make them feel that their minds are becoming out of control, and that they are threatened by insanity; a fear which is not always unjustified, and therefore should be taken seriously by therapists.

The exploration of daydreams is especially important in cases of people with sexual difficulties. People who have been isolated in childhood and adolescence and who have not shared their experience of developing sexual feelings with contemporaries, tend to develop a sexual life based upon masturbatory daydreams, perhaps fuelled by internet pornography (Wood 2011), often of an extremely unrealistic kind. Since masturbation is a partially rewarding experience, and the internet in any case can blur the boundary between reality and fantasy, it tends to reinforce the daydream in such a way that it becomes a fixed pattern which interferes with the patient's capacity to make a sexual relationship with a real person.

There are two entirely opposite kinds of daydream which may have this effect. The first is the daydream of the kind encountered in women's magazines and the works of 'romantic' novelists. Such tales usually end with the heroine being finally able to secure the affections of a virile, masterful hero who, it is implied, will care for her for ever, making few demands upon her other than that she retain her beauty. The second variety of daydream, more often encountered in men, are those stereotyped fantasies of ever-ready sexual availability, pneumatic proportions, and unquestioning acceptance of masculine sexual prerogative which can be found in pornography.

Confession (the very word implies shame and guilt) to daydreams of either kind is often a painful undertaking for patients, but is a necessary precursor to change. The daydream predominates over a 'real' relationship with another person not only because it itself brings at least some pleasure, but because the alternative, actual physical intimacy with a separate individual, is so terrifying. Real intimacy, while ultimately the source of satisfaction and empathy and true warmth, also involves taking another person's feelings, preferences and flaws into account, and exposes one to the risk of failure and rejection.

Such are some of the negative aspects of daydreams. In contrast, many daydreams are not escapist but rehearsals for future actions, or attempts at finding solutions to problems. Some of the greatest achievements of the human mind take origin from daydreams. The special theory of relativity depended upon Einstein's ability to daydream about how the universe might appear to be to an observer travelling at the speed of light. Einstein did not attribute his success as a scientist to his superiority in mathematics or physics, but to his imaginative capacity.

The psychotherapist will frequently have as patients middle-aged people suffering from depression; especially women whose children have grown up, who feel unwanted; or men who have reached a plateau in their careers and feel they have nothing to aim for. It is often useful to ask such people to recall the daydreams they had as adolescents. Often ambitions and interests that were important have had to be discarded during the years in which a family is being raised and a career pursued. Revival of adolescent daydreams may point the way to a new departure which may once again make life into an exciting exploration instead of a dull routine. The way out of a mid-life crisis may be to develop those sides of one's nature which never had a chance to grow during the years of conventional striving.

Creative activities

When patients find it difficult to describe what they are feeling in words, they sometimes find it helpful to draw or paint some aspect of their experience. Some will object that they cannot draw; but since it is not works of art for which one is asking this does not matter. Paintings, partly through the use of colour, are often vividly descriptive of a patient's mood; they may reveal an underlying depression which may not be manifest in the patient's talk or manner. Paintings are not only useful for revealing the present state of affairs, but also have a therapeutic function in themselves. An important antidote to depression is activity of any sort; the act of painting a picture, however aesthetically simple, is an achievement in itself.

Earlier we touched on the helpfully objectifying aspect of putting things into words. Paintings also have this effect; but have the advantage that they can be kept and looked back upon; words are more easily forgotten. Some patients produce serial paintings which most interestingly record their emotional progress. As in the case of dreams, the therapist does not have to feel obliged to interpret every aspect of a drawing or painting. She may see some things which the patient does not; but mostly it is the patient who provides his own interpretation. Paintings also provide a useful variety of 'homework' in between psychotherapeutic sessions, which is especially important for patients who are not coming very frequently. The therapist who is treating a patient who is afflicted by moods of rage and despair may be asked: 'But what can I *do* before the next session? Suppose I get into one of my moods?' Suggesting that the patient should 'paint' or write about their feelings sometimes enables them to master them, rather than continuing to feel at the mood's mercy.

Keeping a diary can be helpful in exactly the same way as painting. However, whereas few patients overwhelm the therapist with too many paintings, too much reading matter for the therapist can inhibit the spontaneous encounter that is the hallmark of the dynamic psychotherapy session. The same is true of inter-session emails or twitters which can be a feature, especially when therapy is infrequent. One way round this is to say: 'Well, there obviously won't be time for me to read all that you have written. Perhaps you can describe what you discovered in the act of writing which you think was most important, and whether there were things that struck or puzzled you… '.

Writing and other creative pursuits help people suffering from psychological illnesses, especially depression, in two ways. First, the sufferer may gain an increased sense of their own competence in being able to produce anything at all. Second, if what he produces is published or displayed, and becomes accepted by others, he will receive a boost to his self-esteem which may be repeated each time he produces something new (although depression is sometimes an immediate aftermath of completing a piece of work). Depression-prone people are particularly vulnerable to criticism. All creative people identify themselves to some extent with what they produce; every piece of work, even if it consists of mathematics or observations requiring maximum scientific detachment, contains part of themselves. Imaginative writers are even more identified with their work than are scientists, and therefore even more sensitive about it.

One of the commonest causes of 'creative block', that is, inability to conclude original work which has been embarked upon, is fear of hostile criticism when it is finally exposed. Virginia Woolf is one example of a successful writer who remained intensely vulnerable to criticism throughout her life. She was almost certainly a bipolar sufferer (Dalsimer 2004). Despite being with her husband Leonard, a psychoanalytic publisher, and having a brother who was prominent in the early psychoanalytic movement in the UK, she always refused to undergo psychoanalysis, in the mistaken belief that it would interfere with her creativity. She had a number of attacks of depression of psychotic intensity, and finally, realizing that another attack was imminent, committed suicide.

AS included the following in the earlier editions of this book:

> I once treated a patient who had recurrent psychotic breakdowns of a very dramatic kind. Whilst she was psychotic, she was beyond the reach of psychotherapy, but, in between episodes was co-operative and anxious for help. Most of the doctors she had seen had encouraged her to ignore the content of her psychosis, and to forget all about her periods of madness once they were over. I took the risk of encouraging her to write an account of her illnesses, taking the view that by this means, she might feel less at the mercy of the illness should it recur. This she did, using a pseudonym, and the book was published. Some fourteen years later during which she had been free of attacks, she wrote to me about another matter, and I enquired whether she felt that writing the book had had any effect upon her health. She has given me permission to quote her reply. 'Yes, it was very good for me to have written the book, and to have done so while the events were vividly in mind. Having done so I'd "got it in the bag" so to speak, and could afford to forget all about it for some years – which was also good for me ... If I hadn't written the book, I might have been frightened to get married. But as A. had read it, and was *still* prepared to take the risk of getting married to me, I reckoned it was OK to go ahead.'
>
> I am sure that her marriage after her series of illnesses was more important than her writing in maintaining her stability; but I am also sure that one cannot afford to 'forget all about' very disturbing things in one's own psyche unless one has faced them. Writing about such things is one way of accomplishing this.

The Nature of the Therapeutic Relationship: Boundaried Intimacy

In this chapter we shall look in more detail at the nature of the psychotherapeutic relationship, from the point of view of therapist and patient. Despite contrasting positions and roles, both are equally caught in the paradox of being in a relationship with someone with whom one is intensely intimate, and yet who is, and must necessarily remain, a stranger. This relationship of intimate strangers is inherently chimerical– neither merely that between a professional and her client, as one might be with a surgeon, solicitor, hairdresser or a plumber – nor lovers. This is perhaps one reason why psychotherapy arouses uncomfortable feelings in society generally – curiosity, suspicion, ridicule, parody – and why the psychotherapist is often seen as a somewhat enigmatic figure. In order to be effective, the therapist has to be something of an outsider – someone who has no direct power or influence in society generally, and specifically in the patient's life. Yet with that detachment goes power – the ability to see things clearly, without prejudice, with no particular axe to grind. It is perhaps not surprising that psychoanalysis was invented by someone who was, by virtue of his Jewishness already on the outside of mainstream society, and whose family circumstances were also somewhat marginal (Makari 2008). The image of the cigar-smoking bearded middle-European psychoanalyst beloved of cartoonists is a token of the fused fear and contempt this role evokes.

Intimacy

In the course of her daily work the psychotherapist comes to know her patients extremely intimately; this is what makes the job so rewarding and interesting. In one sense psychotherapists know their patients far better than they know their friends or colleagues, and sometimes better than they know their own spouses or children.

But this knowledge is strictly limited and boundaried. First, there is an absolute prohibition on any kind of sexual contact: as Adam Phillips (Bersani and Phillips 2008) pithily puts it, psychoanalysis is a conversation between two people who have agreed not to have sex. Many of the ethical and professional dilemmas in psychotherapy flow from this. Also, the therapist only sees her patient in the confined, albeit unguarded, setting of the consulting room. She does not see him in the bar, at work, on the playing field, feeding her baby, or in front of the television. Except in extreme cases of, say, alcoholism, eating disorders, or people who harm themselves, the patient's physical body obtrudes relatively little into the therapeutic space. And the same is true, reciprocally, of the therapist from the patient's perspective.

Thus, although the psychotherapist neither lives with nor sleeps with her patients, she is, if she is at all skilled, likely to acquire a deep intimate knowledge of them. This is in part a consequence of the undivided and focused time which the therapist gives to each individual she treats; a span unlikely to be matched in any other kind of relationship, with the possible exception of mother and baby. It also derives from the fact that the intimacy is necessarily one-sided. During the time of therapy, the therapist puts herself at the patient's disposal and refrains from talking about herself. This feature of psychotherapy is difficult to match outside the confessional. The psychotherapist's purpose is to increase the patient's self-knowledge, both by acting as a reflecting mirror in which the patient may descry himself and also by gradually building up a coherent picture of the patient's personality by making the interpretative connections discussed earlier.

Preconceptions

This chapter is designed to explore some of the factors which may interfere with this process. The first difficulty which the therapist may encounter is the need to rid herself of her own prejudices. However objective we may think we are or attempt to be, we never approach a new person as if he was entirely an unknown quantity. More especially, if we are interested, as the therapist is in her patient, we begin by trying to 'place' him. Suppose, for example, that you are travelling by train and find yourself attracted (or repelled) by the face of a stranger opposite. 'He looks like a business man,' you say to yourself: and, depending upon your imaginative capacity and the degree of your interest, you may carry your speculation further, to include the man's age, family, dwelling place, type of business, and so on. Nature abhors a vacuum; and we fill the Rorschach silhouettes of personality with which unknown people present us from our own experience; the store of memories derived from our previous encounters with which all our minds are furnished. In origin, this 'placing' activity is biologically adaptive; a kind of safety precaution. Primitive man, encountering a total stranger, needed to know whether he was a friend or foe, and wanted all the clues he could get before deciding whether and in what way to approach and address them.

However, basing new encounters on figures from the past cuts both ways. Without it, we should not know how to approach new people at all: with it, we are liable to preconceptions which have to be corrected and discounted if we are to know the person as he really is. To take an absurd example, if we have been brought up to believe that all red-haired men are short-tempered, we may make the wholly unjustified assumption that the unknown red-haired patient who has just sat down in front of us is short-tempered also. If the patient has a 'posh' English accent, we may assume, quite wrongly, that he is arrogant or snobbish. So even at this very mundane, quasi-sociological level we must learn to clear our minds of preconceptions, or at least to bracket them off, and as far as possible to approach each clinical encounter, as Bion (1967) famously put it, 'beyond memory and desire'.

The 'Colombo' stance

One of the fascinating aspects of psychotherapy is that the therapist comes to know a good deal about people from a huge range of different experiences and backgrounds. As we have said, this can often be put to good use therapeutically. The patient can be invited to explain to the therapist the subtlety of the mores, say, of an upper-class Indian family from Delhi, or what it is like to grow up on a tough inner city housing estate in North London. Here the therapist adopts the 'Colombo' position, so named after the fictional TV detective, Lieutenant Colombo, who, while appearing to be bumbling and ineffective, and inviting their help, disarms his suspects to the point at which they unwittingly reveal their crimes. This approach in psychotherapy can be empowering for patients, who feel they have got something valuable to impart, and in the course of doing so may reveal much about themselves in a way that would not happen if the therapist is put into a superior all-knowing role.

Beginners may also be ill-at-ease when confronted with patients who are older, more intelligent, and more gifted than they are themselves. It is helpful to remember that even the most impressive people started life as helpless infants; that very high intelligence may march hand-in-hand with emotional obtuseness; and that the psychotherapeutic situation offers a unique opportunity for self-exploration which the patient, however sophisticated, will never have encountered before, and which the therapist is now able to provide. As she gets to know her patient, the therapist will find that her sense of awe diminishes, and see how it may derive from her own childhood, in which 'grown-ups' seemed inaccessibly powerful and superior. Disappearance of awe does not, of course, involve any diminution of respect, or any loss of appreciation of the ways in which patients may be one's intellectual, social, and moral superiors. Indeed, the more one gets to know other people intimately, the more one respects the ways in which human beings manage to retain courage and dignity in the face of what may be grave emotional hazards. It should also be acknowledged that there does need to be a reasonable 'match' between patient and therapist, who should, especially in difficult clinical situations, be of comparable fighting intellectual and moral weight.

Apart from difficulties of the kind already outlined, the therapist may find herself confronted by other prejudices of her own. Some therapists (Jung was one; Reich another) are prejudiced against homosexuals. Women therapists may find dependence and passivity in male patients hard to tolerate. Male therapists are often put off by dominance and assertiveness in women. In such cases, the therapist does well to take a closer look at her or himself. Most of the traits we most deplore in others are no strangers in the recesses of our own psyches; and this is one of the several reasons why those who wish to practise psychotherapy as a major professional activity should themselves undergo therapy.

The analytic attitude

Perhaps the most common difficulty that therapists in training encounter is that of remaining relatively passive. As we have said, doctors in particular often find it difficult to abandon their traditionally authoritarian role. Doctors may feel ill-at-ease if they are not handing out something to the patient; a regime, a prescription, or advice: and the more inexperienced they are, the more they feel the need of doing something other than just listening. Doctors tend often to be active rather than contemplative; practical people who enjoy manipulating gadgets, using apparatus, changing the external world. They are – to use Liam Hudson's (1973) classification – convergers rather than divergers; scientists rather than artists, albeit with many exceptions. Such people find it hard to tolerate the passivity required of the psychotherapist, whose function is that of a midwife rather than that of a surgeon.

Sometimes beginner therapists suffer from the converse problem. These are those who are *too* passive, merely listening, not daring to disturb the universe of the patient's inner world. As we have said, silence can be persecutory, and although therapy patients do not expect to take something concrete away from their session, there does need to be a sense of something achieved – a feeling validated, new light thrown on an old problem, a current difficulty re-evaluated. Particularly in time-limited therapy an active therapist is essential (Malan and Della Selva 2006). While eschewing problem-solving, the therapist is far from passive: listening, commenting, challenging, re-evaluating, gently and empathically disrupting the patient's habitual patterns of thinking, speaking and relating.

Another not uncommon pitfall for psychotherapists is to be afflicted by a species of humourless earnestness. While it is vital to give the patient one's total attention, to put one's own worries and preoccupations to one side, and take the task of listening and treat the patient's point of view with utter seriousness, none of this needs to be heavy-handed. The therapist should cultivate a light touch, always reaching to counterbalance the patient's frame of mind. If they are gloomy one may want to lighten things up; if manic, to bring them back to earth; if too loud to speak quietly, if inaudible to pump up the decibels a fraction. Humour can be a defensive way of avoiding mental pain, but it also betokens warmth, acceptance, and a degree of detachment, and if patients can be helped to laugh at themselves and their predicaments that can be a first step toward psychological health (Lemma 2009).

Those in training sometimes ask whether it is necessary for them to *like* their patients if they are to help them. This question generally arises during preliminary interviews, more especially when the therapist has a prejudice of the kind mentioned. At one level it is an important question. The mere fact that it arises suggests a particular feeling has been evoked in the therapist. This is best thought about in terms of transference and counter-transference, which we shall discuss in more detail in the next chapter. The patient may have evoked in the therapist an important aspect of their own inner world – a worry about being likeable or not, which may relate to their early attachment experience with a mother or father who for some reason was not able to 'fall in love' with their baby in the normal way, or for whom love was always 'conditional' upon success, rather than unconditional. On the other hand the likeability issue may properly belong to the therapist's own psyche: perhaps the patient reminds her of some difficult situation in their own family – e.g. a patient with alcohol problems may bring feelings associated with the therapist's own alcoholic father – disgust, the wish to rescue at all costs, fear etc.

On the rare occasions when, on serious examination of her own negative preconceptions and their origins, a therapist continues actively to dislike a patient who has been referred, it may be better to cease working with that particular patient and to refer them elsewhere. There needs to be a basic bond of sympathy, concern, wish to help, interest, and acceptance as a preconception for psychotherapeutic work, even if the latter does involve unravelling the component of 'dislike' which the therapist has noted. Coming to know another person very intimately and active dislike are generally incompatible. From an attachment perspective the issue at stake which links therapist and patient is not so much liking or disliking, but the biological propensity to seek help from an 'older, wiser' figure when one is in distress and the complementary impulse to help those who are vulnerable or suffering (Holmes 2010). Liking comes later; and another rewarding aspect of the practice of psychotherapy is that one enlarges one's capacity for liking a wide range of people.

Psychotherapists are far more likely to encounter difficulties because they like their patients too much rather than too little. Finding a patient sexually attractive, fascinating, and exciting needs to be examined under the microscope of transference and counter-transference no less than negative feelings. Here too therapists needs to be alert to the very occasional danger signals that tell them that their motivation for taking this particular patient on is less than purely professional, and to consider onward referral.

The 'special' patient

There is a species of patient familiar to all therapists. This is the 'special' patient – someone with whom one feels a particular affinity or to whom one is challenged to offer help despite one's better judgement and rational self-knowing that such assistance is unlikely to be effective. All this must be factored into the therapists ongoing self-scrutiny. It is not an argument for not having special patients, since all therapists would admit to having them, but rather for being aware of the ways in which with such people one may find oneself 'off-piste', bending the rules and behaving in untoward ways. One needs to be particularly vigilant in maintaining the normal boundaries of therapy with such patients, not acceding to requests for out-of-hours sessions, excessive texting etc. An exemplary illustration of how to work with 'special' patients is illustrated in the film, *The King's Speech*, an exploration of the relationship between the then Duke of York, who later became King George VI (who had a serious stutter) and Lloyd his therapist. Lloyd refused to go to the palace for sessions, insisting that the future King came to his consulting room in the normal way. No boundary breaking, not even for royalty!

One danger here is too close an identification with the patient: the psychotherapist may be so intensely sympathetic with the patient's difficulties, and so entirely capable of putting herself in the patient's shoes, that she loses the objectivity required to see in what way the patient is failing to deal with his problems. In previous editions AS tells the following story:

> Many years ago I took over the treatment of an intelligent woman from a distinguished woman psychiatrist who had been seeing her for some time. For a long time, I could not make out what had been going on in these previous sessions. Finally, I asked her to tell me more about them. 'Oh', she said: 'We just sat and chatted about how dreadful men were.' It was obvious that the therapist had found so much in common with the patient that all objectivity had been lost, and the sessions had deteriorated into a mutually sympathetic exchange in which all possibility of dynamic progress had disappeared. Since both doctor and patient may enjoy such exchanges, sessions of this kind may go on for some time without either party complaining or even realizing that 'nothing is happening'.

Sadly, this is a not uncommon tale, although one should always take with a pinch of salt patient's accounts of their encounters with other professionals. Perhaps this patient was subtly flattering AS, and the reality of the therapy may not have been so collusive as he assumed. 'Nothing never happens' is a psychodynamic watchword; the 'nothing' that was happening is a very definite something!

Sexual exploitation

A passionate desire to help people with whose problems the therapist feels a particular sympathy may sometimes have undesirable consequences. One psychiatrist found himself unable to bear the tears of his women patients, and hastened to comfort them by putting his arms round them. This first step on the 'slippery slope' (Twemlow and Gabbard 1989; Dimen 2012) sometimes led to his becoming sexually involved with them; not, at least at a conscious level, because he was psychopathically setting out to exploit them, but because his intense desire to relieve their misery led to his offering love as a direct way of bringing comfort. The example given shows how easy it is to deceive oneself. By entering into physical relations with his patients, the psychiatrist was obstructing their progress toward finding ways of fulfilling their own needs independently. He was also, implicitly, promising more than he could deliver since, as a result of his actions, his patients would be bound to entertain fantasies of love and marriage, and to be angry and disappointed when their hopes were not realized. Moreover, the psychiatrist, apart from flouting all codes of professional ethics, was gaining sexual gratification for himself without taking the risk of being rejected or facing any of the other hazards and responsibilities which normally accompany sexual involvement between peers in ordinary life. He was a diffident man who had always been uncertain of himself when approaching the opposite sex. The therapeutic situation offered him a 'safe' way of gaining the love of women; a fact of which he was insufficiently aware. The *reductio ad absurdam* of this approach would be the argument that if therapists really feel that their role is altruistically to provide sexual fulfilment and validation for their patients, this should be applied indiscriminately to all patients, irrespective of gender, age, or attractiveness.

This example also makes the point that the corollary of the unique intimacy of the therapeutic relationship is the maintenance of unbreachable boundaries. The patient can only place absolute trust in the therapist and lay bare his or her utter vulnerability if he is sure in the knowledge that such exposure will not lead to exploitation, whether this be sexual, financial or any of the other ways in which power can be abused. This precept is rendered all the more poignant by the fact that many of our patients' difficulties stem from being victims of just such exploitation in the past.

If the therapist has the tact and gentleness to accept love (and hate!) from patients without responding, but, at the same time, without making the patient feel rejected, she will find that, in the course of therapy, the problem usually solves itself. It is possible to interpret these manifestations of quasi-erotic love in the way which Freud did, as referring simply to the past, resuscitations of feelings which belong more properly to the patient's parents. But this is never the whole story, since the loving feelings which the patient experiences as an adult are different from their precursors which he experienced as a child; and it is undervaluing the patient's love to dismiss it as nothing more than a piece of persistent childishness. Through her actions, attitudes and occasionally words, the therapist must communicate the absolute impregnability of the sexual barrier in therapy. This firmness has the same beneficial effect as the incest taboo; indeed, it is a manifestation of it.

The therapist cannot deviate; but that does not preclude playfulness, being able to appreciate the patient's attractiveness; or allowing sexual fantasies to arise in the counter-transference which must then be carefully examined for their meaning. The therapist is in a situation somewhat analogous to parents of adolescent children; the mother or father can see the young person's inherent beauty and sexual potential, and the child needs non-verbally to feel that their parent values them in this way; but this has to be on the basis of a sense of complete safety from any sort of sexual overtones. All this has the effect of making the patient realize that not all his needs can be fulfilled by therapy; that what therapy does is to provide a new base of confidence from which he may go forth better equipped to seek his own fulfilment. It could be said that we all start independent life with a disappointment in love, since the parent of the opposite sex can never be ours. The same is often true of the new start offered by psychotherapy.

In myths and fairy stories, one common theme is the story of the youngest child who is forced by circumstances to leave the shelter of the parental roof to 'seek his fortune'. He usually encounters a great many perils and threats to his life. Often he is required, like Tamino in '*The Magic Flute*', to pass a number of tests of courage. Sometimes, as in '*Sleeping Beauty*', or in '*Siegfried*', his princess is surrounded by protective barriers of fire or thorn which make her difficult of access. Eventually, the hero overcomes all obstacles, and is rewarded by the hand of the princess. In other words, sexual happiness is the reward for having been brave enough to leave the shelter of the parental home, and face whatever dangers an independent life may confront one with.

Dependence

A less obvious way in which therapists can exploit their patients is by unwittingly encouraging dependence. Even the most self-deprecating psychotherapist is bound to acknowledge that she sometimes is gratified by having a number of patients who turn to her, look up to her, and value her as someone in whom they feel able fully to confide. Psychotherapists in full-time practice are apt to collect a number of 'good' patients who come regularly, who are grateful for what the therapist has to offer them, who produce interesting dreams or other 'material', and who pay their bills regularly. As time goes on the patient is apt to overlook the fact that therapy cannot be a substitute for life; while the therapist may turn a blind eye to the fact that the patient's dependency on her is a boost to her own self-esteem. The danger here is that the patient's progress toward autonomy is brought to a halt, while the treatment goes on indefinitely.

Handling such cases is not easy, as Freud himself found out during 1937. Clearly the issue of dependency needs to be discussed, but it has to be done tactfully so that the patient does not feel attacked or blamed. The therapist needs to examine her own part in the impasse, usually in supervision, highlighting those cases in which the patient appears to be making good progress but in which no obvious end to the treatment ever appears to come into view. One way of dealing with this situation is to 'set a date' for ending, perhaps a year or even two years ahead and then work concentratedly on the issues thereby raised – previous experiences of loss; resentment; feelings of being unwanted or not good enough, premature drop-out, fantasies of revenge etc. Another is to think in terms of gradual attenuation. There are a small number of cases in which psychotherapy needs to be extremely prolonged, and even those which last 10 or more years are not necessarily instances of misjudgement or exploitation. An outstanding example is Marion Milner's (1969) account of a psychoanalytic treatment lasting more than 20 years, in which no one could possibly think that the patient was exploited, although they might think that the analyst herself was setting impossibly high standards of professional devotion.

Self-revelation

The patients with whom the therapist is likely to feel the most intense sympathy are generally those whose psychopathology in some way resembles his or her own. The therapist who has herself been lonely will feel particular compassion for the isolated; or one who has had numerous physical illnesses will find it easier to understand the way in which emotional stress can have bodily manifestations. Sympathy of this kind might tempt the inexperienced therapist into telling the patient about some of her own difficulties, past or present, just as she might say to a friend in distress; 'I know how you feel; I've been through it myself.'

There is a recognized school of dynamic psychotherapy, relational psychoanalysis, which argues that self-revelation can be helpful, is ethically appropriate, and there is indeed some research evidence to suggest that limited self-revelation on the part of the therapist produces therapeutic benefit. But, on the whole, we take a contrary position on this point, despite finding much to admire and agree in the relational perspective (Holmes 2010). We hold that the therapeutic relationship is inherently asymmetrical, and although the psychotherapist gets to know her patient intimately, the patient does not, and should not, get to know the therapist in the same way. Some feel that it might be helpful to the patient if they revealed their own problems, since it would convince him that they understood what it is to be depressed or anxious from the inside. Or they feel that it is somehow pretentious not to reveal oneself; setting oneself up as superior; pretending to a state of maturity or balance which one has not, in fact, attained. However, there are a number of good reasons why it is important that the therapist does not yield to the temptation of revealing herself to the patient.

The first is that, if she does so, she will deprive herself of a valuable source of information. For, just as we have seen that the therapist is bound to have fantasies about the patient, so, equally, the patient is bound to have fantasies about the therapist, and exploration of the latter will be an important part of the treatment. If the patient knows too much about the therapist he will not have so many fantasies about him. The therapist cannot be an entirely 'blank screen': she is bound to reveal a good deal about herself by her manner, speech-patterns, clothes, wearing of a wedding ring or not, décor of the consulting room, etc. But she will find out more about the patient if she remains reticent about her personal life than if not.

For example, many patients will want to know whether or not the therapist is married. From the point of view of the therapy, what matters is not the answer to that question, affirmative or negative, but what it *means* to the patient, why it is coming up at this particular point, and what other questions there are that lie behind that seemingly innocent question. Rather than answer such a question directly, it is better to throw the question back, enquiring what the patient imagines, and what difference the patient would feel if the therapist was married on the one hand, or was not on the other. Suppose the patient is a male homosexual and the therapist is also male. The patient may be hoping that the therapist is unmarried because he feels that only another homosexual will be able to understand what he feels. Or suppose the patient is a woman, and the therapist is a male. Her anxiety to know whether or not the therapist is married may be because she has a fantasy that he is exactly the sort of person she would like to have as a life's partner; a fantasy which might never become explicit if she knew that the therapist simply answered the question with a yes or no. Exploration of such a fantasy may lead on to all kinds of discoveries about the patient's wishes and fears about men which would greatly help her understanding of herself and her difficulties in relationships.

Again the *reductio ad absurdam* here is to consider at which point would one stop in one's self-revelation. 'Are you married?' – one might allow oneself to answer that, and in any case the patient could probably find that out by some other means. In these days of Google and Wikipedia, patients can and frequently do find out a great deal about their therapists from the internet, and it is important to bring that into the open in the course of therapy. But few would find it so easy to reply directly to 'are you happily married?', 'how good is your sex life with your spouse?' Where does one stop? There is no escaping the need for boundaries. The important things to recognize are a) that this boundary is therapeutic, and b) that it is non-absolute in the sense that patient and therapist are not a different species, merely playing different roles. The therapist's personal therapy will remind her that she, at one and the same time, is excluded from her therapist's private life, and be excluding her patient's from hers. The 'oedipal' barrier between children and their parents, which means that in order to have sex – or simply an intimate uninterrupted conversation – parents will exclude children from the bedroom, is tempered by the fact that as their children reach adolescence and adulthood, they too will exclude their parents from theirs, as the wheel of the life-cycle gradually turns.

Second, it is inadvisable to tell patients of one's own psychological difficulties and problems in the way one might share one's own experiences with a friend, because, in the end, one is not a friend, but a therapist. Indeed enhancing one's capacity to make the occasional subtle distinctions of this sort is one of the benefits of therapy. Of course one draws on one's own experience of life when trying to understand another person's feelings; one of the several purposes of personal therapy for therapists is to widen their range of difficult experiences and feelings so these can be brought to bear in their work. But it is not therapeutic to say: 'Yes, I know what it is like to be depressed, I've been terribly depressed too', even if this is true. Patients of course realize that therapists have their problems, and the more sophisticated know that it is not by accident that the therapist became interested in psychotherapy; but, while they are in treatment, what they want and need is a therapist whom they can trust, and upon whom they can rely, not someone whom they perceive as wrestling with unsolved problems of her own. This is especially true in the early stages of therapy. When patients begin treatment, they are often extremely anxious and unsure both of themselves and of the therapist. It is only when they become more confident themselves that they can afford to see the therapist as the fallible human being which, like everyone else, she is bound to be.

AS courageously revealed the following anecdote in earlier editions of this book:

> When I was young and inexperienced, a man once came to see me whose principal problem was intense guilt about masturbation. His sessions with me were progressing fairly well, when one day he suddenly asked me, just as he was about to leave the room, whether I had ever masturbated. Without thinking, caught off my guard, I answered 'Yes'. I never saw that patient again.

This is an extreme example of a fairly everyday occurrence, the emergence of significant issues just on the boundary of the therapy, where the therapeutic relationship is changing from one of intense intimacy to that of strangers. There is a number of ways in which one might respond to this question. It is a delicate task; the therapist must neither give a direct answer, nor to make the patient feel blocked, put down, or that such questions are off-limits. One should remind oneself of a basic therapeutic principle: 'nothing human is alien to me' ('*nihil humanum mihi alienum est*'; Terentius).

Wise after the event, here are some possible replies:

> 'That's a really important question, but we are at the end of the session and I think we need to come back to it next time';

> 'That's a brave question, I wonder where it is coming from, and what's made you bring it up today ';

> 'I wonder what reply you were hoping for? Were you hoping I might say 'no', because someone who has never masturbated is a kind of ideal to you, or 'yes', because that might make you feel less odd and abnormal?';

> 'Maybe you are thinking I'm a bit of a wanker, especially as I am just about to throw you out!';

> or simply 'I wonder what you imagine?'

Nevertheless the patient might persist: 'Look, you are being evasive: *do* you masturbate or not?' To this one might have to take a more definite stand:

> 'I can see that you might feel you need to know that, but this therapy is about you, not me, and that is where our focus must lie. I respect you for having plucked up courage to ask the question, and let's think together about what it might mean, but no, I am not going to answer it'.

This gives the message that there is an impregnable boundary between the therapist's private life and her work and on the whole this is reassuring especially as highly disturbed patients often find managing such boundaries problematic (see Chapter 12). The one exception to this is where the patient has experienced some hugely traumatic and life-changing event such as the death of a child, or a cancer diagnosis. Knowing that the therapist, or fellow members of a therapy group, have been through comparable experiences can give hope and help show that there is a way out of despair.

Revealing things about herself is, for the therapist, nearly always contra-indicated, however much she may try to believe that it is for the patient's benefit. Therapists want acceptance and understanding from people just as do their patients; but they should not use a psychotherapeutic session for this purpose. Sometimes it represents a failure of nerve at holding the boundary, an indication that the therapist fears her aggression and does not see how a degree of benign toughness can be just as important as empathy. The therapist's job is to serve the patient; and, although she may legitimately enjoy the gratification of using her special skills, of earning a living and of feeling that she is doing a good job, she should not be seeking any other form of reward. That said, there is some research suggesting that limited self-revelation in the form of anecdotes, stories and jokes on the part of the therapist are associated with good outcomes in therapy (Zur 2007). Perhaps these are best confined to 'phase four' (see Chapter 14) of a therapist's career.

What we have said does not mean however that we are advocating the kind of remote, detached, impersonal attitude which convention associates with psychoanalysts. Research has shown that patients do better if they perceive their therapists as warm and sympathetic; and they are clearly more likely to perceive them thus if they are in fact genuinely warm and sympathetic and not afraid to show their feelings in their tone of voice. If the therapist is too detached, she cuts herself off from an important avenue of understanding what the patient is feeling, and will be less effective as a therapist. Psychotherapy is, and should be, emotionally demanding of the therapist; if, at the end of the day's work, she does not feel somewhat drained, it is unlikely that she will have accomplished much therapeutically. However, she must retain enough objectivity to see in what way the patient is failing to cope with his problems and contributing to them. Empathy without objectivity is as little use as objectivity without empathy. The therapist has to walk a tightrope between over and under-identification with the patient. If she remains critically detached she will not be able to understand her patient as a person or appreciate the difficulties which he faces. For this reason the practice of psychotherapy will always remain more of an art than a science. As Jung put it:

> 'If the doctor wants to guide another, or even accompany him a step of the way, he must *feel* with that person's psyche. He never feels it when he passes judgement. Whether he puts his judgements into words, or keeps them to himself, makes not the slightest difference. To take the opposite position, and to agree with the patient offhand, is also of no use, but estranges him as much as condemnation. Feeling comes only through unprejudiced objectivity. This sounds almost like a scientific precept, and it could be confused with a purely intellectual, abstract attitude of mind. But what I mean is something quite different. It is a human quality – a kind of deep respect for the facts, for the man who suffers from them, and for the riddle of such a man's life' (Jung 1932).

Jung's 'unprejudiced objectivity' is underpinned with a respect for the human being which is never wholly objective. He is on the patient's side, however much he deplores some of the things the patient does, or disagrees with his opinions. Carl Rogers' 'unconditional positive regard' is akin to this stance, and evidence suggests this plays an important part in good therapy outcomes. Just as one is inclined to excuse conduct in members of one's own family which one might condemn in others, so one is inclined to be indulgent towards the faults of one's patients. There is a sense in which all a psychotherapist's geese are swans. One of the factors which helps patients in psychotherapy is the conviction that there is at least one person who is entirely 'on one's side'; and who is, for the time that one is with her, wholly dedicated to one's interests. This can be seen as an extension into the consulting room of the 'healthy narcissism' with which one invests one's own family, and indeed oneself, and which is the basis for good self-esteem (Freud 1914).

Critics sometimes accuse psychotherapists of spending too much time trying to treat people who may be beyond redemption, the 'wretched of the earth' (Fanon 1961).

Since psychotherapy is a scarce resource, and an 'inverse care law' (Tudor Hart 1971) applies, and, from a strictly cost-benefit perspective, those who do 'best' are relatively psychologically healthy in the first place, the critics may sometimes be right. But championing the damaged, the despised, the insulted and injured, is better than an irrational prejudice against them. It is an important ingredient in the moral fabric of psychotherapy, and one that should be upheld in the face of a society whose values are increasingly instrumental and utilitarian.

8

Transference and Counter-transference

Dorothea, a warm and respected middle-aged psychoanalytic colleague, came bursting into the psychotherapy department coffee room one day:

> 'Jeremy', she said, 'transference really *does* exist. I've just seen two patients. The first complained that I looked like a witch, an old hag; the second told me I was the most beautiful woman he had ever seen! They can't both be right.'

The truth that beauty lies in the eye of the beholder was known long before Freud and Breuer discovered transference. In a sense, Dorothea's patients *were* both right, not perhaps about her objective beauty, but about their inner worlds and the role of women in their lives. Psychodynamic psychotherapists see transference as central to their work because evoking and analyzing transference is like an *in vitro* or living experiment. (This is a bacteriological metaphor. Bugs which cause trouble do so *in vivo*, in the wild. They can be studied *in vitro* in glass Petri dishes in laboratories, and so tamed and treated).

Transference puts people in touch with the unconscious assumptions that underpin our daily lives and loves. The therapist's part in this is twofold, both based on the reticence and neutrality that is integral to her role. First, she offers an ambiguous stimulus which the patient then 'fills in' on the basis of prior assumptions. Dorothea's neutrality was what evoked the two very different responses. Second, because therapy is not 'real life', therapist and patient together can look at the images and feelings and assumptions that have come up transferentially and learn from them. Were Dorothea to have felt flattered and sexually interested in response to her admiring patient, or outraged at the rejecting one, this opportunity would have been missed.

In Chapter 7, we saw how getting to know another person consisted of the correction of misconceptions, since we all 'project' upon unknown figures images derived from our experience of others in the past. If, for example, the patient approaches every new person he meets with the expectation that that person will despise him or be critical of him, his capacity for close relationships is likely to be compromised. If a person's early childhood has been one in which he was ill-treated and rejected, he may expect such treatment from any new person whom he encounters, whether they are in positions of authority over him, or potential sources of intimacy and pleasure. We do not approach new people as if they were blank sheets, but 'transfer' what we have already experienced from the past into the present. Directly we treat another human being as an authority, we are apt to endow that person with attributes of the authorities whom we have encountered in the past; and, for most people, these are, of course, their parents.

The tendency to project upon the therapist attributes belonging to the patient's parents will be reinforced by the fact that, in any prolonged psychotherapeutic treatment, revival and reliving of the emotions connected with the patient's childhood is inescapable. Although psychotherapists today do not place as much emphasis as did Freud upon the recovery of buried memories or the recall of forgotten traumata, most would agree that the patient's early years are important in shaping his adult character, and that the emotional climate of those early years significantly determined his attitudes to other people and to the various challenges with which life confronts all human beings.

It is also the case that, whenever we 'look after' another person, we are to some extent taking on the role of a caring, nurturing parent. One of the main objectives of psychotherapy is to enable the patient more effectively to care for himself, and thus obviate the need for parent-figures by becoming his own parent. But the emotional situation which prevails in the early stages of therapy, when the therapist is faced with a person who may be acutely distressed, is bound to have some of the features of a parent-child relationship. For have not all of us, unless particularly deprived, had the experience of being comforted by a parent when hurt or disappointed? And is it not the case that, although the therapist may not offer comfort directly, the fact that she is prepared to listen and to try to understand puts her automatically into a 'parent-figure' category? Attachment theory, originally developed by John Bowlby, especially emphasizes this aspect of the therapeutic relationship (Holmes 2010).

When Freud first encountered and described the phenomenon of transference, he regarded it as an obstacle to therapy. At this stage in his thinking the main vehicle for psychic cure was free association. When he observed that some patients found this process difficult, or suddenly ground to a halt, he attributed this to the emergence of transference – perceiving the analyst as a disapproving figure from the past who would be shocked by their revelations. He wanted to dispose of these transferences and get on with helping the patient's free associations. But his experiences with patients such as Dora (Freud 1905), who developed a strong negative transference to Freud and dropped out of therapy, brought home to him the new idea that if one could analyse and transcend transference the patient would recover. Another aspect is that Freud did not wish to become emotionally important to his patients, but would have preferred to be regarded in the same light as, say, a surgeon; that is, as a technical expert whose field of expertise happened to be the mind rather than the body. However, by 1907, when Jung first visited Freud in Vienna, his views had changed. He asked Jung what he thought of transference; and when Jung replied 'It is the alpha and omega in treatment', Freud said; 'You have understood.'

Transference in its widest sense comprises the whole gamut of the pattern of relationship – verbal, gestural, affective and behavioural – between the patient and the therapist. It can be thought of as the single most important factor in dynamic therapy. Here again, the psychotherapeutic situation is unique. For what the therapist tries to do is to understand and interpret the patient's attitude to her, and by this means to help the patient understand his difficulties in relationship with others. Here is a typical example:

> A young woman of 22 had made a suicide attempt, and was referred for psychotherapy. She was fluent verbally, and was talking about some of her difficulties in relationship with other people when she suddenly broke off. 'Can't you say something?' she asked. 'I'm doing all the talking, and you are just sitting there listening. I can't bear your silence.'
>
> AS said something to the effect that, as she was talking freely, there was no need for him to interrupt her, and then went on. 'But I wonder what you were reading into the silence ... ?'
>
> 'If you don't talk, I don't know what you are thinking of me.'
>
> 'Let's look at what you imagine that I might be thinking ... ?'
>
> 'I think you might be finding me boring, or that you are inwardly criticising me.'
>
> 'It sounds to me as if it is hard for you to think of people as finding you interesting or likeable.'

She agreed that this was indeed the case. Her mother had died when she was very young, and she had never managed to get on with her father. She had not had enough love in early childhood to acquire any sense of being lovable or even likeable. AS and the patient went on to discuss how, if one does not like oneself, one is apt to make the assumption that no one else will like one either, and thus approach other people with suspicion and hostility.

The assumption here is that attitudes to parents and other important figures in a child's early development will tend to be transferred to other people as the child grows up. Psychotherapists deal predominantly with people who have negative expectations; who believe that nobody wants them, or that nobody can understand them; or who are isolated because they have come to believe that intimacy with another person is a threat. If therapy goes well, the patient will come to feel that there is at least one person in the world of whom this is not true. Just as children generalize from their experience of parents, expecting that others will treat them in the same way as their parents have treated them at home, so patients who have come to regard the therapist as understanding and helpful will, one hopes, generalize from their experience with the therapist, and come to regard the people they meet as at least potentially friendly. Psychotherapy thus becomes a 'corrective emotional experience' (Alexander and French 1946), in which negative assumptions about other people are gradually modified by means of the repeated analysis of the patient's changing relationship with the therapist.

Positive and negative transference

It is natural, therefore, that, during the course of therapy, the therapist should, for a time, become emotionally important to the patient. If, for most of one's life, one has felt misunderstood or unappreciated, and then encounters someone who appears to understand and accept one, it is scarcely surprising that this should happen. 'Positive transference' comes to predominate over the 'negative transference', i.e. the assumptions of rejection and hostility already mentioned. If therapy is going to be effective, negative transference has to be 'resolved': that is, dispelled by the therapist continually detecting the patient's negative attitudes, drawing attention to them, and trying to trace their origin from the patient's experience in the past of rejection and hostility. Where negative transference cannot be resolved, therapy may well come to an end because the patient will break it off. Whereas analysis of negative transference is important if therapy is to proceed, it might be argued that analysis of positive transference is unnecessary, or indeed inimical to progress. Is it not positively helpful to the patient to regard the therapist in the light of an ever-loving, all-understanding parent who will heal the wounds of the past, and make up for all the incidents of rejection, misunderstanding, pain and loss which have forced the patient to seek help?

The answer is both yes and no. It is certainly essential to the patient's progress that he regards the therapist in a positive light. But transference projections, because of their origin in childhood experience, are, as Freud recognized, apt to be unrealistic and exaggerated. The more deeply disturbed the patient, and the more he or she is cut off from affectionate relations with others, the more likely is it that the therapist will be idealized and exalted to the position of being 'the only person who understands'. In the early stages of such an intense transference, it is wise not to be in too much of a hurry to disillusion the patient – as Yeats (1968) put it, 'tread softly for you tread on my dreams', a precept particularly advocated by followers of Kohut's (1977) self-psychology. Although the therapist can never replace the patient's parents, or make up for what may have been missing in the patient's early childhood, or obliterate trauma and its residues, the patient's positive feelings about the therapist may have a healing effect which premature interpretation would dispel. A sensitive, self-deprecatory therapist may well deplore being regarded, even temporarily, by the patient as an omnipotent worker of miracles, a faultless parent, when she knows herself to be no more than a fallible human being with her own store of problems. She must realize, however, that, for the purpose of therapy, she is only partly herself. Her function is also to act as a peg upon which the patient can hang the images derived from his own past experience and his present needs and she must be prepared temporarily to accept this role, sure in the knowledge that good and bad are but two facets of a balanced whole. In Kleinian terms, this means that a degree of splitting is inevitable, before reaching the painful, yet healing reality of the so-called 'depressive position' (Waddell 1998).

It is important to note that much of the healing process here is metaphorical; an 'as if' process in which the therapist comes to represent both persons from the patient's past and also a series of possibilities for the future. Real improvement comes about through symbolic playing with these images in the patient's mind, seeing them for what they are – 'just thoughts' – and that, as Hamlet said, 'there's nothing good or bad, but thinking it makes it so'. This is the process which the term 'mentalising' attempts to capture (Allen and Fonagy 2006), and is also central to cognitive therapy.

Internalization

As therapy progresses, a number of changes take place in the patient's image of the therapist, so that she comes to be seen as less remote and more as an ordinary human being. This may be thought of as analogous to the small child's progress in emotional development; a progress from regarding the parents as omnipotent and omniscient toward seeing them as more or less ordinary human beings, albeit with a special, significant place in the patient's emotional life. Concurrently, the patient's experience of the therapist becomes an integral part of the patient's psyche. This is the introjection of the therapist as a 'good object' (Waddell 1998). This process of internalization can also justifiably be assumed to take place in small children. The newborn baby comes into the world in a state in which he is utterly ill-equipped to fend for himself. Without care the child will die. As Winnicott (1971) famously put it 'there is no such thing as a baby, only a mother and baby together'. However robust, the child needs the presence and the care of reliable, trustworthy adults if he is to learn to rely on himself. In fact the 'himself' which the child learns to rely on is something which he has introjected, or taken into, 'himself' from his experience with good parents. Freud (1917) saw this in his idea that the ego is a 'residue of abandoned cathexes' – in other words that our Self, however solid it may seem, is in fact forged from the significant relationships in our life.

Similarly a patient in therapy begins to form within himself a reliable figure to whom he can turn in case of difficulty. Initially this figure may be quite clearly an image of the therapist. Patients report that, when faced with a problem, they often say to themselves; 'What would Mrs Y or Dr X say?' although they know quite well that what Mrs Y or Dr X would actually have said is: 'I don't know exactly what you ought to do; let's try and explore the problem further'. After a while, the therapist's specific image usually fades as a definable entity just as the image of parents as people one turns to disappears as children grow up, and they are left with a more generalized 'good internal parent', or, in attachment terms an 'internal secure base'.

Patients who are going through a phase in which they are very dependent are often apprehensive as to what will happen when the therapy has come to an end. 'What will I do without you?' they ask. There will inevitably be a process of mourning, sadness not untempered by a sense of liberation from the need to devote time and money to therapy. But if all goes well there will be a 'reinstatement of the lost object' in the patient's psyche, so that therapy can be a continuing source of psychic comfort and guidance even when it has physically come to an end. The research evidence shows that this is exactly what does happen when patients are followed up post-therapy (Shedler 2010), in contrast to pharmacological treatments, where the benefits often cease once the pills are stopped.

In some patients the process of introjection is problematic. This has two consequences. First, they tend to remain dependent upon the therapist's actual presence, rather than being able to carry her away 'inside'. Second, they seem incapable of transferring their trust in the therapist to other people, so that the therapist tends to remain as the only person they feel understands or cares about them. It seems likely that these two phenomena are really one, in that if the patient cannot make the therapist's image part of his own psyche, he cannot project this image upon other people. We know that small children who are temporarily deprived of their mother often become depressed because they cannot conceive of her return. They are dependent upon her actual presence to be assured of her continuing existence. In the ordinary course of events, the child's 'emotional object constancy', and ability to tolerate absence gradually increases, but it may be that, where a firm tie with the mother has never been established, the person remains particularly vulnerable to loss. Whatever the explanation, most psychotherapists will encounter a few patients in whose eyes she remains the only person whom they feel they have ever trusted, and of whose continuing interest they feel assured. This discussion will be continued later in Chapter 13.

Erotic transference

Earlier we raised the issue of sexual feelings as they arise in therapy. The concept of transference helps us to think further about this. The temporary idealization of the therapist not infrequently includes an erotic component. It is only to be expected that the patient's feelings toward the therapist should sometimes include sexual feelings, and for their dreams and fantasies to include the therapist playing the part of a lover. How should the therapist respond? First, it is important to disentangle sexual needs and dependency needs. Human beings remain dependent in the sense that, however grown-up they are, they continue to need human relationships. But this 'mature dependence' Fairbairn (1954) is very different from the dependence of childhood. Ideally, the choice of a sexual partner should be made from a position of confidence. Adult sexuality is probably the main force which compels the young to leave the nest of home; and unless he or she have achieved sufficient confidence to do this, they may either fail to find a partner, or choose one in which the parent-child component predominates over that of adult sexuality. A degree of emancipation from parents is a prerequisite for a satisfactory love relationship on equal terms (although it is acknowledged this view may be somewhat culture-bound); and many marriages, which go wrong, do so because one partner treats the other like a parent or child instead of as an equal.

Since the patient endows the therapist with attributes which are predominantly parental it follows that when erotic elements arise, the patient is trying to make the therapist into a combination of parent and lover. Freud's model of infantile sexuality (1905) explains this by conflating dependency and sexuality. Children undoubtedly do have sensual wishes and exhibit the precursors of adult sexuality both in behaviour and in fantasy. But Bowlby and others argue that attachment/dependency needs and sexuality are distinct spheres, and that the latter come mainly into play with the advent of adolescence (Diamond *et al* 2007).

Attachment and dependency account for the transferential need for parental-type love and understanding more convincingly in our view than sexual theories.

Tragically, a history of sexual abuse is common in a significant proportion of psychotherapy patients, especially, although by far from exclusively, in women. Here the child is not only subject to all the dangers which threaten when sexual relations occur between partners of greatly unequal strength and authority, such as being cowed, bullied, frightened, but is also prevented from growing up and leaving home to deal with the external world on his or her own and become autonomous. Such children have often discovered that the only way in which they can be valued, noticed or gratified is by submitting to sexual abuse, often from step-parents, siblings, uncles and family 'friends'. These events often occur within dysfunctional families so that the child cannot confide in her mother, either because sworn to secrecy by her abuser, or because she intuitively feels the mother must be protected from knowledge of the awful pain that is being inflicted under her unseeing eyes. These themes may be transferred to the consulting room, including the feeling that the only route to even a modicum of attention is through becoming the therapist's lover. Facing the pain of abuse is understandably difficult and may be evaded by seductive acting-out or covert invitations to the therapist. Just as Freud originally conceived it, such patients are immobilized by their inability to free themselves from their fixations upon the past. As we have already discussed, therapists need to be especially sensitive to the erotic aspects of transference, and help their patients work through them, without inappropriately responding, or rejecting advances in ways that make the patient feel put-down or shameful.

Therapy offers the patient a chance to re-work these ingrained patters of relating and sexuality. But the task is not easy. The therapist must treat those patients who make declarations of love with tenderness and understanding. It is important to realize that the love which is shown by the patient for the therapist is just as 'genuine', even though it may not be as realistic, as love occurring outside the therapeutic situation. Although the therapist is dealing with aspects of his patient which are predominantly 'childish', he is also dealing with an adult who is as subject as any other to the compulsive need for sexual fulfilment which man's erotic nature imposes upon him.

Gifts

Another, related, manifestation of the patient's feelings toward the therapist which may cause difficulty is the offering of gifts. Gifts from patients may signify a number of different things. Sometimes they are unconscious bribes, hoping that the therapist will feel obliged to the patient and thus to comply with his wishes in a way which she might not do otherwise. Sometimes gifts are an expression of the desire to establish a 'special', intimate relation with the therapist, not shared by other patients; or a wish to show, by flattery, that the patient is especially aware of the therapist's tastes or needs. All of these are best seen in terms of 'transference enactments'. Thus the patient may, through his gift, be 'telling' the therapist about his relationship with his mother whose love was conditional on her children being pleasing and good, rather than accepting and loving them however good, bad or ungrateful they were (which is not to say that boundary-setting, and the capacity appropriately to say 'no', are not vital ingredients in good parenting).

It is hard to refuse gifts however without seeming churlish or rude, especially if it is something which the patient has created himself. To refuse a book which one's patient had written, or a picture that he has painted could be cruel; this is so intimately part of the patient's being that it would be difficult to refuse without causing hurt. Where the gift is of little or no monetary value, one way of handling this is to say:

> 'that's very sweet of you and I am touched … but the important thing is for us to look at the feelings behind the present, what prompted you to make (or buy) it, and to understand what you are trying to express through the medium of the gift. If you really want me to keep it I certainly will, along with your notes, but maybe it really belongs with you'.

Two examples illustrate some of the difficulties that receiving gifts present.

> One day a woman, a devoted and compliant patient who had always felt second best in her parent's eyes to her high-flying brother, brought her therapist a lovely looking fruit cake. For some reason he had an overwhelming counter-transference (see below) feeling that the cake might be poisoned. Remembering the famous Latin tag apropos the Trojan Horse 'I fear the Greeks even when they bring gifts' he felt he must put this feeling to good therapeutic use. 'I wonder lurking in that lovely cake may be a smidgeon of resentment towards me, I am about to go on holiday. Perhaps you resent this, and want to neutralize your resentment with a gift – and a covert message to me that you fear I think you are a bit of a 'fruit-cake''. This led to an interesting discussion in which she admitted that she did feel that I was uninterested in her, and felt devastated at the prospect of the upcoming break. Somehow that defused the cake problem, and she took it home to share with her husband and child.

> Another patient, a wealthy man, arrived at a session and slapped an envelope down on the table containing several thousand pounds. He suffered from bipolar disorder, a condition in which over-spending and money mismanagement is part of the illness. Here the therapist refused point blank to accept the gift, but in the course of time suggested to the patient that he could, if he wished, make a donation to the department's library. The transference meaning of the money was both one of aggression ('all you are interested in is money, not me'), and avoidance of mental pain ('if I give you money you won't make me think about the mess my life is in'). Interpreting the patient's profligacy as a way of trying to escape from his underlying depression was important; but it was also important to acknowledge his genuine wish to express gratitude to the therapist and the hospital.

In general, it is best to refuse gifts, except at the end of treatment, when a gift may not only signify appreciation on the part of the patient, but may also ease the process of parting. Gifts, at this stage, may be an expression of the fact that the patient feels more on equal terms; that he or she also has 'something to give'.

The universality of transference

The emotions exhibited by the patient toward the therapist may be of any degree of intensity. Although transference is a universal phenomenon, there are also those who pass through a period of therapy without showing evidence of profound emotional involvement. However, even in such cases, the therapist should try to make himself aware of the patient's attitudes to himself, and be prepared to investigate these, whenever it seems appropriate. A simple entrée into this is from time to time to ask the patient near the end of a session how he is finding the process. The therapist should also be alert to indirect references to the therapy and the patient's feelings about it.

> Thus a patient might be complaining about the impact of her children's half-term on her routines. The therapist might say 'well of course I was away last week too … '. 'Yes' comes back the reply, quick as a flash, 'and I really *needed* you then, just when you were no doubt gallivanting on the ski-slopes with your family,

or whatever you were doing'. This came from a patient whose parents were, by her own account, 'never there', 'always working'.

Here we find a typical Malan-type triangular transferential pattern connecting the present (children's half-term); therapist (his break); and past/parents (neglect).

Most, if not all, patients who seek psychotherapy show evidence of disturbance in interpersonal relationships. They will, inevitably, reflect this disturbance in their attitudes to the therapist; and it is when they begin to become aware of such attitudes in the here-and-now of the therapeutic encounter that they begin to change. People who approach others with habitual suspicion, for instance; or who are invariably submissive, or who, perhaps, are intellectually arrogant, may be quite unaware (unconscious) that such attitudes interfere with their relations with others. It is only within the therapeutic situation that they are likely to become aware of such things; for it is unlikely that the people they encounter in ordinary life will point these attitudes out without causing offence, and ordinary encounters will not give them the opportunity to change. One reason why psychotherapy is apt to be a slow business is that changing attitudes takes time and repeated correction. Psychoanalysts refer to this as 'working through' (Freud 1911–15); a phrase which acknowledges the fact that, although certain insights may come in a flash, making use of those insights requires patient application.

Counter-transference

Just as Freud initially thought of transference as an interference, holding up the flow of free associations, but gradually came to see it as the key to therapeutic change, so too counter-transference was first seen as an impediment to therapy. If, it was argued, patients could maladaptively bring past perceptions into the present, might not therapists be similarly afflicted? Counter-transference at this stage was seen as a blind spot, a flaw in the therapist's make-up, which could impair her capacity to help her patients. To repeat an example already given, if a therapist had an alcoholic father this might well lead her either to be less than sympathetic, or conversely inappropriately over-solicitous, with her problem-drinking patients. The answer to this dilemma, as true today as it was for Freud, is personal analysis for the therapist.

But there is also a very different sense in which the term counter-transference is nowadays used, alongside this 'classical' account. Psychoanalytic thinking has moved from its early models of the mind in which the unconscious was thought of as a repository of powerful primitive drives, the taming of which fell to the ego, beset also with external prohibitions from society internalized as the superego. In contemporary thought, unconscious and ego are no longer necessarily seen as opposing forces. Psychological health depends on harmonious collaboration between the imaginative, creative, unstructured 'dream-self', and the rational, orderly, reality-oriented conscious self (Rycroft 1985). If this is so, then the therapist's unconscious is not a hindrance to good therapy, but a vital part of it. The therapist needs to be able to tune into her own free associative reactions to the patient and to make use of them in her attempts at understanding. In this sense, the largest part of 'the art of psychotherapy' consists in being able to give one's counter-transference free reign, listen to it, and put it to good therapeutic use.

A good rule of thumb is that if one has a strong 'counter-transference' feeling in the course of a therapy session – e.g. arousal, excitement, compassion, sadness, irritation, boredom, anger – one needs to find some way of weaving that into one's interpretations and comments. Equally one may find one's mind wandering off in an apparently irrelevant way; that too is grist to the therapeutic mill.

> One might notice for example that an indoor plant was looking a little parched and needing watering; the therapist thinks to herself, 'I must get rid of that one and find something hardier'. Let's imagine that the therapy is time-limited and nearing its conclusion, and that the patient is someone whose idyll with his mother came to an abrupt end when a sibling was born. This could then be turned into a comment to the patient at an appropriate moment along the lines of 'I wonder if you are feeling rather undernourished these days ... perhaps you feel that with the end in sight, I have switched off a little, and am already thinking of my next patient, a little bit like when your mother got pregnant with your younger sister'.

Ferenczi (1980) paved the way for the contemporary conception of counter-tranference initiated with Heimann's famous paper (1950) in which she pointed out how the therapist's counter-transference is an important clue to the inner world of the patient. This is often conceptualized in terms of 'projective identification' (Waddell 1998; Hinshelwood 2011), a Kleinian concept based on the idea that people may induce those around them to embody or experience unacceptable aspects of their own feelings or personality. In the above example the therapist's attention shifted momentarily from the patient to the ailing plant. In her inner thought-drama, she enacted at that moment the very trauma with which the patient was wrestling – his feeling of displacement by a rival sibling. From this contemporary perspective the therapist's counter-transference response is viewed as *induced* by the patient's unconscious, rather as a moving magnet induces a current in an adjacent wire. By cultivating the capacity simultaneously to feel such feelings, and to observe oneself feeling them ('mentalising' yet again!), the therapist puts her counter-transference to therapeutic ends.

This capacity for 'binocular vision' (Bion 1968), 'listening with the third ear' (Reik 1922), or bi-hemispheric attention (McGilchrist 2010), in which one simultaneously listens to the patient, while allowing one's counter-transference reactions to arise and flow freely in one's mind, rather as the listener can hear the different voices in a fugue, is a key therapeutic skill. Becoming proficient at using one's counter-tranference is a life-long task. This is one of the many reasons why supervision is so important for therapists, however experienced, as it is primarily in supervision that one can tease apart the relative contributions of transference and counter-transference in both classical and contemporary senses.

Diagnosis and Psychodynamic Formulation

Psychotherapy is rarely people's first profession. Part of its attraction, especially for those in mental-health professions is that it breaks the mould of instrumental 'labelling' and the 'medical model' – symptom, diagnosis, treatment – and considers the person and their life history, the Self, as an experiential, existential, ethical whole.

Nevertheless, classifying and categorizing are both inescapable and essential. In any encounter, we need to know who, and what, we are dealing with, and to adjust our expectations and focus our attention accordingly. The psychoanalyst Wilfred Bion is often quoted as saying that one should approach one's patients 'beyond memory and desire' – but he was notorious for having a photographic memory and an incisive mind both of which he needed to keep in check; also, as Jung said of the search for a Self-free nirvana, before one can lose one's Self, one needs first to find it. Holism and diagnosis are two halves of a dialectic: we need to think about what sorts of problems our patients have and what kinds of people they are to be so afflicted; *and* to be able to respond spontaneously and without preconceptions to their uncategorized being-in-the-world.

Diagnosis

Psychotherapy is no panacea. For people suffering with psychotic depression, schizophrenia, dementia, active addiction to alcohol or drugs, severe eating disorders, serious suicide intent, or life-crippling obsessive-compulsive disorder, the first line of help may well be symptom-focused treatments. These might include pharmacotherapy, cognitive behaviour therapy, general psychiatric management and rehabilitation. As the adage goes – there is no such thing as emergency psychotherapy. Psychotherapy can come later, or as an adjunct, but therapists are ill advised to take on patients with these sort of problems when they are in full flood, or without collaboration and backup from another professional.

That means, like it or not, that diagnosis is important, whether this be made by the therapist or by a co-professional. If the former, that justifies and requires detailed inquiry about the fabric of a person's daily life: sleep, eating patterns, suicidal feelings (where again the 'how often do you beat your wife' procedure works: 'how suicidal would you say you are?'), use of alcohol and drugs, and any psychotic thoughts or experiences, and, where appropriate, their sex life.

Thus far, from the point of view of psychotherapy, diagnosis is mainly a matter of exclusion. If none of the major problems listed above apply, that clears a space within which psychotherapeutic work can be done. The patient may well have some of the symptoms listed above – anxiety, depression, suicidal feelings, difficulties with eating or addiction – but not of sufficient severity, or so overwhelmingly crippling, that they cannot be tackled psychotherapeutically. As always, therapists need to be sensitive to severity and *context*, and to gauge the extent to which the patient's illness prevents them from coping with their daily life – including the capacity to get to appointments on time, pay fees etc.

Therapists use classification in one of three ways. First, as above, in order to make sure that the patient they are treating is suitable for therapy, and does not require a different approach. Second, even within its own terms, the psychodynamic approach makes diagnostic distinctions. A commonly used one is the 'pre-Oedipal/'two person' (i.e. child-mother) versus 'Oedipal/'three person' (i.e. child-mother-father/sibling) dichotomy. The former usually refers to more disturbed clients whose developmental trauma is located in the early mother-child bonding stage.

Another binary classification, attributed to Jung, is that between introvert and extravert. In Chapter 12 we shall develop an attachment-derived tripartite classification of personality into those who 'deactivate' their emotions, those who 'hyperactivate' them, and those whose attachment patterns are 'disorganized'.

Defence classification

Implicit in all these approaches is the idea that a person's character can be understood in terms of how they negotiate the psychobiological challenges of development – the need to be safe, to be nourished, to be able to learn and grow and play, to reach maturity, to reproduce, to be part of a social network, to provide for and rear children, to cope with loss and trauma, etc. 'Defences' represent the often- unconscious strategies and attendant compromises people arrive at as ways of balancing the internal, relational and social forces to which they are subject.

The theory of defence mechanisms has been developed by Valliant (1992). Building on Anna Freud (1936) he classifies them into four groups: *mature* (e.g. humour); *neurotic* (e.g. intellectualization); *immature* (e.g. passive-aggressive); and *pathological* (e.g. denial and projection). Valliant's long-term follow up studies of men classified originally under those four headings reveal that those with mature defences had better adjustment, happiness, job satisfaction, and friendships; fewer hospitalizations and better overall health; and a lower incidence of mental illness. Conversely presence of 'immature defences' is related to poor adjustment, higher divorce rates and marital discord, less satisfactory friendship patterns, higher incidence of mental illness, greater number of sick leave days taken, and poorer health generally.

Thinking about a person's predominant defence style can help the therapist attune to transference and counter-transference reactions. Someone with, say, narcissistic style is likely to find it difficult to see the therapist as a separate person with their own views and thoughts; or those with obsessional defence styles may put pressure on the therapist to give them precise explanations and instructions for living. A key aim for therapy is to help the patient be aware of their defence styles and to move from less to more mature modes.

The formulation

The third way in which therapists think diagnostically is in coming to a *formulation*. Formulation attempts to synthesize the two halves of the dialectic mentioned above. It is both diagnostic/categorical and unique; off-the-peg and individually tailored; *table d'hote* and *a la carte*.

A formulation aims to cover all or most of the following points.

- What are the ways in which the patient feels that things are not right in their life?
- If therapy was successful, how would things be different in their lives?
- What would others notice if they suddenly became 'better' overnight?
- What part has trauma and loss played in their life?

Diagnosis and Psychodynamic Formulation

- Are there current factors in their life that are preventing recovery?
- Are these internal to the patient (self-defeating attitudes and behaviours) or external (pressure from parents, spouse, living circumstances)?
- Are the patient's main difficulties 'internalizing' (e.g. depression, anxiety) or externalizing (e.g. arguments with colleagues, drunkenness, risky sexual behaviours)?
- Are the patient's defences predominantly 'primitive/pathological' (splitting, projection, blaming), intermediate (obsessionality) or mature (humour, 'sublimation')?
- How much 'ego strength' and resilience does the patient display – in terms of being able to weather storms, make their own decisions etc?
- What are their sources of self-esteem? Are there areas of success, competence, and interest in their lives?
- Who is or are the key people, or attachment-figures, to which they have in the past and would now turn to in times of trouble?
- Has the patient had previous therapy or counselling? If so, what went well, what not so well?
- How motivated is the patient to work on themselves, and to turn up regularly for therapy?
- Is the problem 'pre-Oedipal' (two person, e.g. narcissistic) or Oedipal (three person, e.g. excessive jealousy, difficulty with assertiveness)?
- How do they relate to the therapist? Deferential, challenging, avoidant?
- What is their narrative style? Dismissive, rambling, disorganized?
- What were the interviewer's predominant counter-transference reactions, and how might these be related to the patient and his problems?
- Was the patient able to think about themselves, and make use of the assessor's tentative interpretations?
- Was the patient able to get in touch with painful affect in the course of the assessment?
- What would be realistic and desirable outcomes for therapy?
- What difficulties, transferential or counter-transferential, can be anticipated?

Here is a fictional example of the development of an initial formulation.

> The patient, 46, a single mother, had had recurrent major depressive episodes, and sought therapy when she developed depression following the break-up of a five-year relationship with a married man. She herself had been brought up by her lone parent mother, a narcissistic woman who had numerous affairs throughout the patient's childhood. In the initial interview she described how she longed for closeness, but at the same time felt intruded on whenever she did get close to a man, and how she felt this had contributed to the breakdown of her relationship.
>
> She mentioned at the outset that her funds were limited and that she could only afford infrequent sessions.
>
> In the course of the interview she became very tearful, her face distorted with suffering and misery. Without saying much or indeed consciously being aware of any more than adopting a 'witnessing' stance, the therapist mirrored this distress with her physical posture, facial expression and non-verbal murmurings of sympathy. The patient responded to this by seemingly 'seeing' her own affects through the therapist's eyes and ears, and therefore to an extent objectifying them, saying with a wry smile 'by the way, I don't think I'm depressed – just distressed'.
>
> As the formulation began to crystallize in the therapist's mind she hypothesized that it was precisely this kind of responsiveness that the patient's self-preoccupied mother would have found very difficult to achieve. The patient came into therapy with the idea that there was something 'wrong' with her which drove people

away – her intolerance of closeness, 'bad temper' etc. The therapist offered a new set of meanings: her fear of intimacy linked with her mother's neglectfulness (better to be self-sufficient than get close to another and then be abandoned); her choice of partner was a continuation of this pattern; her angry outbursts represented the protest of the abandoned child. Underlying everything was the fear that if she gave up her fragile self-sufficiency things would fall apart, and yet she had to cope with her longing for intimacy.

The therapist suggested that she had learned as a child to keep her distance from her attachment figure, achieving a modicum of security thereby, protecting herself from her mother's narcissistic intrusions, albeit sacrificing intimacy and understanding. She suggested that she had then reproduced this pattern in her relationship, choosing a married man, who was, like her mother, not really available. But now, without him, she was left with her longing and neediness. Her defence of self-sufficiency had broken down, but the result confirmed her tragic view that to expose herself meant rejection. In addition the loss of her man may have revived childhood feelings associated with her missing father. The danger was that this pattern would be reproduced in therapy. Her declaration that she could only manage infrequent sessions meant that here too she was trying to square the circle of simultaneous intimacy and avoidance.

The therapist stated that once a week should be a minimum, but that she would be prepared to see her fortnightly but not less often, as that would then perpetuate her difficulties rather than helping to overcome them. The patient emailed the next day to say that she would like to come weekly. Had the therapist insisted on this from the start she might have decided against therapy; by partially accommodating to her defence-structure, while interpreting it, enabled the patient to think about her decision and begin the long journey from defensive isolation to openness and vulnerability.

She would need in the course of therapy to be able to bear the pain of loss without relapsing into depression. The therapist noted that depressive illness was a real possibility and suggested she consulted her GP with a view to taking antidepressants. The patient found this suggestion very threatening and here too the stark alternatives of self-sufficiency or dependency were played out in relation to drug therapy. She needed to learn to steer a middle course and to discover that dependency did not mean abandonment or abject servitude.

Selection for psychotherapy

There are no absolute criteria both for selecting or excluding someone from a course of therapy. In his papers on technique Freud (1911–1915) laid out a number of guidelines. For example he was opposed to analysis for people with psychosis and those over 40 years old. Neither of these would today be considered absolute contraindications. Each case needs to be considered on its merits, and the answers to the questions listed above taken into consideration. Good outcomes in therapy are not so much a feature of the specific problem or illness from which the patient suffers, but issues such as motivation, the capacity to form a positive working alliance with the therapist, their ability to make use of sessions, especially as revealed by affective responses to interpretations. With disturbed people therapy can be highly beneficial, provided other mental health workers or a supportive spouse are available to provide backup between sessions and during breaks.

Therapists need also to be conversant with other forms of therapy such as cognitive therapy, couple therapy, art therapy etc, and to consider whether one of these approaches might not be more appropriate than dynamic therapy for the particular patient with his specific difficulty. Thus severe obsessive-compulsive disorder (OCD) on the whole responds better (although not all that well!) to cognitive behaviour therapy than to analytic therapy.

Diagnosis and Psychodynamic Formulation

People suffering from schizophrenia generally need medication and friendly support rather than intensive therapy. Uncomplicated depression is often first treated with cognitive therapy and only when the result is poor, or there is a history of childhood adversity, referred for psychodynamic therapy.

Many therapists work in third-party funded services where diagnosis is seen as important. Here dynamic therapy has to compete with other forms of therapy and prove its worth and that, despite the costs of training therapists, and relatively long treatments, it is good value for money. In the next few chapters we shall look at working with some of the main diagnoses patients bring into the consulting room, starting with one of the commonest; depression.

10

Depression

Depression is a very common condition, and, worldwide, one of the foremost causes of suffering and disability. A number of different depressive patterns exist. Depression may range in severity from a temporary state of low morale which anyone is likely to experience in the face of commonplace setbacks, to a tormenting condition of melancholic hopelessness which may result in suicide. As in the case described in the previous chapter, depression is sometimes clearly a response, though perhaps an excessive response, to definable events like bereavement, a broken love affair, failure in an examination, loss of a job or a financial reverse. In major depressive disorder low mood is likely to be accompanied by insomnia, loss of appetite and consequent loss of weight, and other physiological manifestations. Some people feel chronically 'down' and are persistently dysphoric. In bipolar disorder the sufferer swings between episodes of elevated mood and depression, although even when 'high' there are often traces of depression. Mania can be helpfully thought of as a 'manic defence' against misery and depression, especially as the manic patient often causes chaos around them, and facing up to the consequences of that is depressing in itself.

The origins of depression: contextual and developmental

Contextual as well as developmental factors play a big part in determining whether or not a traumatic event produces clinically definable depression or not. Depression seldom comes out of the blue without any precipitant, and people who react to traumatic events with depression are generally contending with a variety of difficulties that render this response more probable. Thus, those who are struggling with an unsatisfactory marriage or with poor housing are more likely to become depressed. So are women who lost their mother before the age of eleven. Other factors which make them more vulnerable are having three or more children under the age of fourteen at home; having no other adult in whom to confide; and having no employment outside the home (Brown and Harris 1979). Working-class women are more likely to become depressed in response to precipitating events than their middle-class counterparts. Those who have to cope with chronic physical ill health are also more vulnerable to depression; and in underdeveloped countries, chronic depression is common as the result of malnutrition, disease, and infestation with parasites. In our own culture, certain infections, for example glandular fever and influenza, are notorious for leaving the sufferer depressed, as are the biochemical changes which follow upon the end of pregnancy, or which occur at the menopause. Pre-menstrual tension and depression are sometimes associated.

It is important that therapists take into account all the circumstances of the patient's life, both past and present, if they are to understand the condition. In addition, they must study the personality of those who are particularly liable to depression; even if they believe that there is a significant genetic contribution to this liability, which in some cases is undoubtedly so. Blatt (2008) makes an important distinction between people who suffer from 'anaclitic' (leaning-on or dependent) depression, and 'introjective' (self-absorbed; isolated) depression.

These represent different strategies of defences against feeling mental pain, species of 'affect phobia' (McCullogh *et al* 2003). In anaclitic depression the pain is partially transferred to, or shared with, the person on whom the sufferer is dependent (in therapy often the therapist). In introjective depression the sufferer tries to isolate himself from others so as to suffer no further losses, and experiences the medicalized symptoms of depression rather than the sadness, helplessness, and misery of loss.

Some of those who are temperamentally inclined toward depression are, except when actually suffering from the condition, robust, aggressive personalities who, most of the time, cope successfully with their underlying tendency by being overactive, and may exemplify subclinical bipolar disorder. Balzac and Winston Churchill were both examples of this type. However, most of the depression sufferers who come the way of the psychotherapist belong to the more passive, dependent anaclitic group.

In the face of adversity, people with this kind of personality tend to feel both helpless and hopeless. Instead of imagining that, by their own efforts, they can improve their condition, they believe themselves to be at the mercy of events. On the surface, they may display not only misery, but hopeless resignation, affirming that whatever adverse circumstance is making them depressed was not only to be expected, but also, in some way, their own fault. Their resignation is more apparent than real; for, like the rest of mankind, they not only suffer, but also resent what has caused their suffering, However, instead of their resentment being mobilized to make an effective response, it is repressed and turned inward, showing itself only in self-blame and self-depreciation.

Such people, therefore, often seem far more ineffective and inadequate than in fact they are; and the psychotherapist's task is not only to reinforce the glimmer of hope which has brought the patient to seek help, but also to disinter the active, aggressive aspect of his personality which, being largely repressed, is unavailable to him.

Self-esteem

The most striking characteristic of most depression sufferers is the absence of built-in self-esteem. When a person is actually suffering from depression, it is usual for him to feel, and to refer to himself as, worthless, no good, hopeless, not worth bothering with, a failure, a 'waste of space'. Although the patient's depression may have been initiated by bereavement, a broken love affair etc, his feelings of hopelessness and his self-castigation seem to the observer to be out of proportion to the event which sparked them off. The respiratory tract of an asthmatic is unduly sensitive to certain allergens which cause a degree of bronchial spasm and outpouring of mucus comparable to that induced in a normal person by poison gas. Similarly, the psyche of the depressive is unduly sensitive to events which lower self-esteem, reacting profoundly to reverses which, to the normal person, seem minor or at least endurable. Thus, a quarrel that to some might seem no more than a passing episode, seems to the depressive to be the end of the world. Failure in an examination which, to most students would involve no more than a transient annoyance at having to repeat some work, may spark off feelings of total worthlessness.

People with a tendency to depression often take the view that, in their periods of depression, they have greater insight into the true nature of things than when they are cheerful, and that periods of freedom from depression are no more than mirages which obscure reality. Most therapists take the opposite view, believing that the patient's depressed mood distorts his vision. However, there is a sense in which the patient is right: a great part of his life is determined by efforts to avoid depression; to establish defences against this dread condition by over-activity, gaining esteem from external sources, or any other manoeuvre which will prevent descent into the abyss. It seems that the state of depression underlies all the fronts which he may present to the world, rather as a house may beneath the surface be in a sad state of decay despite presenting a brightly painted exterior.

Although the depressed person's protestations of his own worthlessness may seem exaggerated, he is right when he affirms that his state of depression is more real, more truly reflective of his essential self, than his state of mind at other times: it is so for him, however it may seem to anyone else.

From what source is self-esteem derived, and why is it that the depressive has so little of it? The psychodynamic account of the origins of self-esteem runs as follows. The human infant is born into the world in a helpless and dependent state, and remains so for a period that, in comparison with his total lifespan, is longer than that of any other creature. It is reasonable to assume that the human infant has, at first, but little notion of his own capabilities or lack of them. As he matures, however, he becomes increasingly aware of his dependency and helplessness relative to adults. If he is brought up in a home in which he is welcomed, played with, cuddled, and delighted in, the likelihood is that he will come to feel himself sufficiently a worthwhile person to counteract his realization of his own inevitable inadequacy compared with adults. Loved children are generally praised for every new accomplishment; for every word learned, for the beginnings of manual skills, for all kinds of achievements which, only a year or two later, will be taken for granted. And the more that parents are 'irrationally' adoring, the more is a child likely to grow up thinking well of himself, irrespective of his accomplishments. Unconditionally loving parents habitually, and rightly, overvalue everything that their infants do. Because his parents value him so highly, the child comes to have a good opinion of himself. Whereas his self-esteem originally depended upon repeated affirmations of his worth from outside sources, it gradually comes to depend upon something within himself which has become built-in as part of his own personality. The process is not unlike that of the formulation of conscience, in which prohibitions originally promulgated by parents become the person's own conscience or super-ego.

Contact with the mother may be interrupted by her illness or death. Research into the development of subhuman primates has confirmed the hypothesis that some forms of depression may be related to severance of the mother-child tie in infancy (Suomi 2008). Monkey infants brought up in isolation for six months are fearful and insecure when introduced to their peers; are unable to play; and, later, are unable to mate. Infant monkeys which are separated from their mothers for short periods even when they have already become somewhat independent, not only become depressed at the time, but show after-effects which persist for years, for example, less social play and greater fear of strange objects. Similar processes may operate in humans, although research suggests that the long-term effects of childhood bereavement result from the consequent social disruption rather than the loss itself (Rutter 1981).

Depression precursors are as much to do with the subtleties of parent-child relationships as with major trauma. Parents may not proffer enough irrational adoration; or may tend to keep the child over-dependent, thus depriving him of any sense of his own achievement. A child may be born with a physical disability, or may suffer so much ill health that he continues to feel inadequate compared with his peers. Or the parents may set such high standards that the child comes to feel that he will inevitably fail to live up to them. Depression-prone people do not necessarily feel disregarded but rather that they have been weighed in the balance, and found wanting.

The absence of an inner sense of worth has a number of consequences. First, such a person may become more than usually dependent upon the good opinion of his fellows. Depressed people are highly attuned to what others think of them, since repeated assurance of their good opinion is as necessary to his psychic health as are repeated feeds of milk to the physical well-being of infants. They are 'hungry' for approval (which some psychoanalysts take as evidence that depression is related to an 'oral' regression), and need recurrent proofs of their acceptability in the shape of repeated reassurance from others, recurrent successes, or other bolstering devices to prevent them relapsing into despair. Being so dependent upon the good opinion of others and so vulnerable to criticism means that the depression-sufferers are less than normally assertive with other people, and overanxious to please them. Some become expert at identifying with others, and are exceedingly sensitive to what the other person is feeling. Because they are so anxious to avoid blame, and to obtain approval, they develop antennae which tell them what might upset, and what might please those with whom they are associated.

This kind of adaptation to others carries with it obvious disadvantages. The habit of deferring goes hand-in-hand with a kind of passivity and can be looked upon as a prolongation of one aspect of childhood. Children defer to their parents because they need to in order to keep their parents' approval; and also because, for many years during which they are growing up, the parents do in fact 'know better' because of their longer experience. Depression sufferers often defer to persons who, in reality, are their equals or even inferiors; and this habitual mode of behaviour has the effect of reinforcing their sense of their own worthlessness.

Moreover, habitually to be so orientated to what others are feeling, often has the effect of making people uncertain of their own feelings; of dissociating them from their inner selves. Since they are always guided by the opinions of others, they end up by having no identifiable opinions of their own. Always adapting to the emotional state of others, they become progressively less conscious of what they themselves are feeling. Because of this habitual suppression of the independent, executive aspect of their personalities, such people feel themselves to be more helpless than the average person, and turn to others to tell them what to do in any situation in life requiring decision. An underlying conviction that whatever choice they themselves make is likely to be wrong, and a desire to avoid blame if things in fact turn out badly, supports this tendency; with the consequence that they not only feel themselves helpless, but often are so in reality. Someone with good self-esteem assumes that whatever they decide it will probably turn out well. Someone with low self-esteem believes that their happiness turns on making the right decision, leading to agonies of indecision, believing that their whole future rides on the decision, rather than focusing simply on the pros and cons of the specific choice to be made.

Recent non-psychoanalytic work has emphasized the role of helplessness in depression. Helplessness and hopelessness march hand in hand. The depression-prone feel themselves to be powerless to affect the course of events, and therefore 'give up' and adopt a passive role. In the histories of depressive patients, it sometimes emerges that the individual did far less well at school or university than his intellectual gifts would warrant. This is generally because, at some point in his development, he became convinced that his own efforts would be useless. Later in life, when experience has taught them that some measure of success does in fact follow from their own efforts, they may substitute ceaseless striving for passivity. This is why achievement of a goal is often followed by depression. The writer who completes a book, the businessman who brings off a deal, the person who is given promotion, may all find that depression rather than euphoria follows their success. If one has been striving very hard to achieve a particular end, completion of the task actually involves a loss; a loss of the endeavour to which so much energy has been devoted, and which, during the effort, may have contributed to self-esteem by making the individual feel effective or important. People not prone to depression feel the need of a holiday on completion of a demanding task; the depression-sufferer often finds that holidays precipitate depression.

We have seen that, in their personal relationships, people liable to depression tend to suppress their own opinions, and covertly or overtly defer to others. This lack of assertiveness involves considerable repression of what may be called the aggressive side of the depressive's personality. But it is impossible to separate entirely the violent, destructive, hostile aspect of aggression from the constructive, effective, assertive aspect, without which no decisions would be taken, no leadership proffered, no action to alter events embarked upon. Without a certain assertion of his own personality, a person ceases to exist as definably distinct. In his relationships with others, the depressive personality generally feels defeated. What he is usually unaware of is that there is another side to his masochistic submission of self; a violent, hostile and destructive side of which he is usually so frightened that he has erected formidable defences to make sure that it does not emerge. No human being can experience repeated defeats at the hands of others without resenting them. What the depressive has done, albeit automatically and without conscious intent, is to throw the baby out with the bath water. By repressing his destructive hostility, he has at the same time deprived himself of those positive features of aggression which would allow him to assert himself when necessary, stand up to other people, initiate effective action, 'attack' difficult problems, and make his mark upon the world. Helplessness and hopelessness march hand in hand: let us add hostility to make a triad of 'h's.

Therapeutic strategies

In sum, people suffering from depression are wrestling with all or some of the following issues: loss and avoidance of the pain associated with grieving; lack of unconditional acceptance and consequent feeling that they must please others; deficient inner sense of worth or self-esteem; passivity; perfectionistic generalization from temporary or minor faults to global condemnation; suppressed anger.

If this outline is accepted, it is possible to delineate what the therapist is aiming at and to suggest how positive results may be achieved. First, the fact that the therapist is willing to continue to see a depressed patient over a period of time in itself reinforces hope and counteracts despair. Second, the therapist's acceptance and understanding of the patient tends to counteract the latter's negative view of himself, and may over time become internalized as a good internal object. The patient, because he comes to feel that there is at least one person in the world who genuinely appreciates him, may alter his attitude towards others, assuming that they are more likely to be friendly than critical. This can stimulate benign circles of reinforcement and activity, as opposed to the vicious ones of depressive passivity and isolation. Third, the therapist may be able to mitigate the depressive's negative view of his own accomplishments and effectiveness (often referred to as a 'punitive superego') by drawing attention to the many occasions on which he has behaved intelligently and competently. Fourth, the therapist will try to validate and mobilize the assertive side of the patient's personality, partly so that he is less frightened of his angry feelings, and also in order that he may be able to 'attack' life more successfully.

The psychotherapist who undertakes the treatment of people suffering from mood disorders may find it helpful to bear in mind the following considerations. First, nearly all episodes of depression resolve themselves one way or another. Close examination of such recoveries usually discloses psychological factors of a more or less subtle kind which have prompted recovery, just as it is usually possible to uncover the precipitants of the attack. Loss triggers depression; 'new start' events help people overcome it. These factors seem to be of three kinds.

First, the patient, especially if he manages to remain at work, may find that his self-esteem is partially restored by discovering that he is not entirely useless. It is inadvisable to reinforce a depressed person's desire to 'give up' and retire to bed or to hospital unless he is exhibiting clear-cut psychotic symptoms, dangerously suicidal, or is so depressed that he cannot function.

Second, a depressed person may recover because he has been able to re-establish a loving relationship with people who are emotionally important to him. People who are vulnerable to depression may be thrown into a state of profound despair by the kind of transient quarrel which we all may have with people who love us and whom we love. The depressive has no certitude that he is worthy of love or that love will last. Its temporary disappearance is, to him, a confirmation of his pessimistic convictions. However, if a tactful spouse or other loved person manages to convince him that he is still loved, or if, more importantly, he manages to admit that he too was angry, his depression will often lift, at least for the time being. Such a 'flight into health' however is likely to be short-lived, and may be misinterpreted by therapists, who may erroneously flatter themselves that it is the consequence of their ministrations. It also may mean that the patient breaks off treatment prematurely. Ultimately it is the patient's decision whether or not to continue in therapy but it is worth pointing out that the aim is for relapses to be less frequent or less severe; and that learning how to deal with such episodes more effectively takes time and patience.

Because of this dependency, passivity, and anxiety to please, people with depression quickly form a positive transference. Or rather, they will rapidly appear to do so, for such patients seem to be more compliant and grateful than actually they are. Psychotherapists are easily deceived into thinking that such a patient has accepted an interpretation when, in fact, he may disagree or have reservations which he does not yet dare to express. It is particularly important for the therapist to be alert to this possibility, and to interpret excessive politeness, deference and over-eager compliance with the therapist's remarks. It is vital that the patient should learn that it is possible to be quite different from other persons and yet retain friendly relations with them – to 'agree to differ'. A certain amount of healthy aggression is required to maintain differentiation of oneself as a separate entity.

The third and most difficult task is to help the patient get in touch with his hostility. And yet it is by means of the disinterment and expression of this that recovery often comes. Since the depressive adaptation almost certainly began in childhood, it will be particularly difficult to uncover and to help the patient to accept hostile emotions to his parents, whom he is likely to have idealized. A child who is a poor mixer and who cannot stand up for himself is prone to idealization since he may feel that his parents are the only persons in the world who care for him, and that his very existence depends upon maintaining an image of them as 'perfect'. The persistence of such a belief in adult life impairs the patient's capacity to achieve independence and make new relationships.

One opportunity for disinterring hostility is when the therapist goes on holiday, or unavoidably has to cancel an appointment. The more dependent the patient, the more he will resent being abandoned. His depression is likely to increase while the therapist is absent, and he will probably complain of this while carefully refraining from criticizing the therapist in any way for leaving him. But his complaints are likely to be phrased in such a way that criticism of the therapist is implicit, for instance by employing a querulous tone of voice. Or else the patient may fall silent, saying that he has nothing to say, or that therapy is useless. This is a form of 'sulking', and if the patient can be brought to see this, he will be one step on the way to discovering that hostility can be expressed without his relationship with the therapist being compromised or even terminated.

Suicide

The risk that a depressed patient may commit suicide should never be ignored. Most people working in the field of mental health have known or worked with someone who goes on to kill themselves, and it is normal to feel guilty and depressed when this happens (Michel and Jobes 2010). As after any bereavement, one searches one's mind for occasions where one may have said the wrong thing or failed the dead person in any way. On the other hand it is very rare, although sadly not unknown, for patients to take his or her life while actually in regular treatment. Nevertheless it is important to have a sense, or explicitly to ask, how far ahead in terms of minutes, hours or days the patient can visualize themselves continuing to live, despite feeling suicidal. The next session needs to be within that interval, and that may mean a period of very frequent sessions, or possibly referral for admission or to a crisis team. Suicide in the context of therapy is more likely if the patient has had to discontinue treatment because of moving elsewhere; if the therapist unexpectedly cancels a session, however good the reason; or where the therapist has seen the patient only once or twice and has not had time to establish a relationship.

There is a difficult balance to be struck in assessing suicide risk in patients who are in therapy. If psychotherapy is to achieve one of its main objects, that the patient shall become more independent and autonomous, the risk of suicide has sometimes to be taken. Here the therapist must listen to and trust their intuitions. Worry about suicide should always be discussed openly with the patient, and where necessary lead to specific actions on the part of the therapist. At an initial consultation, if the therapist feels that suicide is an imminent possibility, she may decide that she cannot take on the case, and take steps to ensure that the patient is admitted to hospital, or treated by some other means than psychotherapy. But if the patient is coming regularly, and a psychotherapeutic relationship has been established, it can be difficult if the therapist suddenly changes from a person who is encouraging independence and freedom of choice into a risk-driven mental health monitor. But patients who threaten suicide must be taken seriously.

The meaning and implications of those feelings need to be thought about. Some may be desperate for the therapist to give them more time. Some are seeking revenge upon those they feel have not loved them; and it is important to seek out and make conscious the hostile motive in suicide, which is almost always present. Others may be seeking oblivion, which often seems to represent a final wish for complete merging with an idealized mother of the kind portrayed by Swinburne (1992) where 'even the weariest river, winds somewhere safe to sea'. It is often appropriate gently to point out that, if the patient really wants to take his own life, ultimately no one can stop him: and it is the task of therapy for patient and therapist to try together to understand the reasons why death might seem so attractive, life hold so little joy.

In general, suicidal people need at least two mental health professionals: a therapist, whose job is to help the person understand why life no longer seems worth living, and another, more in the role of case manager, whose job it is to take the steps needed to keep the patient alive, including, occasionally, admission to hospital. Another relevant point is that the distinction between deliberate self-harm and suicidality is best thought of as one of degree, not kind. Even in the most determined suicide attempt there is somewhere a longing to be saved and to find hope. Conversely deliberate self-harm objectively greatly raises the risk of dying, and although often dismissed as 'attention-seeking', it is a good principle to consider that embedded in what looks like 'manipulation', there is part of the person that is truly seeking oblivion as the only conceivable way of escaping from mental pain.

The 'depressive position' and the 'manic defence'

Melanie Klein and her followers make a useful distinction between what they call the 'depressive position' and the 'paranoid-schizoid position'. While finding such psychopathological language distasteful, we endorse the basic idea that a degree of 'depressive position' acceptance that the world is made up of a mixture of light and shade, that love and hate can and usually do co-exist, and that a degree of sadness about this is appropriate and healthy. The 'paranoid-schizoid position' is a developmentally earlier state in which the world is divided into good and bad, and one blames others or circumstances for one's unhappiness, rather than taking full responsibility for one's own faults and failings and contribution to vicious circles one finds oneself in.

Another useful Kleinian concept is that of the 'manic defence' (Waddell 1998), in which one escapes from underlying sadness in a number of ways: overwork, spending sprees, hypersexuality, or by finding legitimate enemies upon whom to vent aggression.

An example of such a person is Winston Churchill (Storr 1989).

Churchill became depressed when he was immobilized, as during his brief imprisonment by the Boers, and when confronted by failures, such as the campaign which he initiated in the Dardanelles during the First World War. His neglectful background gave ample reason why he should be vulnerable to what he called his 'Black Dog'. But, during most of his life he was adept at staving off depression. While he was awake he was seldom idle, and when he stopped working he immediately went to bed. He had, for much of his life, the sustaining influence of holding great office. When he was out of office, he turned to creative activities such as painting and wall building (the latter of which might be seen symbolically as wanting to 'wall off' his misery). He was at his best during the Second World War in which he had in Hitler an entirely appropriate object for his aggression.

Another example of a famous depression-sufferer was the philosopher John Stuart Mill (1873), whose upbringing clearly predisposed him to this condition.

Mill was remarkable in his intellectual precocity. His father, James Mill, himself undertook his education, with the consequence that Mill started to learn Greek at 3-years-old; he recalls: 'my father, in all his teaching, demanded of me not only the utmost that I could do, but much that I could by no possibility have done.' Mill was kept from mixing with other children so that he had no idea, until he was over the age of 14, that his achievements were in any way remarkable. Measuring himself against his father, he had always found himself to be wanting. Moreover his physical skills were minimal, and he remained 'inexpert in anything requiring manual dexterity'. Far ahead in intellectual matters, 'the deficiencies in my education were principally in the things which boys learn from being turned out to shift for themselves, and from being brought together in large numbers'. Moreover, as Mill observed: 'The children of energetic parents frequently grow up unenergetic, because they lean on their parents, and the parents are energetic for them'.

Mill suffered from a major depressive breakdown when he was 20-years-old. The first ray of light broke in upon his gloom when he was reading some memoirs in which the author relates his father's death:

> 'the distressed position of the family, and the sudden inspiration by which he, then a mere boy, felt and made them feel that he would be everything to them – would supply the place of all that they had lost' (Mill 1873).

Mill records that he wept at this affecting account; and clearly believes that it was because the book made him able to feel emotion again that he started to improve in spirits. A comparable turning point occurs in Coleridge's *Ancient Mariner* when the protagonist finally feels empathy for fellow creatures (in his case, sea-snakes), and is at that moment relieved of the burden of his depressive guilt (symbolized by the albatross). Mill's 'bibliotherapy' marked the end of his 'affect phobia' and he could begin to experience the emotions of sadness, grief and anger which, ironically, his depression had blocked. Another interpretation would be that this passage made him aware that sons can sometimes aspire to replace, or even surpass, their fathers; and this realization helped him to feel less inadequate. Some patients recount similar experiences when listening to music, or watching films that resonate with their own situation.

Mill's upbringing clearly demonstrates that a child may receive the most devoted attention from his parents but fail to acquire a proper sense of his own value. And both Churchill's life and Mill's demonstrate that great achievements may in part come about because an individual, who in early life believed himself to be inadequate, is driven to make especial efforts to prove the contrary.

11

Anxiety

Inevitably, going to see a therapist is anxiety provoking. Will the therapist understand me? Is it safe to lay bare my hang-ups, conflicts and shameful secrets? Can I rely on her not to gossip or laugh about me? Will she be there for me when I want her, or will she be on holiday at the crucial moment of need?

All these are normal, healthy and expected feelings. We need anxiety to stay safe, and to tell us whom to trust, when to hold back. Just as sadness and grief are normal responses to the loss of a loved one, so fear is an adaptive and protective response to external threat, helping us avoid danger. But if fear is a good thing, anxiety-disordered patients suffer from too much of a good thing. They are overwhelmed with anxiety rather than unable to benefit from it. In this chapter we shall look first at anxiety disorders in general, and then focus on one in particular, obsessionality.

Freud on anxiety

As in depression, where the source of the loss is veiled (although almost invariably present if one looks in the right place), in anxiety the source of the threat is often obscure. Thus anxiety and depression have in common either the absence of an obvious stimulus, or a seemingly disproportionate response to a trivial one. To account for this, Freud put forward two radically different theories of anxiety. In his first attempt (Freud 1905) he argued that since in anxiety disorders there is no evident *external* source of fear, the source must lie within: people are made anxious by their inner feelings – in his model predominantly sexual or aggressive. These id-impulses are repressed, and the result is anxiety. But Freud later saw that anxiety can result not just from the presence of threat, but also from the absence of someone with whom to mitigate and modulate that threat:

> 'Missing someone who is loved and longed for is the key to an understanding of anxiety' (Freud 1926).

Here the cause of anxiety is to be found as much in the absence of a protective relationship as the presence of a threat. Bowlby (1973) argues that we appraise external threat not just for its intrinsic danger, but its danger *in relation to the presence or absence of appropriate protection*. In the absence of a secure base, a child alone is wise to treat strangers with suspicion; if accompanied, the child can rely on the mother to evaluate the stranger and, with the help of her visual cueing, afford to be more exploratory and forthcoming.

Attachment theory

A basic postulate of attachment theory is that anxiety is a normal, expected and adaptive response to physical or emotional separation from a secure base. Anxiety becomes pathological when relatively trivial separations trigger intense anxiety responses. From an attachment perspective this can be understood in terms of early developmental experience which instantiate expectations of abandonment and/or difficulties in assuaging anxiety when in the presence of a base whose capacity for security provision is sub-optimal.

Secure children become anxious on separation, stop playing, express angry protest, are soothed and assuaged on reunion and will then return to exploratory activities. If the commitment of the caregiver (e.g. due to maternal depression) is intermittent, partial, or in the rare but pathogenic circumstances where the caregiver is also the source of threat, defensive or compromise processes necessarily come into play.

The resistant or ambivalent child's anxiety levels are hyper-aroused as she becomes clingy and exploration-inhibited for the sake of the security provided by the inconsistent caregiver. By contrast the avoidant child dampens down anxiety, thereby achieving a measure of security even from somewhat rejecting caregivers. The disorganized child faces a difficult approach/avoidance dilemma and may resort to various pathological self-soothing measures to reduce anxiety and build up an illusory world of self-sufficiency.

Klein

Melanie Klein (1935) postulated that the infant in the early weeks and months of its life suffers from *persecutory anxiety*. Klein, like Freud, concentrates on the 'enemy within'. She imagined the infant to have a praeternatural Oedipal sense of being usurped by the father in the mother's affections. The consequent frustration and envy leads to the defensive projection of these potentially disruptive emotions into the mother, which are then seen as persecutory.

For Klein the presence of a 'good object' is the main mitigating factor in overcoming anxiety. The role of the good object is to neutralize the anxiety aroused in the infant by his or her projected hatred and aggression.

But this in turn stimulates a second cycle of anxiety-generation. To the extent that one is able to love, the idea that one might damage the loved object with one's aggression becomes unbearable. One is now prey to *depressive anxiety*. Here mitigation flows from reparation – 'making good' the imagined injury by acts of generosity, construction and repair. In Bion's (1970) extension of Klein, the role of the good object now is to contain the projected aggression, to hold it and name it without retaliation or incomprehension, and eventually to hand it back, when the child reaches a sufficient level of maturity for this to be tolerable.

All this is clearly relevant to the work of the therapist, whose job is to be the secure base the patient turns to when anxious. Since anxiety inhibits exploration it is only when the patient feels safe that he can be expected to start thinking about himself and his inner world. The therapist is alert to ways in which she may disturb this trust – lateness, unexpected breaks due to illness, preoccupation with her own worries – all these may precipitate fear and withdrawal in the patient.

An aim of therapy is to foster the capacity to mentalise (Holmes 2010). The anxiety sufferer is encouraged to move from a non-mentalising 'teleological' perspective (e.g. 'if I go to the supermarket I'll get a panic attack') and to begin to think in interactive relational terms ('if I go to the supermarket on my own I may lose a sense of who I am and panic, since I have always relied on my mother or husband to be there for me and give me reassurance'). There is also a negatively reciprocal relationship between mentalising and anxiety – the more anxious one is the less easy is it to 'think'.

The anxiety-aggression cycle

A useful working hypothesis in the therapy of anxiety disorders is that behind every manifestation of anxiety there lies unexpressed anger, and behind every act of aggression there is latent anxiety. From an attachment perspective, separation triggers anxiety, which in turn stimulates angry outbursts in attempt to re-establish attachment. But this, as Klein suggests, may then trigger a new round of anxiety, based on the fear that the object may be damaged by one's 'demandingness' – leading to more anxiety, further aggression, and so on.

The caregiver of the securely attached child is able to accept the child's angry protest, to see it for what it is, soothe the anxiety which underlies it and so assuage anger – 'a gentle answer turns away wrath'. The anxious patient needs to learn that it is OK to feel angry and that the object of their anger will listen and survive an angry attack – as Winnicott memorably put it: 'hello object, I just destroyed you!' (Winnicott1971). A major component of Busch, Milrod and Sandberg's (2009) evidence-based treatment model of panic disorder is based on working with unexpressed aggression.

Role of control

The two fundamental defences in anxiety disorders are a) avoidance and b) control. But in the absence of a secure base, internal or external, both are doomed to failure. The world's vicissitudes cannot be entirely avoided, and we live in an inherently uncertain universe, so complete control over the unexpected is impossible.

The agoraphobic person avoids exposure to anxiety by staying within the confines of his home. The behavioural treatment approach is to help the sufferer to expose himself to fears of the outside world, in the presence of trusted other – the behavioural therapist. As we shall see, obsessive-compulsive disorder sufferers attempt to control anxiety by rituals and ruminations. Again, learning to tolerate anxiety and uncertainty in the presence of a trusted other – through, for example, 'response-prevention' in the case of obsessive hand cleansing (where the behaviour therapist literally stands over the patient and forbids him to wash his hands more than once after going to the toilet) – is the essence of therapy. Similarly when the source of the threat is one's own thoughts, as in the case of the young woman discussed on page 23 who had morbid fears of harming her relations with her thoughts, one needs a trusted other, or the internal representation of one, to be able to tolerate and normalize one's thinking.

Learning to tolerate ambiguity and uncertainty is a crucial feature of the psychotherapeutic process. The patient will observe the therapist's tentative formulations, will see her tolerating not-knowing, probing and exploring possibilities on the basis of a trust that solutions will be found. Informal cognitive challenge is as integral to psychodynamic work as it is formalized in CBT. One patient with a fear of flying was helped when his analyst, in contrast to the usual reassurances that flying is far safer than crossing the road etc, pointed out, seemingly without undue anxiety, that it is indeed the case that aeroplanes sometimes crash, albeit very rarely. With the help of a secure base, uncertainty and the reality that every contingency cannot be controlled become tolerable.

For a psychoanalytic psychotherapist, working with patients with anxiety disorders presents a particular challenge because the patient is usually manifestly distressed and often on a desperate search for an 'answer' to their feelings of panic, somatic symptoms etc. A convincing case can be made for a symptom-reduction strategy preceding psychodynamic exploration of the meaning of symptoms, in that the greater the patient's state of arousal, the less likely he will be to be able to reflect or free-associate. Hence meditation or mindfulness training, yoga etc can be recommended in parallel with psychodynamic therapy.

However, the analytic therapist can all too easily get caught up in symptom-chasing, rather than sticking to his or her last – a regular, reliable, predictable and accepting therapeutic relationship, helping the patient to tolerate and mentalise transferential anxiety, and using cognitive processes to down-regulate panic by giving meaning to symptoms.

> A woman in her late 50s had been prone to anxiety for most of her life, for which she had had a number of only partially successful short-term treatments, including CBT. She was now asking for help with incapacitating anxiety symptoms following a series of life events which included the deaths of both her parents and a close friend, retirement from her job as a local government officer, and the re-homing of a puppy which she had felt unable to manage, despite as a childless woman, having built huge hopes around this 'baby'.
>
> Outwardly controlled and calm, she said that inside she was in extreme physical pain due to muscle tension and feared constantly that her symptoms of anxiety would take over and she would collapse into a 'shaking babbling mess'.
>
> She described herself as having been moulded by a mother who, frustrated herself, wanted her daughter to be everything she herself had been unable to achieve. She felt throughout her childhood that her mother's approval turned almost exclusively on top exam grades and fulfilling her expectations.
>
> In the initial consultations there seemed an urgent need to help the patient control her symptoms. Adopting a cognitive model, mood diaries and suicide and physical pain rating scales were suggested. She dutifully brought back beautifully constructed spreadsheets showing the variations in her symptoms. She described a number of agonizing moments during her week and questioned the therapist about various techniques for managing anxiety she had found via the internet.
>
> On the fifth session she arrived apologetically confessing that her printer had scrambled the rating scales and handed over a sheet of incomprehensible numbers. The therapist intuitively felt that this was a message to be heeded, and decided to change tack. He said that she was far more expert than he in techniques for managing anxiety-symptoms, and indeed that he would be interested to learn from her more about them. He said that he saw his skills in helping her to understand the deeper meaning of symptoms, and that the best way to do this was psychoanalytic psychotherapy, and invited her to ascend the couch.
>
> Within minutes, or so it seemed, and certainly within a few sessions, she was far more able to manifest both in the transference and in her relationship with her husband, not mention her mother, the anxiety/aggression cycle that kept her trapped. She felt angry with the therapist for failing to rid her of her symptoms and for, like her mother, expecting her to 'achieve' with his charts and rating scales; angry with her husband for his 'stubbornness' about domestic matters; angry with her mother for the conditionality of her love. At the same time, and in the same breath as expressing discontent, she would immediately back-track, excusing the therapist by saying he was doing his best, her husband for having his own problems, and similarly excusing her mother. This punch-pulling 'strategic defence' (Malan and Della Selva 2006) – based on a fundamental fear of abandonment – meant that she never felt confident enough to express anger and to know that her object would survive. The job of therapy was both to redress that and help her to begin to mentalise this bind.

This patient illustrates both persecutory and depressive anxiety. She had a fundamental sense that the world was a dangerous place, and that only avoidance or control would mitigate its dangers. Such people need to learn to 'trust the universe', first in the presence of a secure base, and then with an inner confidence that they can successfully negotiate the pathway between risk and desire. Her task in relation to depressive anxiety was rather different. Here the need is to lessen an omnipotent sense of one's destructiveness. Control is an issue, but in a different way from the persecutory anxiety sufferer. Those with depressive anxiety often are over-controlling of others rather than themselves, compulsively caring towards their objects, vainly attempting to mitigate the effects of their imagined destructiveness. Their need is to learn to tolerate the ambivalence that is integral to all relationships, and that 'good-enoughness' rather than perfection is the goal, and that a degree of 'failure' is inevitable, but not necessarily catastrophic.

Tracking the differences between the various categories of relational anxiety is important. Severity is an equally important dimension. Severe childhood disturbance may permanently compromise anxiety and hormonal neural pathways, leading to chronic hyper-reactivity when faced with minor stress or ambiguity. It is important for the therapist to recognize how deeply ingrained maladaptive stress responses may be in such cases.

Obsessionality

Persons with obsessional personalities are meticulous, scrupulous, accurate, reliable, honest, and much concerned with control, order, and cleanliness. Many of those who have made outstanding contributions to Western culture exhibit these traits. Indeed, most people of considerable intellectual accomplishment need to be somewhat obsessional to achieve their results. Who would not choose to be operated on by an obsessional surgeon who counts his swabs in and out of the operating field? On the other hand, a GP who tears up a dozen prescriptions before handing over the final version is to be avoided, especially if one is in a hurry. Only when these traits become exaggerated into compulsive rituals or tormenting thoughts do we speak of obsessional neurosis.

Freud described his own personality as obsessional, and once said to Jung that, if he were to suffer from neurosis, it would be of the obsessional variety. He described obsessional personalities as:

> 'noteworthy for a regular combination of the three following characteristics. They are especially *orderly, parsimonious* and *obstinate*' (1913).

A minority of people with obsessional personalities may go on to develop obsessive-compulsive disorder. These take the form of unwanted thoughts which intrude upon the patient's consciousness; or ritual actions which the patient feels compelled to carry out against his will. The line between pathology and normality is often hard to draw. If a man exhibits occasional anxiety as to whether he has closed his front door or turned off the gas taps, we do not take this too seriously, for we have probably experienced the same phenomena ourselves. But if he always has to check the door and the taps ten times before he leaves the house, there is clearly a problem to be thought about. Writers ought to be meticulous in their choice of words; but those who, like Dorothy Parker, say 'I can't write five words but that I change seven' are in difficulties. However, the majority of obsessional patients referred to dynamic psychotherapists exhibit traits and behaviour which are not more than slight exaggerations of valuable aspects of the obsessional personality; scrupulosity, reliability, self-control, and honesty. They seek psychotherapy because of tension and anxiety, or because of difficulties in interpersonal relationships.

Whatever its causal origin, the obsessional personality is double-faced; when present in moderation, it is valuable, indeed essential to the more complex pursuits of civilized life. When exaggerated, it is destructive of spontaneity, and may eventually paralyse action. Obsessionality can be seen as an attempt to defend oneself against feelings of failure and chaos. But, since the world is inherently somewhat disappointing and chaotic, obsession-sufferers are doomed to disappointment. This is one reason why obsessionality is a risk factor for depression. However fiercely we discipline our unruly minds and bodies, there is always much about ourselves and the world we can never entirely control. Even those who dislike the processes involved, need both to eat and excrete; sex is so urgent a drive that it, too, cannot be entirely subdued. Much of our mental life, from dream to inspiration, is beyond the reach of the will. We have to fit in with our own natures, just as we do with those of other people; and the idea that control over ourselves can ever be absolute is an illusion. In Book IX of *The Republic* Socrates says that 'in all of us, even in good men, there is a lawless wild-beast nature, which peers out in sleep'. People plagued with obsessionality behave as if the beast was straining at the leash. Moreover, they are apt to assume that other people are similarly constituted; and therefore look on the world as a jungle in which the unseen hosts of Midian are forever on the prowl.

The philosopher Kant is a good example of a scholar whose whole life was ordered with meticulous exactness. The obsessional scholar's ideal, which can never be wholly realized, is that the world shall be an ordered place in which everything is understood and everything is predictable. Such also is the vision of the scientist. The progress of science depends upon the invention of hypotheses which, by bringing an ever-increasing number of facts into causal relation with each other and under one heading, impose order upon chaos, and enable more and more accurate predictions to be made. It is the discernment of anomalies, of facts not covered by existing hypotheses, which leads to new discoveries and new theories. Anomalies are a form of disorder which spur the scientist on to create a more comprehensive order; just as dirt or disarray may impel an obsessional to arrange and rearrange his room.

The wild beast which obsessionals fear is principally an aggressive animal. Although sexual impulses often constitute a part of the forces which obsessionals are trying to control, aggression plays a larger part than love in their psychology. Instead of perceiving other people as persons with whom they can make relationships on equal terms, obsessionals tend to relate in terms of domination versus submission, or superiority versus inferiority. The weaker the child feels himself to be in relation to authority, or the more dominant that authority is in fact, the more resentment will equal or outweigh the love he feels.

Many people of obsessional disposition show precocious intellectual development in childhood. This is especially true of the type of intellectual mentioned earlier. When such a child perceives his parents as restrictive authorities, he learns to relate to them by means of his intelligence rather than emotionally. In adult life he treats others as if they were authorities who might suddenly become angry; this betokens the persistence of aggressive feelings from childhood, and demands he exercise control over such feelings. In adult life, obsessionals tend either to be authoritarian and often irritable; or else unduly submissive. Either attitude is one in which the object is to disarm the other party. Faced with possible hostility, he either conquers or submits. In neither case can he achieve equality and mutual respect.

Obsessional types entering psychotherapy often appear to be especially mild, compliant characters who are anxious to please the therapist and who agree too readily with everything which she may propose. Fear of aggression from others dominates their adaptation to their fellows. They are usually carefully and neatly dressed, in order to forestall any possible criticism of their appearance. They are punctilious in keeping appointments for which they often arrive early. They show gratitude toward the therapist before she has had time to do anything to help them, and are overanxious about causing him any possible inconvenience.

Whereas this variety of obsessional is primarily concerned with warding off the aggression of other people, there is another type who is more concerned with controlling his own. When his defences fail, he becomes naggingly critical, and may be extremely difficult to live with. Tense, irritable, obsessional parents who want to keep everything under tight control extend this wish to those with whom they live. They insist upon cleanliness and tidiness; upon locking doors, being polite, keeping up appearances, not offending the neighbours. For such people – popularly known as 'control freaks' – living in a family is difficult. They may be able to order their own behaviour so that things will not 'get out of hand', but they cannot entirely control the behaviour of other people. Their anxiety leads to anger, and it is small wonder that their wives and children rebel against what they feel to be an irrational tyranny.

Thus the obsessional person's failure to integrate or control his aggressive impulses may lead in either of two directions; toward submission, on the one hand, or tyranny on the other. Extreme submission leads to his virtual disappearance as a separate entity. Extreme tyranny leads to the annihilation of the other, and hence to isolation.

These observations explain how the obsessional defences may be employed against depressive states. If the subject stays close to people, he may become angry with them because he cannot control them; or depression may result from his turning his anger against himself. Alternatively, he may detach himself from people. It is possible to live with a family and remain uninvolved emotionally. When personalities of this kind develop overt symptoms, there is usually evidence of aggression in their psychopathology. Some cannot ascend to a high place, or even travel on top of a bus, without being beset by the thought that they might drop something on passers-by. Clergymen if obsessionally inclined, whose profession requires that they be kind and understanding, frequently fear that swear words or obscenities will escape their lips at inappropriate moments, such as when they are preaching. Housewives may anxiously feel compelled to put all food which they serve to their families through a sieve, in case some minute particle of glass might do someone an injury. Such symptoms represent a failure of defence in that the repressed, underlying aggression of the subject is allowed to peep through.

The psychotherapist's task with such people is twofold. First, she must facilitate the emergence of the instinctive impulses against which the patient is defending himself. Second, she must present herself as someone with whom the patient can experiment in trying to reach a new kind of relationship on more equal terms; a relation in which the question of who is dominant and who is submissive is no longer crucial.

Obsessional patients are generally described as difficult subjects for psychotherapy because of their capacity for intellectualization. Since their whole defensive system is one designed not to allow the free expression of emotion, they find it just as hard or as dangerous to 'let go' during psychotherapy as they find it in other situations in life. They will be anxious to understand exactly what the utterances of the therapist mean. Often, they will accept her interpretations as likely to be reasonable, without giving any indication that they have struck home in a meaningful way. Such people tend to understand with their heads rather than with their hearts. Since intelligent patients of this type are often verbally fluent, they are able to use words as a way of distancing themselves from their true feelings, rather than as a means of expression. When the therapist says something which might be expected to produce outrage, like 'You must have wanted to *murder* your mother!' the patient mildly replies: 'Perhaps you're right. I suppose something of the kind must be involved.'

Such patients become much more accessible when they are depressed. It is often helpful to pick up any tiny instance of spontaneous reaction to the therapist in the here-and-now, since this may give access to the spontaneous feelings which the patient tries so hard to control. It is also useful to explore dreams, since these may be the quickest route into another side to his personality which he is attempting to suppress and banish. Some obsessional patients find that they can let go better through painting and drawing than they can by using words.

Of all patients, the obsessionally-inclined are the most likely to persist in psychotherapy even when showing little evidence of improvement. It is part of their problem that they tend to live in the future rather than in the present. Their habit of anticipating danger leads them to take all sorts of precautions about the future and to be preoccupied with it to the exclusion of the present. While at a cinema or the theatre they may be so preoccupied with imagining how they are going to get home afterwards that they fail to appreciate the performance itself. The same tendency manifests itself in therapy.

Interminable analyses may represent obsessionality in both parties: the therapist as well as in the patient. Cases of obsessional personality combined with mild compulsive symptoms are suitable for psychotherapy and rewarding to treat. However, there are also cases of severe obsessive-compulsive disorder which are beyond the capacity of the psychotherapist to ameliorate, and which are so extreme as to suggest that the causal factors are not purely psychogenic. These are the patients whose lives are so dominated by rituals that they can scarcely find time for any normal living. Some patients of this kind are even more disabled than if they were suffering from chronic schizophrenia.

Samuel Johnson is a famous example of a person who throughout most of his life employed obsessional defences to control aggressive impulses and to ward off the depression which constantly threatened him. Boswell wrote:

> 'He had another particularity, of which none of his friends ever ventured to ask an explanation ... This was his anxious care to go out or in at a door or passage by a certain number of steps from a certain point, or at least so as that either his right or his left foot, should constantly make the first actual movement when he came close to the door or passage ... I have, upon innumerable occasions, observed him suddenly stop, and then seem to count his steps with a deep earnestness; and when he had neglected or gone wrong in this sort of magical movement, I have seen him go back again, put himself in a proper posture to begin the ceremony ... ' (Boswell 1799).

This clinical description could not be bettered today. We can see how Johnson was defending himself by his obsessional rituals, and what kind of thoughts he was attempting to expel. Johnson was subject to recurrent depression; what he called 'a vile melancholy', and was plagued by constant guilt. Throughout most of his life he feared insanity. He hated going to bed because, once alone, morbid thoughts were sure to plague him. He was preoccupied with death and said that he never experienced a moment in which death was not terrible to him. He condemned himself for indolence, for having sensual thoughts, for indulgence in food and drink. This marvellous writer and lexicographer, who accomplished so much, wrote of himself, 'I have lived totally useless'.

Johnson is a fascinating and sad example of a man who kept depression at bay with obsessional defences during most of his life, but which failed at times, so that he was precipitated into a slough of despond. It is interesting that Johnson prescribed intellectual activity for a fellow-sufferer who was plagued with guilt. He himself turned to arithmetical calculations in order to divert himself; an early example of 'thought stopping'.

12

Patterns of Personality

According to the advertising of a well-known manufacturer of trekking equipment, there is no such thing as bad weather – only bad weather gear. Although this chapter could well be entitled 'the difficult patient', one could equally say that there is no such thing as a difficult patient, just ill-prepared therapists.

Reprise

Before proceeding to discuss some of the difficulties which the psychotherapist may encounter with her more challenging patients, let us summarize the three key tasks which the therapist must undertake: two fairly straightforward, the third more subtle.

Her first duty is to provide a secure, reliable background of personal concern against which the patient can develop. Just as children grow best if they are fortunate enough to live in a stable home in which continuing care is taken for granted, so psychologically troubled patients are more likely to learn to understand themselves and to cope better with their problems, if provided with a secure base in the shape of a therapist to whom they can turn as a caring, concerned person.

Her second duty is to get to know her patients sufficiently intimately to make sense both of their symptoms and personality as a whole – which can be encapsulated in the 'formulation' discussed previously. This involves having a clear picture of how the patient developed from early childhood onwards. Although such understanding does not necessarily abolish all symptoms, nor bring about radical or sudden changes in character structure, it enables the person to stand back from himself; to look at himself, modelled on the therapist, with an eye both critical and sympathetic. This capacity for self-reflection – for self-mentalising (Allen and Fonagy 2006) – is a prerequisite for change. People who seek psychotherapy do so not because they are very different from the rest of humanity, but because they are overwhelmed or demoralized by their psychopathology. When they can stand back from their own personalities and problems, and apply critical understanding to them, they are on the way to some degree of recovery.

The psychotherapist's third duty is more complex. It is to provide the patient with a laboratory in which he can see himself in action in the world of interpersonal relationships. The therapist does this by offering herself as a more or less unknown quantity upon which the patient will project the images of those who have been emotionally significant to him in the past. She then helps patients become aware in the here-and-now of how those images, and the assumptions on which they are based, influence how he currently relates to others. The therapist is both like, and unlike the patient's previous experience of significant people in his life; negotiating this discrepancy is the lever that generates change (Holmes 2012e). For a while he tries to hang onto the old while trying out the new; eventually, all being well, he can let go of past patterns and defences, and trust that new relationships will be sufficiently safe and satisfying to justify the risk involved in change.

Classifying personality

The two previous chapters have considered the common symptoms of anxiety and depression not so much as problems in themselves, but more as pointers to a developmental history, modes of defence, and ways of being in the world. In contemporary mental health practice the first line of treatment for anxiety or depression tends to be CBT or psychopharmacology. The cases we are concerned with here are those who have failed to respond to these forms of therapy, often where there is clear history of childhood adversity. These are people who want to understand themselves as whole persons, rather than abolish particular symptoms.

Thus the aim of dynamic therapy is to address this more global aspect of the personality. This takes us into the contentious area of 'personality' and 'personality disorder' and their nomenclature; in terms of DSM IV, so-called 'Axis II Disorders' (APA 1994). In the past, including previous editions of this book, 'abnormal' personalities were characterized as discrete categories – 'the' hysterical personality, schizoid personality, obsessional personality etc. This approach is now outmoded, for a number of reasons. First, such categorization has an implicit labelling quality which implies immutability, and self-perpetuating denigration. Second, we know that psychiatric symptoms are widespread in the population (Benthal 2010), and that, for example, people 'with' schizophrenia probably represent an extreme end of a spectrum in which a cascade of developmental factors – social, environmental, and genetic – have combined to produce a mental illness. 'Personality disorders' too are increasingly seen in dimensional, rather than categorical terms (Tyrer 2007). Clearly, people vary in their personalities – some are introverted, some extroverted; some neat and tidy by nature, others more chaotic; some warm, others cool; some gushing, others reticent; some risk-taking, others cautious by nature; and so on. These patterns are largely inherited, but their implications, whether they represent advantageous features or handicaps, depends on the environment in which the individual grew up. People who are 'difficult' or who 'have' personality disorders are no different in kind from the rest of humanity. We all have odd traits and self-defeating aspects to our personalities, but some are more afflicted by extreme versions than others. People suffering from 'personality disorders' need to be seen as lying at one end of a spectrum, rather than in a class of their own.

A third reason to reject a simple categorical approach is that there is a great overlap between the different categories both in terms of symptoms and etiology. Most patients fit into several of the pre-determined DSM Axis II categories, which weakens the concept of discrete 'personality disorders', and at worst leads to an absurd mélange of pseudo-diagnoses. Finally, over-simplified categorization takes no account of severity. From a clinical perspective, more important than the specific personality disorder assigned, is the severity of that disorder and the extent to which their psychological health is compromised by it. It is not enough to label someone as, say, 'Borderline' (see below); we need to know just how incapacitated they are, and in what ways, before we can get a good picture of what their life is like and how psychotherapy may or may not help.

That said, clinicians unavoidably use prototypical categorizations – as we do in everyday life, 'a typical narcissistic politician' etc – to help make sense of the varying personality types that present to psychotherapists (Westen *et al* 2012). In earlier editions, AS devoted four chapters to what he called 'the depressive', the 'obsessional' the 'hysterical' and the 'schizoid' personalities. The first two of these we have covered already. The latter two are to an extent obsolete, both in their denigratory social implications and questionable theoretical and evidential underpinning. Here we shall adopt an attachment-derived classification centred on the three types of insecure attachment (Cassidy and Shaver 2008). No doubt this too can be questioned by classification purists, although there is a remarkable overlap between these three attachment categories and Westen *et al*'s (2012) tripartite typology derived from factor-analysis of randomly selected patients attending mental health professionals. Attachment insecurity is currently described (Mikulincer and Shaver 2010) in terms of the *hyperactivating, deactivating,* and *disorganized* strategies, the implications of which will be explored in each section. These correspond with Westen *et al*'s (2012) *externalizing, internalizing* and *borderline-dysregulated* groupings.

Note that from an attachment perspective these are 'strategies' rather than categories – i.e. defence-like modes of being, ways of dealing with, and surviving psychologically in, sub-optimal developmental situations. They can be seen as solutions for growing up in a difficult environment persisting inappropriately into the present. Taking account of the severity vector, extreme versions of these strategies can be thought of in terms of the categorical approach adopted in earlier editions of this book. It is the task of therapy to help people delineate this story, and to find more appropriate ways of relating; loosening the hold of rigid or maladaptive methods of achieving security, thereby widening the repertoire of their personality.

Hyperactivating; extreme version: 'Hysteria'

The pejorative ring of the terms 'hysteria' and 'hysterical personality' means that the heart of the psychotherapist is apt to sink when he hears that a patient with such a label is being referred to him. She may imagine that she will be unable to understand or identify herself with this type of personality. While most therapists are ready enough to admit that they themselves can become depressed, suffer from various forms of anxiety, exhibit some obsessional traits or symptoms, or an avoidant detachment, they are usually reluctant to recognize or admit the existence of any 'hysterical' components within themselves. And yet these were not only those upon whose psychopathology the early structure of psychoanalysis was built, but were also those who seem best to have responded to treatment.

Today the psychotherapist is unlikely to see the dramatic cases of hysteria so vividly described by nineteenth-century psychiatrists. Gross hysterical paralyses, blindness, deafness, 'glove and stocking anaesthesia', fits, tremors and faints have become rare presentations. Fugue states, in which the subject experiences massive amnesia for large areas of the past and may find himself in a strange place without knowing how he got there, are not phenomena which the average psychotherapist is likely to encounter often. Nevertheless hysterical symptoms of a less dramatic kind are common enough. In earlier editions AS approvingly quotes Slavney and McHeigh (in Nicholi 1978):

> 'The hysterical personality is dominated by the urgent need to please others in order to master the fear of being unable to do so. This results in restless activity, dramatisation and exaggeration, seductiveness, either social or overtly sexual in manner (often creating disappointment in the other person), and immature and unrealistic dependence upon others.'

Today we would note the labelling implicit in this definition, and its negative connotations. These symptoms are best seen in terms of hyperactivating attachment strategies. Children whose caregivers' capacity to provide the undivided attention a small child needs is compromised (often by social stress, poverty, being a single parent, an abusive relationship etc) may exaggerate their emotional needs and resort to clinging relationships in order to maintain some sort of attention from their caregiver. These tendencies can then persist into adult life.

Psychotherapists who believe themselves free of hysterical potentialities should search through their memories of childhood. They are likely to find examples from their own experience of a physical symptom which conveniently let them off some boring or alarming occasion, and as conveniently disappeared again when the occasion was safely past. Hysterical symptoms serve a purpose of which the patient is unaware, or only partially aware. It may represent the normal protest which one feels towards a caregiver whose attention is distracted, and therefore exposes one to danger. It may serve the purpose of attracting sympathy or at least attention.

Patients presenting such symptoms are divided selves in that, to the observer, there is an obvious discrepancy between what the patients say they want and feel and what their symptoms make clear that they actually want and feel. 'I wanted to go for a walk, but my legs wouldn't let me.' 'I love my husband, but I can't bear him to touch me.' 'I wanted to die when I took the tablets' (but took obvious precautions to ensure that she would be found before there was any chance of dying).

This type of discrepancy arouses in the mind of the therapist the possibility of play-acting, which may be reinforced if the patient displays emotions of an exaggerated, 'histrionic' kind whether of distress, gratitude, love, or anger. In spite of Freud's description of repression, the suspicion remains that the patient is somehow playing false, simulating emotions which she does not feel, denying others which she does feel, and generally making herself out to be someone quite other than she truly is.

It is this characteristic of histrionic patients which those around such people, including their therapists, find so irritating. It is easy to feel sympathy with the despair of the depressed patient, with the isolation of the schizoid, or with the compulsions of the obsessional. Such patients are obviously 'genuine', however unconscious they may be of their less admirable aspects. But with hysteria, the doubt remains. If such a patient tries to please, he or she overdoes it in such a way that the therapist feels that she is being 'manipulated', another pejorative phrase which is often applied to such patients.

Therapists rely on the honesty of their patients. Confronted by a patient of whose honesty they feel uncertain, they tend to be nonplussed and then angry, believing that their authority is somehow being undermined, and that their role is to pander to the patient's obvious falsehoods.

It is understandable that, in such cases, the therapist should be suspicious and prone to resentment. However, she will never be able to help her patient if she continues to feel such emotions. What she has to do is to control her immediate response sufficiently to penetrate a short way beneath the façade presented by the patient. When she is able to do this, two things happen. First, she will find a deeply unhappy human being with whom she will be able to sympathize and whom she may be able to help. Second, she will see that her own resentment, irritation and anger are projections or mirror images of the emotions that belong with the patient but which he has not felt safe enough to experience. If the developmental origins of hysteria lie in anxious attachment, anger at an inconsistent caregiver is a normal biological response of a care-seeker who feels exposed and unprotected. But overtly to express such emotions runs the risk of further alienating the caregiver, hence the 'manipulative' or exaggerated symptoms, which express anger indirectly and do not threaten the caregiver's role and power.

Hysterical patients are defeated. They do not consider themselves capable of competing with others on equal terms. More especially, they feel themselves to be disregarded, and, as children, often were disregarded or neglected in reality. If a child finds that grown-ups do not appreciate his needs or try to meet them when they are made manifest, how does he behave? He becomes demanding, and attention-seeking, exaggerates his needs dramatically, or adopts subterfuges in order to get what he wants indirectly. In trying to understand this, it is useful to picture a child who has repeatedly attempted to get his parents to treat him as a person in his own right, but who has repeatedly failed in this endeavour. Many parents pay very little attention to their children's needs, or treat them simply as extensions of their own personalities rather than as individuals with separate identities and requirements.

The deafer parents are, the more the child has to shout to gain their attention. A child who is desperately frightened of going to school, but who knows that, if he were to admit such a fear openly, his parents would dismiss it as 'silly', may shout, scream, or threaten to run away or threaten suicide in order to have his feelings taken seriously. Or, if direct appeals prove ineffective, he may find that indirect ones will work. Physical illness is generally accepted as a valid reason for not attending school, and also has the advantage of ensuring at least some additional attention from adults. No wonder that children in desperate straits develop illnesses which serve this double purpose.

Patterns of behaviour of this kind are adopted by children because, at the time, they were the only ones which worked; the only way in which they could persuade adults to pay attention to their needs. Often they then set up vicious circles of maladaptive behaviour. The more neglectful the caregiver, the more the child will demand attention, and the more demanding the child, the more annoyed and neglectful the parent, until his shouts become so loud they cannot be ignored. And so the cycle perpetuates itself. When such patterns persist inappropriately into adult life, we label them 'hysterical'. Since in adults sex and attachment are closely intertwined (Diamond *et al* 2007) the client may use their sexuality as a way of gaining attention and a measure of security. Since women are allowed more exhibitionistic licence than men in our culture, these efforts are more obvious in their case. Psychotherapists become accustomed to the phenomenon of a female patient who dresses and makes up like a model, but who complains that she has little interest in sex itself, and finds it hard to enjoy making love. Promiscuous 'lady-killer' men may be embarking on a similar quest, but because society, even in a post-feminist era, condones male promiscuity more readily, their behaviour goes more easily unnoticed. It is easy to label these phenomena as 'narcissistic' (another term which has come to be used abusively), and to forget that beneath it is a person who feels that relationships have failed and therefore can only love him or herself in the absence of anyone else. Those who have never received enough attention lavish it upon themselves *faute de mieux*.

'Holding up a mirror to nature', the theatre is one of the highest of human achievements. The developmental origins of this may lie in the concept of 'marked mirroring', developed by Gergeley (see Allen and Fonagy 2006), in which the caregiver reflects back to the infant his facial expressions in a 'marked' or exaggerated way. This is the basis on which, as Winnicott suggests (1971), the mother's face is the mirror in which the child first finds himself. By seeing the mother *act* his feelings, the child can begin to *represent* them within his own psyche and thus begin to know himself. It is possible that when this process goes awry, due for instance to maternal depression, children may have to develop ways of recruiting others as 'mirrors', long beyond the normal stage at which this process is internalized. The stage as a profession has a particular appeal for the kinds of people we are discussing, and some of the most successful actors and actresses belong to this personality type, although it is dangerous for psychotherapists to generalize about particular groups since by definition they see only those who are troubled members of that class.

There are a number of reasons why this should be. First, the stage provides an opportunity for the dramatic display of emotion; something at which people with hysterical tendencies are often expert, since they learned the techniques in childhood. Second, actors and actresses, if at all successful, are applauded by their audience. This collective adoration is extremely gratifying to someone who has no inner conviction of worth. To be a public figure is rewarding even though the rewards are superficial and the fidelity of the public fickle. Third, actors are, by definition, playing parts; being someone other than themselves. People with hysterical tendencies, because they have failed to gain what they want by being themselves, are prone to adopt masks and roles in the hope that they will be more acceptable to those around them. The danger is that they may lose touch with a sense of continuity in their own personalities; to be alienated from a sense of an inner core which constitutes the 'real me'. Such people may feel that they do not exist as individuals in their own right, and dread being alone because they are then confronted with an inner emptiness. Paradoxically, they only come alive when acting a part.

Successful psychotherapy with patients of this type depends a lot on establishing a positive transference. But this does not come overnight; and there are often many ups and downs and tests along the way. Because these patients are passionately anxious to find someone who understands and cares for them, and, at the same time have almost lost hope of ever finding such a person, they may behave 'badly' in order to find out whether the therapist will be able to tolerate this. Appointments may be missed without good reason; accounts overlooked or payment postponed. During sessions patients often accuse the therapist of lack of sincerity. 'You don't really care about me, it's just a job to you, a way of making a living'. If the psychotherapist is young and relatively inexperienced, the patient may pick this up and use it against her, and one may easily become depressed at one's own inadequacy as a therapist. One must hold on to the realization that the patient's accusations spring from a deep unhappiness, and that one's induced counter-tranferential feelings of inadequacy reflect the patient's own feeling that he is not fully qualified for living, and finds it hard to establish deep caring relationships.

Some patients alternate between idealization of the therapist and global denigration. During one session they may extol her as uniquely kind, understanding, perceptive and sympathetic; at the very next launch a vicious attack on her as useless, cruel, insensitive and altogether hateful. Then, terrified of dismissal, they may write deeply apologetic letters after every 'negative' session.

Such people are profoundly deprived and unhappy people who are generally suffering from the effects of neglect throughout their early childhood. When they do form attachments, they repeat over and over again the disappointments of their childhood, making impossible demands upon their chosen objects, and then become furiously angry when those demands are not met.

Psychotherapists may find themselves confronted with emotions of an extremely violent and primitive kind which they themselves may find disturbing. Provided that the therapist remains calm in the face of abuse, she will usually find it possible to understand and sympathize with the patient's feelings, and to interpret them in terms of the patient's actual experience in childhood. Thus, if the patient accuses the therapist of neglect or rejection, the therapist might say:

> 'What you are saying is, I have to admit, quite painful for me. And I can see that our brief hour together once a week leaves you feeling abandoned and neglected for long periods. And it is true that, at one level, I am 'only' doing my job – although I do try to do that to the best of my ability. But I sense that your disappointment in me arises out of a deep feeling of pain and neglect in you. I'm sure that you have felt rejected in this way by others before me. Can you remember when you first felt as you are feeling now?'

This overlong speech breaches the precept that interpretations should be short and to the point. In a real situation only one or two of the sentences would be appropriate at any given time. But the aim here is to convey the spirit of what might be said. The final question may disclose a long history of repeated patterns of hope followed by despair, and to show the patient that in part it is because his hopes are so exaggerated that they are always doomed to failure.

It is always important to focus on the ways in which the therapist's actions in the here-and-now may have given rise to the patient's misinterpretation that he is rejecting, especially when there has been a sudden switch in the patient's attitude. Very often, some seemingly trivial but actually significant variation in the therapist's behaviour may trigger off feelings of rejection. For example, a patient may say: 'You didn't smile when you opened the door for me'; or, 'Your voice sounded different. I was sure that you were fed up with me'; or 'You yawned whilst I was talking'.

Although psychotherapists try to remain calmly and reliably the same, their demeanour is bound to vary from day to day to a minor degree. Perhaps the therapist is tired or worried or has a hangover. Patients who are hypersensitive to rejection pick on these subtle yet real changes in the therapist's behaviour. It is unwise to dismiss the patient's complaints as figments of their transferential imagination. Although there are good reasons why the therapist should not talk about her own feelings, there are times when it is right and proper to admit to being human, without going into details. Thus, in response to the patient's accusation that she seems 'different', or looks tired she might say:

> 'Yes, I suppose I do vary from time to time, and it has been a long day. You are very sensitive to pick that up. I suspect you are very alert to other people being self-preoccupied and out of touch with your feelings – just as your mother was in your childhood. I wonder if that doesn't lie at the basis of a lot of the rows you have with your partner. Anyway I am fully awake now – let's work on this issue together'. (Again overlong – but conveying the gist.)

If the therapist has really been at fault; that is, if she has actually yawned, or missed something the patient was saying, or forgotten something which the patient told her previously, it is always best to admit it. Psychotherapy can only be conducted on the basis of honesty on both sides, and to pretend to be better than one is means falsifying the relationship.

Provided the therapist has the fortitude and tact to hold on through the difficult times, the patient's good image of her will come to predominate. This may be an idealized image. The therapist may be seen as impossibly good, understanding, loving; a paragon of all the virtues, an idealized parent who will solve all problems, heal all hurts, make up for past unhappiness. It is difficult to obtain objective evidence of what has actually been missing in the patient's early development, and one must guard against the tendency to blame all on the patient's parents; nevertheless evidence does point to the link between early developmental trauma and adult psychopathology. It seems that, if we have not been given what we need at the appropriate stage in development, there is a residue of compulsive hunger which drives us to try and obtain what has been missing. This explanation certainly helps understand the kinds of patient we are discussing. He or she is driven to demand from the therapist the total acceptance, protection, care and love which mothers give their newborn infants at the stage when nothing can be expected from the infant in return.

The therapist cannot, of course, fulfil such unrealistic expectations. Even if she were to abandon all other work, and take up residence with the patient, be available at any hour of the day, minister to their slightest requirement, she still could not make up for the past, nor wholly fill the aching void which the patient carries inside. Such patients have to come to terms with the fact that, although the therapist may have been able to help them to make new and better relationships, she cannot wholly replace what has been missing in early childhood. To accept this is comparable to coming to terms with a physical disability. If one has lost a leg, one has to make do with an artificial substitute. If the patient can accept this, compulsive demands lessen, and the patient will find ways to look at life in a more realistic light. The patient needs to be helped to become depressed; to mourn for the ideal caregiver who never was, and, rather than pursue a never-ending and fruitless search for reversing past failures, to accept the present and look to the future.

Viewed in this light, hysteria is a defence against depression. In trying to avoid pain – possessed by the 'affect phobia' mentioned before – the patient makes things worse rather than better. It is only when the therapist can appreciate what lies behind the façade of demanding 'difficultness' that she can help such patients.

Avoidance; extreme versions: autistic spectrum disorder; 'schizoid'

The people we have designated as hyperactivating are predominantly extraverted, and share an obvious concern with their relationships with other people. They fear being abandoned by those upon whom their happiness seems to depend, and therefore spend much of their time in psychotherapy discussing their interpersonal relationships.

People with obsessional personalities, on the whole, are more independent. As we have seen, obsessionality can be construed as a defence against the emergence of hostility in interpersonal relationships, and they therefore tend either to placate others, or else to tyrannize them in the same way that they exert tyrannical control over themselves. Unsurprisingly, this tends to keep others at a distance; in therapy they will spend time discussing their work and other relatively impersonal topics. Some are more concerned with controlling their own hostility, and thus closer to the depressive end of the scale: while others are more perturbed by the supposed hostility of other people, and are closer to becoming paranoid. Either way, obsessional defences mean hostility is generally controllable; and people employing them are able to maintain their relations with others, albeit often in a rather rigid and formalized manner.

There is, however, another strategy in which the fear of involvement with others means that a person withdraws into himself. In mild cases this is little more than a matter of dampening down emotions – whether strong desire and love or hostility – in order to maintain a connection, albeit distant, from a necessary but feared other. But in extreme cases, which used to be labelled as schizoid, the sufferer attempts to do without human relationships as far as possible. Today they may be seen as suffering from Asperger's syndrome or as part of the autistic spectrum disorder (Baron-Cohen 2003). Such people come to the attention of psychotherapists in a variety of ways. Because they have little faith in the ability of others to understand or help them, they may be pressed into seeking help by those who are near enough to them to realize that there is something wrong. An undergraduate who is failing at his work and who shows no signs of being able to make friends or enjoy university life may be steered into psychotherapy by a tutor. Or if self-referred, such a patient will complain of not being able to make relationships, especially with the opposite sex; or of being unable to concentrate or complete work; or of what he may call 'depression'.

Although such people do indeed become depressed, their mood is often more of apathy and emptiness than melancholia. For Fairbairn (1976) the 'characteristic affect of the schizoid state is undoubtedly a sense of futility'. Although severely avoidant people may at first sight resemble depressed patients, one quickly comes to realize that their kind of depression has a quality of meaninglessness which is not present in the ordinary case of depression. One feels that their mood of futility is integral to their ordinary adaptation; almost as if their lives never had had much meaning. Such people, especially if intellectually gifted, may substitute power for love in actuality or fantasy, but the satisfaction which they obtain from this is both limited and precarious; it is primarily the feeling of loving and being loved which gives meaning to life and dispels a sense of futility.

Therapy with such people can be difficult. The therapist feels that she and the patient are not on the same wavelength. The patient may induce in the interviewer the feeling that, in answer to every query, he is really wanting to say: 'what on earth is the point of asking me that?' Some affect an air of superiority, especially if they are in fact intellectually superior, and have made their chief adaptation to the world by means of their brains rather than their feelings. It is important not to allow oneself to be put off by this. The therapist's skill is in the world of feelings not intellectual contest. But therapists like to have their efforts appreciated, and it is disconcerting to be faced with an individual who appears to repudiate every attempt to get to know and understand him.

It is important to realize that patients of this kind are deeply frightened of any kind of intimacy. Their defence is to withdraw as far as possible from emotional involvement. If the therapist can tolerate being repudiated and made to feel useless by such patients, she will find them of great interest, and, if she manages to penetrate their defences, richly rewarded by winning the confidence of someone who for years has found it difficult to trust any other human being.

Why are people of this kind so reluctant to allow anyone to become close to them? There are at least three ways in which fear of intimacy might arise. First, a person may be reluctant to embark upon a relationship because he fears that it will end, and that he will therefore be worse off than if he had never taken the risk of involvement. This fear is often based upon an actual experience of loss in early childhood. Isaac Newton, for example, showed many schizoid traits of character. He was notably isolated, and never made any close emotional relationships with anyone of either sex. He was extremely suspicious, reluctant to publish his work, and prone to accuse others of having stolen his discoveries. When he was just over 50, he had a psychotic breakdown in which paranoid ideas were prominent. At least some of his emotional difficulties may reasonably be assumed to have taken origin from the experience of his early childhood. Newton was a premature child whose father had died before he was born. For the first three years of his life, he enjoyed the undivided attention of his mother. Then, when he was just past his third birthday, his mother remarried. She not only presented Newton with an unwanted stepfather, but added insult to injury by abandoning him, leaving him to be brought up by his maternal grandmother while she herself moved to live in a different house with her new husband. We know from his own writings that Newton felt this to be a betrayal. He seems never entirely to have trusted any human being again.

A second reason for avoiding intimacy is the fear of being dominated and overborne by the other person, to the point of losing one's identity as a separate individual. We all begin life being at the mercy of adults who are much more powerful that we are, and we strive, in varying ways, to reach a degree of independence. Although some people wish to continue to be subject to the authority of others, and to have decisions made for them, even the most masochistic prefer to retain a degree of autonomy. Many children's games are concerned with demonstrating that they can be 'king of the castle'. As children grow up, most learn that they can make their voices heard, and exercise some influence over events, even with people more powerful than themselves. They discover that, although they may not be able entirely to have their own way, they can at least make others take notice of their wants and opinions. The people we call avoidant or schizoid, on the contrary, conceive that they can only retain autonomy if they withdraw into isolation. They do not imagine that they can exert any influence over others, whom they think of as being both more powerful and more ruthless than themselves. In extreme cases, they think of other people as being so entirely oblivious of their needs and wishes that they might as well not exist, and so come to feel that their very being is threatened. R. D. Laing (1960) gives a good example.

> Two patients are arguing in the course of a session in an analytic group. One breaks off to say: 'I can't go on. You are arguing in order to have the pleasure of triumphing over me. At best you win an argument. At worst you lose an argument. I am arguing in order to preserve my existence.'

Although at first sight such a statement might seem metaphorical or even delusional, there may be literal truth in it. Bruno Bettelheim (1961), the psychoanalyst who was for a year confined in Dachau and Buchenwald concentration camps, observed that those prisoners who surrendered autonomy entirely and acquiesced in letting the guards determine their whole existence became like automata – Mussulmen, as they were called – and soon died. Survival seemed to depend upon preserving some tiny area in which decisions could still be in the hands of the prisoner himself.

The fear of being overborne or engulfed, as Laing calls it, sometimes seems to be the consequence of having been treated with particular lack of consideration as a child; more particularly, of having been treated as a doll or automaton or as an appendage to the parents rather than as a person with a separate existence.

Impotence in the face of authority are vividly depicted in Kafka's classic novels *The Trial* and *The Castle*. According to his biographer (Brod 1948), Kafka continued throughout his life to attribute almost magical powers to his father. When he was 36 he wrote a long *Letter to my Father* in which he exposed his continuing sense of inadequacy and his feeling of always being in the wrong. The same sense of powerlessness is evident in Kafka's religious attitude. There is an Absolute, but so remote from the life of man that misunderstanding and lack of comprehension is inevitable. Kafka considered that parents were tyrants and slave-drivers. He agreed with Swift that 'parents are the least of all to be trusted with the education of their children'. His novels are concerned with authorities who are so arbitrary and unpredictable that it was impossible to understand them or work out ways of dealing with them.

We suggested earlier that neurotic symptoms were exaggerations of anxieties that everyone feels to some extent. Even the most 'normal' people fear revealing intimate secrets to others; for they realize that to do so is to put oneself in the power of the other person. Real intimacy is not lightly embarked on, even by those who are not habitually suspicious. The common fear of getting married – more prevalent in men than women, as is emotional deactivation – is often rooted in the idea that to do so might threaten autonomy to a dangerous extent. Many people who pass for normal are unable to conceive of a human relationship in which the partners are on equal terms, in which giving and taking are reciprocal, because they have never experienced such a relationship, and may feel that they themselves have nothing much to give.

A third reason for avoiding intimacy is the subject's fear that he will harm or destroy the person to whom he becomes attached. At first sight this kind of fear may seem to contradict the other varieties since it seems to imply that the subject is more, not less, powerful than the other person. However, the power concerned is of a kind possessed by every child; the power to exhaust or empty the parent. Kleinian analysts would trace such a fear to fantasies arising in the earliest months of life, when a frustrated or greedy infant might suppose that his urgent need had emptied or destroyed the breast upon which his existence depended (Waddell 1998). Children may easily get the impression that their capacity to exhaust a parent outweighs the pleasure which they take in them, especially if the parent is elderly or ailing. There are many parents who feel all too easily drained by their children because they themselves cannot play or enter into a child's world through their imagination. A child may thus be faced with a parent who does not give him the affection and understanding which he desperately needs, but also conveys to him that his needs are potentially destructive of the person to whom he turns to fulfil them. This may lead to the conviction that fulfilment through love is unattainable except in fantasy. Close relationships are regarded as mutually exhausting rather than mutually rewarding; and so the safest thing is to avoid them as far as possible.

As we have seen, hyperactivating and depressive patients are generally anxious to please and therefore tend to make an agreeable first impression upon the therapist. Obsessional patients may be more reserved; but their fear of aggression usually makes them polite and respectful of convention. Some schizoid patients, on the other hand, often make little attempt to please, and may proclaim their disdain for convention by eccentricity in dress, disregard for good manners, and what may often seem to be deliberate lack of response to the utterances of the psychotherapist. Others conform to a fault, presenting an impeccable persona which may make their acquaintances, guests, and psychotherapists feel uncomfortable at their own lack of social polish. This pose of superiority compounds the difficulty which schizoid people have in making relationships; for others detect it, and, quite naturally, resent it. However, when people of this kind are faced with emotional demands, a child in trouble, or a wife who is depressed, their only recourse is to retreat. The emotions of others are as threatening as their own unacknowledged feelings, so that, instead of trying to understand or empathize with the person in distress, they shy away and recommend their own prescription, the only one known to them, redoubled self-control.

Once again, if the therapist understands what lies behind the mask of indifference or superiority and is prepared to control her own resentment at being disregarded or treated cavalierly, she will gradually be able to penetrate her patient's façade.

Some avoidant people often develop a realm of fantasy to compensate for their lack of fulfilment in the real world. In this make-believe zone one can be admired, envied, or regarded with awe. Some attain what may appear to be good relations with others by going to the opposite extreme of the disdain for convention described above. They will be punctiliously polite and exaggeratedly considerate, but those who are the recipients of this attention will tend to feel that his consideration comes from the head and not the heart. Avoidant people sometimes make quite conscious decisions that it is morally right to be tactful, or generous, or virtuous; and strive to behave in accordance with their adopted principles. However, they will still convey to others their unconscious intention of keeping them at arm's length and fail to meet them on the common ground of shared humanity. St Paul's best-known passage on love, from the first epistle to the Corinthians, is relevant:

> 'I may speak in tongues of men or of angels, but if I am without love, I am a sounding gong or a clanging cymbal. I may have the gift of prophecy, and know every hidden truth; I may have faith strong enough to move mountains; but if I have no love I am nothing. I may dole out all I possess, or even give my body to be burnt, but if I have no love, I am none the better.'

Trust is a major issue for the avoidant or schizoid individual. Phobias of operations, the dentist, or even the hairdresser are not uncommon; they conceive that if they go so far as to let anyone do anything to them, they will be in danger of being totally destroyed. Such ideas are delusions in embryo. But instead of exhibiting frank delusions, they may be touchy, suspicious or litigious. Very often, they refuse to put their fantasized superiority to the test. Some schizoid people who, in youth, were brilliant passers of examinations, fail to live up to their early promise because they dare not expose their real, but inevitably limited, talents to the light of criticism.

As with severely obsessional people, relationships are conceived of in terms of superiority versus inferiority, so the sexual fantasies of schizoid people are often sadomasochistic. Unable to conceive of being loved, they can imagine being admired for their strength, or think of themselves as dominating a partner who might otherwise disregard them. Sadomasochistic fantasies are certainly not confined to schizoid people, as their widespread occurrence in pornography demonstrates; perhaps it appeals to a schizoid aspect of human nature which is ubiquitous. But schizoid people often make use of fantasies which belong to a childhood phase of development before the child had discovered what sexual intercourse was actually like. Fetishistic and other fantasies of a deviant kind belong to this category. Freud (1938) thought of fetishism in terms of a splitting of the ego, in which one part denied reality, while the other continued to accept reality at least in part. The difficulty which schizoid people encounter in establishing ordinary sexual relations may also be described in terms of their alienation from the body, both of others and their own bodies.

Avoidant patients often use intellectual defences to maintain a fragile equilibrium and self-esteem. They identify themselves with their minds and are apt to regard their bodies as mere appendages with needs and desires which are often regarded as a nuisance; alien demands which interfere with the true reality, the life of the mind. Proust (1970), who showed both obsessional and schizoid traits, wrote: 'Indeed it is the possession of a body that is the great danger to the mind, to our human and thinking life . . .'. Freud (1923) defined the ego (i.e. the Self) in terms of the body: 'The ego is first and foremost a body ego, i.e. the ego is ultimately derived from bodily sensations, chiefly from those springing from the surface of the body.'

Schizoid patients, possibly because of some very early failure in relation with the mother, become 'out of touch' with the body, and regard being closely 'in touch' with another person as potentially threatening. It is touch which gives most of us our sense of reality, as well as conveying closeness to another person. Although we regard being out of touch with the body as a symptom of disorder when we see it in our patients, it should be remembered that man's greatest intellectual achievements depend upon the possibility of disassociating oneself, at least temporarily, from the world of the body. Indeed a degree of avoidance is probably obligatory for certain kinds of creative achievement. Those who have achieved most in the fields of abstract thought have often been solitary people, disinclined to make close relationships with other human beings (Storr 1972).

Descartes refers to the body as possibly illusory, and distrusted the evidence of the senses. The first principle of his philosophy, 'I think, therefore I am', makes mind more certain than matter, and, as Bertrand Russell (1955) pointed out, 'my mind (for me) more certain than the minds of others'. Scientists confine their objectivity to the laboratory, and are as humanly subjective as anyone else where personal relationships are concerned; but their capacity for detachment could reasonably be described as avoidant although their total personalities are not. Baron-Cohen (2003) has argued that a degree of schizoid withdrawal, or benign autism is intrinsic to the being of the male of the species!

Whatever the ultimate cause turns out to be, schizoid individuals develop a mask, or 'persona' as Jung called it, which conceals their feelings both from themselves and from others. It is as if their most basic, primitive, physical needs had somehow been repudiated at a crucial time in their development, with the consequence that they had adopted a pose and a manner of relating which pretended that these basic needs were unimportant. This way of looking at schizoid individuals is closely related to Winnicott's (1971) concept of the False Self versus the True Self. Civilized life demands that we all develop a persona. Indeed, social life would be impossible if we were unable to be polite, show consideration when we ourselves may be tired or out of temper, or sometimes defer to the opinions of others for fear of provoking embarrassingly vehement dissent. But with our intimates, and especially with our partners in love, we ought to be able to shed the mask and risk being our vulnerable, emotional selves without constraint. This the schizoid/avoidant person cannot do. He is terrified that his True Self will be rejected, repudiated, or even annihilated. Over many years he has built up a False Self, until he himself finds it hard to recognize what his own deepest feelings really are. This may enable him to get by for many years, with no one recognizing that there is much wrong, although people may complain that he is difficult to know, or that he does not reveal much of himself. Winnicott (1971) describes one such patient, who had had unsuccessful previous therapies:

> 'My work really started with him when I made it clear to him that I recognised his non-existence. He made the remark that over the years all the good work done with him had been futile because it had been done on the basis that he existed, whereas he had only existed falsely. When I said that I recognised his non-existence he felt that he had been communicated with for the first time. What he meant was that his True Self that had been hidden away from infancy had now been in communication with his analyst in the only way which was not dangerous.'

Schizoid individuals often feel most real when they are alone. Then their true selves can be allowed to flourish without danger of harm from others. If they happen to be gifted in one of the arts or sciences, they may find that creative activity is an effective compensation for their lack of close or genuine relationships with other people, and thus avoid suffering from a sense that life is futile or meaningless. Winnicott again:

> 'It is creative apperception more than anything else that makes the individual feel that life is worth living. Contrasted with this is a relationship to external reality which is one of compliance, the world and its details being recognised but only as something to be fitted in with or demanding adaptation. Compliance carries with it a sense of futility for the individual and is associated with the idea that nothing matters and that life is not worth living.'

By 'creative apperception' Winnicott means a whole attitude to life; one in which the individual feels that he is able to bring his whole personality into relation with other people and the world. Creative people vary very considerably in personality, and by no means all are predominantly schizoid, and their work need not primarily represent a retreat from real life (Storr 1972). But, provided they have the necessary talent, creative work does have a special appeal to those of schizoid temperament because its solitary practice means that they can pursue their own thoughts and fantasies without encountering the withering, shrivelling effect of others' scrutiny. If they then publish a book, or exhibit a picture, they will of course be sensitive to its reception; since it is bound to reveal something of their inner life, their 'True Self'. But the work in which they are thus revealed will display only selected aspects, never the whole person. Moreover, it will have been prepared and polished in such a way as to make it as acceptable as possible. Many creative people feel so sensitive about 'work in progress' that they will not discuss it with anyone else or show it to anyone until it is entirely finished. Some, like Newton, keep their discoveries or their works to themselves; or may profess themselves incapable of finishing them. Newton feared that others would steal his discoveries. Those who cannot complete a book are generally protecting themselves against criticism.

Of course the majority of schizoid patients who come the way of the psychotherapist are not exceptionally creative except in fantasy. The therapist's task is first to recognize the patient's isolation and then so to gain the patient's confidence that the defences which maintain his isolation need not continue. Often the therapist will find it necessary to make a relationship with the patient in what may seem rather an intellectual fashion to begin with. Schizoid patients are easily frightened by a direct approach to their emotional life. Educated patients of this type will often reveal an interest in literature or the other arts, since these afford an opportunity for emotional expression which does not involve other people. One can explore with such patients what books or music or painting particularly appeal to them. This can lead to a feeling of shared emotional experience which may form a basis upon which the patient feels safe to proceed further.

It is important that the therapist is not prematurely discouraged because the patient does not show any immediate response. Progress is bound to be slow; but, very often, a great deal more is happening during the course of psychotherapy than the patient at first acknowledges or even realizes. The most difficult thing for the schizoid patient to give up is his fantasized superiority. Indeed, he may never quite be able to relinquish this, since his whole self-esteem has for years depended upon it. We see this even more clearly in the case of patients who are frankly psychotic. The delusions of the schizophrenic cannot be argued with, because their maintenance has become essential to the patient's conception of himself as a person. If one's only source of self-esteem is the belief that wicked persecutors have deprived one of one's birthright, that belief will not be susceptible to argument. It is only when the schizoid person comes to believe that other people really care for him that he can afford to abandon his fantasy of superiority: that is, when he has been able to discover that love is a better source of self-esteem than power.

Disorganized attachment; borderline personality disorder (BPD)

Psychotherapists often use the term 'borderline' as a shorthand for their 'difficult' or 'complex' patients. The phrase was first coined in the 1930s by psychoanalysts in an attempt to capture the essence of people whose psychological function lay on the cusp between neurotic and psychotic patterns. BPD has been incorporated into the DSM classifications to describe people with some or all of the following characteristics: unstable relationships; fear of abandonment; fragile sense of self; impulsiveness e.g. binge eating; suicidal and self- injurious behaviours; mood instability; substance abuse; feelings of futility and emptiness; angry outbursts; dissociation and paranoia. The reader will recognize aspects here already discussed under previous headings: feelings of emptiness and futility afflict the 'schizoid'; mood disturbance and suicidality are features of depression; unstable relationships often a feature of hyperactivation/hysteria.

This serves to emphasize the overlap between the different personality disorder categories, and to strengthen the case for a dimensional and severity-oriented approach. We need to distinguish between, say, someone who has never held down a stable job, is chronically hospitalized, with unremitting desire to injure himself and suffers recurrent dissociative episodes; and a four-times married high-flying executive who secretly abuses cocaine, and has an inner sense of emptiness. Both might be described as 'borderline', but are clearly at different ends of the severity spectrum.

The origins of BPD are far from fully understood – genetic and developmental factors, and their interactions are both important (Bateman and Fonagy 2004). Here we shall adopt the attachment framework already outlined, suggesting that BPD can usefully be seen developmentally in terms of disorganized attachment. The previously described hyperactivating and deactivating attachment strategies can be seen as 'organized' forms of insecure attachment, in the sense that they enable the growing child to find a way of relating to, and getting a modicum of security from, their caregiver, albeit at a cost. In the case of hyperactivation the price paid is a degree of alienation and dependency; for deactivators, a suppression of feelings and diminution of the pleasures and satisfactions of intimacy.

In disorganized attachment no such coherence is possible. The child is exposed to a caregiver who is either emotionally 'absent' (perhaps 'freezing' when the child cries, or going into a state of dissociation, reminded of her own abusive childhood), or incapable of 'reading' /'mentalising' her child, seeing the child's feelings and actions only in terms of her own needs (e.g. '*stop crying*; you are only doing that to wind me up'). The distressed child is then in a dilemma, since the very person to whom they might turn to for comfort when distressed is the source of that distress. The child then resorts to a number of apparently self-defeating strategies such as going into a dissociated state, curling up in a ball, banging his head, seeming disoriented and lost, or exhibiting apparently senseless violence.

A crucial feature of disorganized attachment is that the caregiver's difficulty in thinking about her own or the child's inner world, means that the child himself may be unable to 'read' himself and others. We are dealing therefore with a 'deficit' state, as opposed to, say the 'conflict' states of the depressed person who is trying to manage two incompatible impulses: the need to be looked after, and his aggression.

If we transpose these underlying features into the adolescent or adult life of the BPD sufferer, we find someone who finds it very difficult to understand his own and others' inner world. His deficit lies in being able to mentalise. He also oscillates between wanting closeness to others and then finding that proximity threatening and so going to the other extreme of emotional isolation. The unbearableness of that state of isolation and alienation impels him once more to seek others, and so the cycle repeats. Unable to soothe himself when distressed by finding a secure base, the BPD sufferer resorts to various forms of 'pathological self-soothing', including seeking oblivion through suicidal acts, transposing mental pain to physical pain through self-injurious behaviour and then getting a modicum of comfort through attention in hospital casualty departments; drinking or drug taking; or through sex without emotional involvement.

Psychotherapy for BPD is never easy, and such patients should not be taken on without careful thought and preparation. There is some suggestion that standard therapies, whether cognitive or psychodynamic,may even make things worse (Bateman and Fonagy 2008) by interfering with the natural tendency of borderline phenomena to lessen with age. The features of successful treatments for BPD are described by Bateman and Fonagy (2004). Here we will confine ourselves to a number of key practice principles.

- A lot of time needs to be spent in engagement. Given the process of oscillation between seeking an object and evading one ('*claustro-agoraphobia*' (Rey 1994)) described above, it is not surprising that BPD sufferers have difficulty in settling into a regular rhythm of therapy. They may miss sessions, turn up late, or conversely ring between sessions, refuse to leave at the end of them, and/or shower the therapist with letters or texts between them. Finding a way to accommodate to this pattern, while remaining properly boundaried, is a challenge for therapists.

- On the whole it is advisable to have at least one other professional involved in the case. The therapist's holidays or illness can be very difficult for BPD sufferers, who take them as a sign that they are unwanted and that no one is to be fully trusted. Having a backup person who can be seen during breaks is helpful. It also gives the message to the patient of a 'combined parent' in which at least two people, working in tandem, are concerned about their welfare. There can be useful division of labour in which the therapist concentrates on helping the patient to understand himself and his behaviours, while the case-manager attends to medication, hospital admissions when necessary, suicidal or psychotic episodes, housing difficulties etc.
- The main focus of therapy is to help with patients mentalising deficit. Since they find it hard to understand their own and others' inner world, 'deep' or historical interpretations make little sense. The therapist needs to take day-to-day occurrences, in or out of the consulting room, and try to dissect them from the point of view of the actors' motivations and plans. For example, if the therapist is a bit late, and the patient then goes very silent, that might be a starting point for discussion. 'Do you think you might have felt quite rejected when I kept you waiting … ?' 'Yeah, you therapists think you can turn up whenever you like, but if I am a second late you go on and on about it'. 'It sounds as though you feel really pissed off …'. 'Well, I am, wouldn't you be … ?'
- Underlying much of the patient's sometimes dependent or insouciant demeanour is a deep feeling of shame: that they are somehow 'wrong', worthy only of contempt. Therapists need to be highly alert to the ways in which psychoanalytic interpretations can reinforce this feeling of failure.

> One patient, an able and enthusiastic student, suffering from depression with borderline features, could barely finish her course at university, her employment prospects were blighted, her social life restricted, her capacity for pleasure and fulfilment curtailed.
>
> JH painfully discovered that his assumed opacity and efforts to 'interpret' her depression in terms of childhood trauma (for which there was much evidence) and unexpressed anger merely served to reinforce the patient's feelings of shameful failure and her conviction that she, the victim, was to blame for her illness. What she needed was validation and understanding that to be depressed is at best to live only partly. It was only when JH moved into a more supportive therapy mode that the patient began tentatively to trust him. At times she hated him and what he stood for. But through 'learning from the patient' (Casement 1985) he came to respect and acknowledge that hatred and its legitimacy, despite knowing that such strong feelings are coloured by a depressive world-view. Painfully, she taught him how corrosive the 'division of suffering' between patient and therapist can be. By acknowledging our own vulnerability we can lessen the need to project our disturbances into our patients.
>
> Staying the course with this patient over many years showed him how favourable life events form the new beginning that can be the starting point for recovery from depression and BPD. Meeting her third husband, and the joys (as well as the tribulations) of motherhood made an enormous difference as she gradually emerged from the darkness of her depression into a sense of light-heartedness and possibility. The patient moved over a period of 20 years gradually from weekly to fortnightly and then monthly sessions, to 6-monthly with occasional extra meetings if required. An attenuating long-term therapeutic relationship can provide a secure base where psychological illness can be explored, accepted and sequestered, enabling the sufferer to live with near-normality in the outside world.

- BPD patients often suffer from hair-trigger arousal and anxiety. Anxiety is inimical to mentalising and for good reasons: when just about to be eaten by a lion, thinking about what is going on the lion's mind is not adaptive; a 'fast' track response seems in order! But most of the time, 'slow' strategies in which one ponders on one's own and others motivations, desires and needs is essential for negotiating the world of interpersonal relationships. Adjunctive anxiety-reducing strategies such as meditation, mindfulness, yoga, physical exercise etc can be beneficial alongside dynamic psychotherapy.
- BPD sufferers are highly sensitive to various forms of psychotherapeutic inauthenticity, such as defensiveness and patronizing remarks. It is even more important than in routine practice to be open and honest with such patient's about one's faults and mistakes.
- Gabbard (2012) makes an important distinction between 'boundary crossing' and 'boundary violation'. The former implies a degree of flexibility and opportunism on the part of the therapist; the latter paves the way for exploitation (perhaps sexual, financial, or emotional). Given that many BPD sufferers have been abused as children, and often live in abusive relationships, it is no surprise that these issues play a part in their therapy, and the therapist may find herself being induced into a potentially abusive situation, often looking quite benign at first sight. As we have discussed, a female patient might ask a male therapist for a 'hug'. He might feel that this would help to validate and redress the loveless world she comes from. But this can well be the first step on the 'slippery slope' to sexual exploitation (Dimen 2012). The whole scenario needs to be mentalised, neither repressed in a 'super-egoish' repressive way, nor acted on. One might say an abbreviated version of something like:

  > 'I can see what a deep feeling of being unacceptable and unlovable that request comes from; and that you see me as someone who really could help you to feel validated. But your past experience has shown you how what looks like love can end up as exploitation and hate. We need to find ways to help you disentangle your need for hugs from your need for self-understanding, and how to carry that into the rest of your life, and that's what our main job is'.

- Another aspect of BPD illustrated by this imaginary scenario is the way in which BPD sufferers find it difficult to keep the different compartments of their life separate. They may approach their boss as though they were a potential sexual partner, and conversely treat their husband as a business partner rather than an intimate. Part of the role of the therapist is to help the patient, as Rey (1994) puts it, to 'render unto Caesar that which is Caesar's and unto God that which is God's'. What Rey meant by this is that in BPD everything becomes conflated and confused – mouth and genital, heart and head, sex and security, intimate and stranger. If therapy is successful, they can differentiate and distinguish, rather than symmetrize and muddle (Matte-Blanco 1975), everything begins to find its rightful place. The background to this, at least for those who have been sexually exploited by caregivers in childhood, is a confusion between sexual and attachment needs; exploring and restoring the damage done by this is a fundamental task in the therapy of BPD sufferers.

13

The Science of Psychotherapy

When AS first wrote AOP the *science* – as opposed to the art – of psychotherapy was in its infancy. Psychotherapy remains an art or craft, but there is now a substantial body of scientific knowledge about its effects, side effects, mechanisms of action and wider contribution as an intellectual presence. We have already touched on some of these aspects. Nevertheless, despite being viewed by service users as an essential component of mental health care, psychodynamic psychotherapy has become something of an endangered species, especially in the public sector. Some argue that the psychoanalytic world-view is inherently subversive and will therefore always be on the fringes of the medical and scientific mainstream. One astute observer (Stepansky 2009) argues that the best hope for dynamic psychotherapy is to opt for 'optimal marginalization'; that is to find a role comparable to chiropractic, a respected, much used, but essentially marginal discipline. In this brief survey we review a number of developments that make this view seem unduly pessimistic (Fonagy and Lemma 2012; Holmes 2012a).

Freud was a Darwinian, and saw psychoanalysis as an evolutionary science (Sulloway 1979). Although his papers on technique are as useful today as they were a century ago, his main preoccupation was to theorize about the mind and its relations. The 'assault on Freud' (Grunbaum 1984) in the late twentieth century centred mainly on the purported scientific credentials of psychoanalysis which, it was claimed, had more in common with the arts, religion and philosophy than science. Psychoanalysis, however, we suggest, will outlive its obituarists. Contemporary psychoanalysis is increasingly compatible with a scientific world view. The new psychoanalysis is evidence-based, effective, and can make a significant contribution to contemporary medical science.

Developmental psychopathology and the science of intimacy

The standard 'diathesis-adversity model' views mental disorders as resulting from the confluence of genetically susceptibility with environmental trauma. A psychodynamic viewpoint combines with recent research to gloss this in two distinct ways. First, environmental susceptibility can be health-enhancing as well as illness-promoting. Here is one example. At a given genetic locus a number of different versions of genes are possible; this is known as allele polymorphism. In DRD4 polymorphism, in the presence of maternal insensitivity, the 7-repeat allele is a vulnerability factor for externalizing (i.e. behavioural disinhibition) disorders in toddlers. But with sensitive mothers, the 7-repeat allele confers *less* deviant behaviour (Belsky *et al* 2009). These findings are best seen in terms of 'plasticity' rather than 'vulnerability' genes, which confer *reactivity* to environmental context, with potential for negative health effects in adversity, but positive effects under conditions of sensitivity and support, the latter including the kinds of health-promoting relationships inherent in psychodynamic therapies. Here we see how 'personalized medicine' can be applicable to psychoanalytic therapy, modern genetics predicting which individuals will best respond to psychodynamic approaches.

Implicit in this model is the need for measures of the relational environment equal in sophistication to those of modern genomics. Attachment-informed psychodynamic approaches provide just such a 'science of intimacy'. An example is the Adult Attachment Interview (AAI) (Hesse 2008), which, in contrast to crude pen-and-paper checklists beloved of non-psychoanalytic researchers, taps into people's perception of their relational environment, both current and developmental, and can be used to track the kinds of changes in the inner world brought about by psychotherapy.

Neuropsychoanalysis

A second growth point for psychodynamics is in the new-minted niche of neuro-psychoanalysis (Solms and Turbull 2002; Panksepp 2004). Psychoanalysts in search for scientific credibility can now visualize physical correlates of their black-box postulates, while neuroscientists learn from psychoanalysis how meanings emerge from brain biology. There are numerous areas of mutual interest.

Neuroscience makes a distinction between the declarative or episodic memory ('my first day at school'), and implicit or procedural memory (the way things were done: 'how my parents handled things when we were growing up'). Traumatic childhood events, inaccessible to declarative memory, may be encoded in the procedural memory system, and inscribed in a person's physiology via changes in the amygdala and hypothalamic-pituitary-adrenal (HPA) axis (Renn 2012). This helps to explain why BPD sufferers, the majority of whom have undergone trauma in childhood, may be so resistant to psychic change.

'Mirror neurones' (Rizzolatti *et al* 2006) refer to the neurons that are activated in a person's motor cortex when they observe another carrying out an action also dependent on the same neural pathway. Thus our brain is induced to 'feel' what the other is doing by a parallel, or mirroring, process in our own brain. The implications for empathy and 'projective identification' (Waddell 1998) have not gone unnoticed by psychoanalysts.

Another important neuropsychoanalytic concept is that of neuroplasticity: the idea that the brain is never in a static fixed state but is constantly changing, growing, pruning, remaking connections and circuits (Schore 1991; 2011). Clearly these processes are at their peak of activity in childhood and adolescence, but they continue throughout life. The neuro-ameliorative impact of psychotherapy can now be tracked using neuroimaging techniques such as functional magnetic resonance imaging (fMRI) which show how the brain changes in response to therapeutic intervention (Holmes 2012d; Karlsson 2011). Endorsing the hopes and projects of neuropsychoanalysis, neuroscientist, psychiatrist and Nobel Prize winner, Eric Kandel (1999) has called for an approach based on the 'rigorous empirical framework of molecular biology yet incorporating the humanistic concepts of psychoanalysis'.

Evidence for psychodynamic psychotherapy efficacy

A twenty-first century *cri-de-coeur* by leading researchers about the crisis in credibility of psychoanalysis called for major research effort to establish its efficacy and relevance (Gabbard *et al* 2002). A number of meta-analyses of dynamic psychotherapy published in high-impact journals have since generally shown that psychoanalytic therapies are indeed effective. Meta-analysis uses sophisticated statistical methods to amalgamate the results from as many relevant studies as possible to gain an overall consensus of the usefulness or otherwise of a particular treatment. Effect size is a statistical method for measuring the impact of a particular treatment by comparing the difference between a group receiving a treatment, and controls.

Leischenring and Rabung (2011) found that long-term psychodynamic psychotherapies (LTPP) produce large within-group effect sizes (average 0.8–1.2) comparable to those achieved by other psychotherapy modalities; that gains tend to accumulate even after therapy has finished, in contrast to non-psychotherapeutic treatments; and a dose-effect pattern, with longer therapies producing greater and more sustained improvement. Two key mutative factors are a secure, sensitive and interactive working alliance; and facilitating experiencing of previously avoided painful feelings (Shedler 2010) – i.e. overcoming affect-phobia. Psychodynamic therapy although expensive, is able in some circumstances to pay for itself (Bateman and Fonagy 2003) thanks to reduction in offset-costs (medication, hospital stays, welfare payments etc). Not all meta-analysis has found major therapeutic benefit from psychodynamic therapies (Smit et al 2012), but on balance the current evidence seems to favour psychodynamic therapy, suggesting that downplaying its role is as much a reflection of political and social forces as of scientific evidence.

Psychodynamic therapy in specific disorders

The role of psychodynamic therapy in a number of specific disorders is beginning to emerge. Anxiety disorders are typically the preserve of cognitive therapy, so it is noteworthy that Busch, Milrod and colleagues have developed a time-limited, evidence-based psychodynamic therapy for anxiety, concentrating particularly on the role of unconscious unexpressed anger, demonstrating good outcomes in 21 sessions compared with controls (Busch et al 2009). Similarly, there is now a number of tailored short-term therapies for depression, for which a recent meta-analysis found within-group effect sizes of 0.69, and pre-/post 1.34, both maintained at one year follow-up (Driessen et al 2010). Compared to CBT there was a small (0.30) immediate advantage to CBT, but no differences at three months and one year follow-up.

As we have already discussed, the complexity posed by people suffering from borderline personality disorder (BPD) represents a major problem for psychiatric services. Two manualized and modified psychodynamic therapies, mentalisation based therapy (MBT) (Bateman and Fonagy 2004) and transference focussed therapy (TFT) (Clarkin et al 2007), have demonstrated significant improvements for BPD sufferers compared with treatment-as-usual controls. As discussed in the previous chapter, MBT sees BPD patients as suffering from difficulties with 'mentalising', i.e. in 'reading' ones own and others' thoughts and feelings, leading to recurrent interpersonal conflict. MBT encourages reflection on everyday affective crises, including those with the therapist, rather than offering 'deep' interpretations. Without the capacity to mentalise the latter are often incomprehensible or may precipitate feelings of shame and humiliation.

We have said little in this book about the psychotherapy of psychosis. The history of psychoanalytic approaches to schizophrenia illustrate in microcosm the rise, fall, and tentative rebirth of psychodynamic psychotherapy. Freud thought that schizophrenia was untreatable psychoanalytically, because, wrongly as it turned out, he believed on theoretical grounds that these patients were suffering from a narcissistic disorder which meant they were incapable of forming and working in a close relationship with a therapist (Freud 1940). Despite Freud's misgivings, psychoanalytic treatment for schizophrenia was widely practised in the 1950s and 60s, especially in the USA. The picture changed as effective drug treatments for psychosis became available and it was shown that many patients dubbed 'schizophrenic' in the USA were in fact suffering from BPD. Eventually McGlashan (1988), in a much-publicized follow-up study of schizophrenic patients showed that psychoanalytic therapy could lead to deterioration and was contraindicated.

At this stage it seemed that psychodynamic therapy for psychosis was obsolete. However, the Scandinavian 'needs adapted' approach to schizophrenia now provides a model in which the uniqueness of each patient is recognized, medication kept to a minimum, the family dynamics around psychosis charted, and a long-term one-to-one relationship with a key worker seen as vital to improvement (Alanen *et al* 2009). The needs-adapted approach is not strictly speaking psychoanalytic, but contains analytic ingredients in attempting to help patients understand the nature and meaning of their symptoms, rather than simply seeing them merely as manifestations of a biologically based 'disease'.

To repeat our opening credo, throughout this text we have tended to use the terms psychoanalytic and psychodynamic interchangeably. Implicit in this is an integrative viewpoint which distinguishes psychodynamic therapy from its parent discipline of psychoanalysis in a number of ways. Rather than espousing specific psychoanalytic ideologies – Kleinian, Relational, Lacanian, Kohutian etc – we have emphasized a 'common ground' (Wallerstein 1990) approach, which argues that when in the consulting room with the patient, the best of the different schools of psychoanalysis differ less than they have in common. If the therapist is skilful and humane, our proverbial fly-on-the-consulting-room-wall would be hard put to know whether it was witnessing a Lacanian or a Kohutian therapy.

For specific mental health problems – depression, anxiety, BPD etc – we advocate treatments which are tailored to particular disorders, drawing on the best and most effective psychoanalytic approaches. We also believe that psychodynamic psychotherapists need to be conversant with and respectful of other psychological therapies – CBT, interpersonal psychotherapy (IPT), family therapy – and to understand their indications and different roles (Bateman *et al* 2010); and to be skilled in working with patients who are taking medication, ever alert to the ways in which managing medication may enact a transference relationship rather than a medical need.

Although the practice of psychotherapy will always be an art, the practitioner of the future will be increasingly buttressed with the knowledge and outlook of science. To take a very practical example, it is now well known that therapists vary in their effectiveness. Some are 'super-therapists', getting almost all of their patients better; a few are highly ineffective and tend to have deteriorating or drop-out patients. The majority of us lie somewhere in between. A scientific study looked at the impact of offering therapists feedback after each session on how their patients were progressing. Simply informing therapists whether their patients were getting better, staying the same, or deteriorating had a major impact, bringing the less effective therapists in line with the average, with marked overall benefit to patients (Lambert *et al* 2010).

14

The End of Therapy

The title of this chapter is a deliberate pun. We are going to discuss different ways of ending therapy, or 'termination' as it is infelicitously called; but also the aim, or 'end' which one might expect to achieve in the course of therapy. The previous chapter used the language and ideology of medicine to assert that psychodynamic therapy is an effective treatment for a number of psychiatric disorders, and that the only way to avoid the 'optimal marginalization' (Stepansky 2009) is to enter into the language and procedures of modern medical and social evaluative practice. The research on which this is based entails 'manualization' of psychotherapy procedures – i.e. specifying in a reproducible way the kinds of interventions therapists' make, and using standardized 'outcome measures' which enable change in psychotherapy to be quantified. This is based on the 'drug metaphor', in which therapy is likened to a drug which is 'administered' to selected patients, and the researcher observes whether or not his interventions have been successful by comparing them with the changes that occur in people who have had no such treatment, or, better still, a dummy intervention of some sort. All this is antipathetical to many psychotherapists who feel that these procedures are far removed from the real world of psychotherapy practice; that the kinds of changes they are hoping to achieve are essentially unmeasurable; and that their aim in therapy is only subsidiarily symptom-removal, and what really matters is an existential change in the way people experience and signify their lives (Lear 2003). In what follows we shall highlight this latter viewpoint, especially as it relates to the question of completion, cure or termination in psychotherapy.

In medical practice, treatment is brought to an end either when the patient is cured, or else when the doctor decides that as much as can be done has been done to relieve a disability. In the case of diseases like diabetes, asthma, or many forms of heart disease, in which alleviation and control, rather than cure, are the doctor's aim, treatment may be prolonged indefinitely.

'Cure' and the early days of psychoanalysis

Occasionally psychotherapy can produce rapid and permanent change. Freud is said to have cured Gustav Mahler's impotence after a four-hour therapeutic walk around the streets of Leiden (Weber 2009). There are cases which centre around some painful or shameful experience which haunts the patient, but which he has been unable to face. AS recalls a man who was cured of his symptoms of anxiety in a single psychotherapeutic session in which he revealed that he had left his parents behind in Europe to the mercy of the Nazis, while he himself escaped. His confession brought considerable relief, and at follow-up some weeks later revealed that he was symptom-free.

In the early days of psychoanalysis, it was hoped that all neurotic symptoms could be abolished in a reasonably simple way, provided that the emotions connected with their origin could be recollected and worked through. In *Studies on Hysteria* Breuer and Freud (1893) wrote:

'For we found, to our great surprise at first, that each individual hysterical symptom immediately and permanently disappeared when we had succeeded in bringing clearly to light the memory of the event by which it was provoked and in arousing its accompanying affect, and when the patient had described that event in the greatest possible detail and had put the affect into words.'

Freud was keen that psychoanalysis should be regarded as a legitimate branch of medicine, and sometimes approached symptoms as alien intruders which could be banished by psychotherapy in rather the same way as the bacteria causing an infection can be eliminated by an antibiotic; in such cases, it is legitimate to speak of 'cure'.

Some patients certainly have appalling childhoods; and adult difficulties are undoubtedly related to their childhood experiences. But it is important to remember that what one child finds traumatic, another may not, to acknowledge the role of genetic and contextual factors, and to dispel the notion that psychotherapy is primarily a kind of treasure hunt for traumatic incidents. Although very occasionally hysterical symptoms may immediately and permanently disappear when the therapist has linked them to a traumatic event, the more generalized symptoms of unhappiness and difficulty in interpersonal relations which most of our patients bring to us do not improve in this way.

Character analysis

Freud soon discovered that symptoms were not always easily reducible to repressed emotions having a particular origin at a particular time. The majority are intimately bound up with the patient's personality, attitude to life, and his relationships with those close to him. These came to the fore once Freud had moved on from hypnosis to free association as his main technique. If the patient is encouraged to take the lead, and to say everything which comes into his head without concealment or the exercise of choice, it is inevitable that he will not only talk about his symptoms, however troublesome these may be, but also about his aspirations, goals, relationships with others, interests, hopes, fears, achievements, and disappointments; in short, about everything which constitutes him as an individual and distinguishes him as a unique person.

Moreover, as psychoanalysts began to take into treatment a wider range of sufferers than those with hysterical symptoms, they realized that many who presented themselves for psychoanalysis did so because of difficulties of character rather than definable neuroses. It was partly because of this that lengthy analyses became the rule. In the early days of psychoanalysis, treatments were brief; but in his *New Introductory Lectures* (1933) written in his late seventies, Freud says : 'The analysis of character disorders also calls for long periods of treatment; but it is often successful.'

Today, many of the patients who seek psychotherapy are suffering from 'problems in living' (Szazs 1965). Here what psychotherapist and patient are aiming at is not so much the abolition of specific symptoms, as changes in attitude toward others and life in general. This has a number of consequences. One is that, in spite of Freud's aspirations to make it so, psychotherapy can never be a purely scientific enterprise. Although the psychotherapist needs to retain a measure of objectivity, she must allow herself to be affected by the patient if she is to understand him. Since the therapist forms part of a reciprocal relationship, albeit of a specialized kind, she cannot maintain the detachment which characterizes the scientist conducting a experiment. Understanding people is, inescapably, a different enterprise from understanding things; and those who attempt to bring toward people the detached attitude they might adopt toward things, are suffering from the very disease which they purport to cure.

Another consequence is that what constitutes 'cure', or even 'improvement', becomes open to debate. The changes in attitude that lead to increased confidence, competence and enjoyment are imponderables which, although qualitative measures can be devised to capture them, are much harder to measure.

Because the presenting symptoms which bring the patient to seek psychotherapy cannot be regarded as extraneous, but are closely bound up with the patient's whole personality, they often fade into insignificance once the psychotherapeutic process is under way. This is consistent with the view that therapy is essentially about the capacity to understand oneself and others, and to lead a meaningful life. These are difficult concepts to define, but not impossible. Shedler and Westen (Shedler 2010) for example have devised a rating scale which taps into many of the things that most people would consider make life worthwhile. These include the ability to use talents, abilities and energies effectively; pleasure in accomplishment; capacity for genuine intimacy and caring; being part of a community; empathy; assertiveness; humour; enjoying one's sex life; coming to terms with and growing through past pain; and the capacity to see others' point of view.

Is it possible for psychotherapy to effect such changes? As we have outlined in the previous chapter, there is strong evidence that it can. But at the same time it must also be accepted that psychotherapy may not be able to alter basic character structure. A person's tendency toward depression, or his use of obsessional or avoidant types of defence will not be abolished, however much he learns to understand, control, and make use of these fundamental aspects of his personality. Indeed it is important for the patient to understand those features of his personality which are *not* amenable to change. Psychological difficulty is not so much a matter of possessing a particular type of character structure, as of being overwhelmed by that pattern, or of being unable to make effective use of it.

The main focus of psychotherapy is in the monitoring and control aspect of the personality. In classical metapsychological terms this resides in the 'superego'. When therapy is effective, the superego typically becomes less harsh, more forgiving and understanding (Strachey 1934; Holmes 2012e), coming to accept that we all make mistakes, are all driven by base motives such as envy, hatred, rapaciousness, and that these need to be understood and come to terms with rather than eliminated. This control function is also a feature of the ego and its ability to self-scrutinize, or mentalise. If we can 'see ourselves from the outside , and others from the inside' (Holmes 2010) our capacity to make and sustain and repair intimate relationships will be enhanced. The training ground for this process of skill-acquisition is the therapeutic relationship itself. The patient learns through his relationship with the therapist how he typically reacts, acquires new interpersonal skills, and can then apply these to his outside life.

We all, whether patients, therapists, or men and women in the street, have the same varieties of psychopathology, in varying degree. Therapists need to remind themselves from time to time that the majority of people get through life happily and successfully without psychotherapy. The key vehicle for benign cycles leading to psychological health is life itself, especially the role of intimate relationships. Women who experience adverse life events, and have a close confiding relationship, are buffered from depression (Brown and Harris 1979). Disturbed delinquent girls who make good partner choices do not become psychologically ill (Moffitt *et al* 2001). The role of therapy is to nudge the patient towards the benign cycles of psychological health, and minimize the self-defeating malign ones that have brought them for help. This is psychotherapy's butterfly effect, the 'difference that makes a difference' (Bateson 1972).

Much of the effect of successful psychotherapy depends upon the patient feeling that he is no longer at the mercy of his unconscious being, but able to experiment with his own nature and make creative use of it. The therapist, through her understanding, acts as a mirror, reflecting back to the patient aspects of himself which he had not seen or accepted. The therapist becomes the patient's temporary 'auxiliary ego' (Strachey 1934). If one is faced with an unfamiliar task of which one is frightened, the fact that someone else seems to regard the same task as manageable helps one to tackle it. Patients come into therapy demoralized by the problems with which their own psychology confronts them. The fact that the therapist is familiar with such problems, understands them, and regards them as issues which can be dealt with, gives the patient the courage to approach them in the same way. The effect of 'suggestion' can never be excluded from any kind of psychotherapy, nor should it be. This kind of indirect suggestion is essentially an instillation of hope, implicit, or occasionally explicit, conveyed solely by the therapist's attitude of confidence. The paradoxical psychiatric mantra runs 'where there's depression there's hope'. It is a reminder that the majority of depressions remit given time, and that attempts to evade one's depression through manic over activity, drugs, intellectualizing etc, are doomed to reinforce rather than solve the problems that are driving them.

What is a good outcome in psychotherapy?

Those states of perfection labelled 'emotional maturity', 'integration', 'self-realization', 'full genitality', or the achievement of 'mature object relationships' are largely mythical. All these terms refer to goals toward which we may legitimately strive, but at which we never arrive. There are no 'and everyone lived happily ever after' moments in psychotherapy; rather, psychotherapy helps people progress upward on a developmental helix, and be able to tackle life's challenges with a wider range of understanding and in more complex and less rigid or stereotyped ways. If we dispense with myth, can we attempt to define what improvement or 'getting better' in the course of psychotherapy really is. Interestingly, there is quite a consensus of opinion between psychotherapists of very different approaches.

Jung used to say that analysis was for people who found themselves stuck; and his objective was to get them moving again.

> 'In the majority of my cases the resources of the conscious mind are exhausted (or, in ordinary English, they are 'stuck') … . My aim is to bring about a psychic state in which my patient begins to experiment with his own nature – a state of fluidity, change and growth where nothing is eternally fixed and hopelessly petrified' (Jung 1931).

This is very similar to Carl Rogers' (1967) statement that

> 'clients seem to move toward more openly being a process, a fluidity, a changing'. He quotes Kierkegaard as saying that 'An existing individual is constantly in process of becoming … and translates all his thinking into terms of process'.

Travelling hopefully toward the future, instead of being stuck in the past, means to be able to modify and make use of one's psychopathology rather than getting rid of it.

Another change which occurs as the result of successful psychotherapy is that the patient feels increasingly more confident in his own judgement. Szasz defines the aim of psychoanalytic treatment as being

> 'to increase the patient's knowledge of himself and others and hence his freedom of choice in the conduct of his life' (Szasz 1965).

Szasz is particularly insistent that the therapist should not give advice or do anything else which might interfere with the patient's autonomy. It is characteristic of depressed and dependent people that they often value others' judgement above their own; this is why the therapist tries to help patients to find their own answers rather than giving direct advice. It is frightening but invigorating to realize that one's own thoughts and feelings are trustworthy guides, and that ultimately one knows more about oneself that anyone else, including one's therapist.

Fairbairn (1958) refers to 'the maintenance of the patient's internal world as a closed system' as being the greatest of all sources of resistance. He emphasizes the fact that patients seem very often to have given up hope of finding relationships with real people in the external world satisfying; and hold on instead to fantasied relationships derived from childhood to which they attempt to make real people conform. Fairbairn sees the analyst's task as penetrating the internal world of the patient and making it accessible to reality. Rogers is surely expressing a similar idea when he says that change is manifested by an increased ability to experience the world more nearly as it is, instead of in terms of preconceived categories; an increased openness to experience. Both are consistent with Freud's view that neurosis is a 'turning away from reality', and that the task of analysis is to re-connect the sufferer with reality, including the reality of their mental pain, traumatic, self-inflicted or self-perpetuating.

All these formulations have in common the idea that change and development are part of human existence, and that psychotherapy can help people liberate the creative part of their personality and embrace rather than resist change. It is this kind of formulation which leads some therapists to see their work not as confined to the treatment of the psychologically ill but as part of the quest for meaning and change, applicable to anyone, however 'well functioning' they appear to be.

Termination; when is enough enough?

Ending psychotherapy (Salberg 2010) is either chosen (i.e. agreed in advance as in time-limited therapies), or contingent (the result of patient or therapist moving away; imposed by funding bodies etc). There are several obvious questions surrounding termination. *When* should one end – when the analyst decides, when the patient decides, or when a fixed term is 'up'? *How* should one end – abruptly, or with a gradual winding down of frequency of sessions; with or without allowances for follow-up, and 'top-ups'? *Why* should one end – what is the theoretical justification for an ending, how does one know that the job is done, how does a decision to end emerge? *In what way* can one discern if an ending is good enough (analogous perhaps to a 'good death'), premature (as in the Dora case, Freud 1905) or overdue (as with the 'Wolf Man', Freud 1918)?

In an ideal world, psychotherapy ought to go on for as long as is necessary for the patient to feel that he understands what kind of a person he is and what forces have helped to shape him; that he can face the ordinary challenges of life as competently as anyone else; and that he is capable of fulfilling relationships with other human beings on equal terms. But of course in practice, psychotherapy is often time-limited, for a variety of reasons.

Time-limited therapies

If 'third party funded' (e.g. National Health Service; health insurance) this will be because only a limited number of sessions is permitted; if privately funded because the patient's resources are limited; or for various other contingent reasons such as the patient or therapist relocating. Time-limited therapy is a discipline in its own right. The rationale informing brief dynamic therapies begins and starts with termination. A time limit is implicit from the first moment of therapy. The therapist will 'count-down', usually starting each session by announcing 'this is our seventh session' or, 'we've another three sessions to go'. Termination hangs over the therapy from the start – conspicuous either by its absence (the patient pretending it does not exist, sometimes collusively with the therapist); or by its inhibitory presence ('what's the point of going into all this, I'm only going to be seeing you for another six times'); but always grist to the transferential mill (e.g. 'I wonder if the fact that you know you are going to lose me means that you cannot fully make use of me, rather as you never really let your weekends-only Dad know how angry you were with him for leaving your Mum').

Different varieties of brief dynamic therapy handle endings in different ways. Balint (1968) realized that for psychoanalytic psychotherapy to reach out from the ivory couches of Hampstead to the masses, it must perforce abbreviate itself, suggesting that at the end of therapy the patient should feel both very much better and very much worse, and that what mattered was that this could be acknowledged. Mann's 12-session take-it-or-leave-it approach (Mann 1973) is justified as an analogue of the existential unavoidability of death. If the pain of loss can be experienced it can be transcended; follow-ups and interminable therapies are simply attempts to evade the reality of irreversible separation. Ryle's (1990) CAT therapists provide a good-bye letter, a memento that can mitigate termination, thereby activating an internalized good object imago, comparable to the 1960s tennis ace Jimmy Connor's letter from his grandmother, kept in the sole of his shoe, taken out and read at crucial moments in his matches.

Chosen endings: when is the moment?

Ending therapy is a real loss: a significant aspect of the client's life is no longer there. A secure space and time where distressing events and feelings can be digested is now empty. A person who focuses her attention and sensitivity on one's inner world is now absent. One is on one's own again, with one's story, feelings, and life history. But, like every aspect of psychotherapy, an ending's significance is always specific and unique. Depending on mood and perspective, the meaning of an ending can be like a death, a bereavement, a completion, a liberation, less a funeral (with or without a convivial wake) than a joyful moment of maturation and the excitement of 'leaving home'.

Ending brings gains as well as loss: the time and money invested in therapy is now available for other projects; the client no longer feels so dependent; autonomy and maturity are reinforced; he or she feels more psychologically robust, more able to provide security for others and less in need of it himself. Just as the bereaved are sometimes said to have 'earned' their widow- or widower-hood, the discharged therapy client may likewise feel he has earned his liberation from the obligations, mysteries and miseries of therapy, without having to deny its now-absent comforts and gifts. The point at which ending enters the therapeutic frame is when the balance sheet of benefit and obligation shifts away from the former towards the latter, the investment begins to outweigh the return.

This has a number of clinical implications. First, therapists must bear in mind the client's predominant character style. Avoidant/deactivating clients may well appear to take an ending in their stride, apparently seeing it as inevitable, natural and appropriate, presenting themselves as eager to move onto the challenges of 'real life' now that their symptoms have diminished and they feel stronger. Regret, doubt, anger, and disappointment may be conspicuous by their absence, gratitude superficial and conventional rather than deep-rooted. The therapist should direct the client's attention to these possibilities as manifest in dreams, missed appointments, seeking other forms of treatment, manic cheerfulness, fulsome gratitude, or being Pollyannaish. Premature ending is a not infrequent occurrence with such clients. It is always worth pushing hard for at least one final goodbye session, in which disappointments and resentments can be aired, rather than simply letting a client slip away.

Clinical folklore holds that as the end of therapy approaches, the client's symptoms, even if alleviated during the course of therapy, may re-appear. This is perhaps particularly likely for hyperactivating clients who may overestimate the negative impact of ending. The therapist may be tempted into premature offers of further therapy, or suggesting an alternative therapist or therapy modality (such as a group). Therapist self-scrutiny is needed to differentiate counter-transference-induced guilt from clients' real clinical need. Such post-therapy arrangements may sometimes be appropriate, but should not be allowed to divert therapeutic focus from working through the ending.

Second, the client's social context should be taken into account when deciding on either offering time-limited therapy, or finding an appropriate moment to conclude open-ended treatment. Time-limited therapy is much more likely to succeed when the client has a good social and emotional network to which they can return once therapy is over. For more disturbed clients in long-term therapy, if treatment has not managed to facilitate the capacity to generate outside attachments, post-therapy relapse is likely. Such clients may need further therapeutic arrangements such as group therapy or key-worker support, and the reality of this needs to be discussed as a period of intensive individual analytic therapy draws to its close.

Winnicott (1971) argues that in any developmental process, however healthy, there are repeated failures of 'fit' between mother and child – a mother is, can, and should only be 'good enough'. There is therefore a necessary 'disillusionment' with the breast if the child is to move towards independence and new attachments, and to avoid the narcissism which finds intolerable the inevitable discrepancy between wish and reality. Resistance to termination can be seen as an impediment to this developmental process. The therapist and therapy are invested with indispensability, an illusory and anachronistic carry-over of infantile needs and wishes into the present. Because the therapist fails to meet the client's overweening need he cannot be relinquished. The therapist may be able to provide only the caring half of the parental imago, and be unable to offer the necessary challenge pointing the client towards independence. Hatred and need might be so stark that they cannot be brought together into the depressive position. As Novick (1988) puts it:

> 'Seldom mentioned in the literature is the necessity for gradual disillusionment in order to begin the process of giving up and mourning the omnipotent mother-child dyad. To a certain extent, the analyst must be experienced as a failure for the patient to respond fully to the treatment as a success '.

The therapist's job is to 'be there' for the patient during the period of therapy. But the therapist is also, albeit in a regular and predictable way, *not* there. During separations, including the final separation that is termination, a secure base figure holds the care-seeker in mind, and stays in the mind of the care-seeker. A client has the right to expect his therapist to hold him in mind between and after sessions, and to refer back to things said and felt in previous sessions. Weekly therapy patients often report in the early stages of therapy: 'what we were discussing last week stayed in my mind for a couple of days afterwards and then seemed to fade'. As suggested in discussing suicide, the appropriate frequency of sessions is dictated by the time it takes for these memories to fade; the shorter the time, the more frequent sessions are needed. Similarly, ending therapy is only likely to be successful if the patient has managed to 're-instate' the therapist in his inner world, and to be able to draw on the therapist even in the absence of her physical presence.

Reich (1950) compares the ending of analysis with mourning in a patient who came to her for a second training analysis:

> 'His description of his reaction to the termination of his first analysis was quite revealing: 'I felt as if I was suddenly left alone in the world. It was like the feeling that I had after the death of my mother ... I tried with effort to find somebody to love, something to be interested in. For months I longed for the analyst and wished to tell him about whatever happened to me. Then slowly, without noticing how it happened, I forgot about him. About two years later, I happened to meet him at a party and thought he was just a nice elderly gentleman and in no way interesting.

The ending of a therapeutic relationship entails dissolution as well as disillusionment, and gratitude for the (albeit professional, and professionally rewarded) love and attention which the analyst has provided. The 'work' of mourning consists of the dissolution of this investment. The conscious awareness of someone who was once 'everything' begins to fade into the background; eventually all that is left is a scar which, like a healed physical wound, imposing its restrictions, great or small. A lost parent, partner, or worst of all a child, inhabits the psyche forever; but as the pain of loss gradually lessens, new investments become to an extent possible. When this process is incomplete there may be an inconsolable effort to replace like with like, eternally in search of what is irretrievably lost, so condemned to everlasting disappointment. Only when this 'transference' from the past onto the potentially new object becomes less compelling are new beginnings possible.

In psychotherapy coming to terms with loss – 'in my beginning is my end' (Eliot 1953) – starts with the establishment of a professional as opposed to an informal relationship; moves into the all-important transferential investment reactivating past attachments and losses; ends with acceptance of separation, loss and the fading of the transference, and the 'reinstatement of the lost object' in the psyche. Now the analysis becomes part of the self, no longer an absence. Faced with some life-problem, the patient may ask himself 'what would Dr X say in this situation', drawing on the inner resources that have stayed with him.

Handling the ending

The suggestion that as much as can be done has been done, may originate either with the patient or with the therapist. The first may say; 'I think I've got about as far as I can', and, if the therapist agrees, plans for termination can be made. In other cases, it may be the therapist who tentatively suggests that the end of therapy is in sight by saying something like, 'How would you feel about the prospect of ending these sessions at some point?' This will often have been stimulated by the patient bringing material that seems indirectly to refer to ending – the death of a pet, a friend who has moved away, a building project completed, etc.

When agreement has been reached, it is usually important that therapy is not too suddenly terminated. Even if the patient announces that they have had enough and that this is their last session, as occasionally happens, the therapist should insist that they have at least one 'goodbye' session where they can review what has happened: what has been achieved, and what not. In planned endings a reduction in the frequency of visits is a common pattern: from twice a week to once, and then to once a fortnight, once a month, and so on. Where the patient has been coming for two or more years, the period between deciding upon termination and putting it into effect may need to be as long as six months. It is good practice to offer patients a follow-up appointment six months after the termination, partly in order to satisfy the therapist's wish to know about their progress and welfare; partly to reassure them that the relationship, while professional, is genuine.

Some patients are anxious to have done with therapy as soon as they possibly can; and these present no problem in termination other than that of deterring them from ending treatment prematurely. Such patients are not likely to keep follow-up appointments; possibly because they have found the position of being a patient humiliating, and do not wish to be reminded of it. Their reluctance to let the therapist know how they are progressing may also be related to what has been described as 'post-analytic improvement'. This phenomenon is particularly likely to occur in people who have been very dependent, but who find, to their own surprise, that after psychotherapy they can be much more independent than they had thought possible. For such people, re-involvement with the therapist, even if it is minimal, represents a threat to their new-found freedom.

There are other patients who, if they could, would go on with therapy forever. Therapists need to learn how to detect when a patient insists upon going on because of his dependency rather than genuine clinical need; a skill more likely to be acquired when the therapist has no financial interest in his patient continuing to come and see her. Careful weaning is a good policy here, perhaps setting a definite 'clean-break' date, without follow-up, at least a year or even two ahead. A small number of patients will remain who have not succeeded in incorporating the therapist within their own psyche, and who continue to need to have the therapist, or some substitute for her, as an actual person in the external world to whom they feel that they can have recourse when this is really needed. Infrequent sessions or *ad hoc* availability provides a sheet anchor which enables such patients to manage their lives without depending too much on other supportive agencies. Like the rain-deterring value of carrying an umbrella, the knowledge that the therapist is still available means that they can carry on without her; and the fact that they can see her occasionally reassures them of her continuing existence and interest.

Some patients, usually those of obsessional personality, tend to persist with therapy indefinitely because they feel that there is still more fascinating exploration to be undertaken. They need to be reminded by the metaphysical poet Andrew Marvell that 'had we but world enough and time', additional enthralling revelations and profounder insights would no doubt be obtained, but also that 'the grave's a fine and pleasant place, but none I think do there embrace'. Patients can become stuck in psychotherapy in the same way that they were stuck in the neurosis which brought them for help in the first place. It is possible to make the therapeutic situation a substitute for life; and it is not only patients who fall into this trap. It is not unknown for therapists similarly to get excessively caught up in their work and the therapeutic ideology of their profession. Like politicians, for them to carry full conviction, therapists need a 'hinterland' of family, hobbies and talents unrelated to their work. Which homily brings us to our concluding chapters.

15

The Life and Work of a Psychotherapist

Since individual psychotherapy depends upon an interaction between two personalities, it follows that we ought to make some attempt to understand the personality of the psychotherapist. What kind of people are attracted toward the practice of psychotherapy, and why? What are the effects of their work upon the therapist? What kinds of support and help do therapists need? Is there a life cycle in the work of a therapist and how might it be characterized?

The personality of the therapist

Psychotherapy is generally viewed, in the UK at least, as an eccentric occupation. Most people find it inconceivable that anyone, all day and every day, should choose to listen to stories of distress. Some imagine that, were they in the shoes of the psychotherapist, they would become intensely impatient; others that they would succumb to despair. In their eyes, the psychotherapist is either as mad as his or her patients, or else as a kind of secular saint, able to rise above ordinary human limitations. Neither view is true. Although some psychotherapists are eccentric, the majority are not, and none, at least among those we have so far met, is a saint.

It is probably true that the majority of therapists have had some difficulty, conflict or trauma in their childhood or early adulthood, and many lead, or have led, quite difficult interpersonal lives. One of the attractions of psychotherapy as a profession is that it provides one with a sphere – the consulting room and the relationship with the patient – where one can be at one's best, even if in the rest of one's life one is some distance from mainstream contentment.

Most will admit that their interest in the subject took its origin from their own emotional problems; but this is too banal and general a statement to be illuminating. There can be few intelligent adolescents who have not read something about psychology in the hope of understanding themselves better, and the fact that psychotherapists have often done the same does not tell us much about them. AS reports a conversation with the director of a monastery: 'Everyone who comes to us', he said, 'does so for the wrong reasons.' The same could be said of psychotherapists of whom a similar quip runs: 'the main trouble with psychotherapy is that most therapists are no good'. We shall look later at ways in which that proportion can be reduced! However, it is not simply because they want to understand themselves better that people take up psychotherapy professionally. It is because certain features of their personalities make the practice of psychotherapy rewarding. Let us first look at some of the personality traits of those who seem to be successful psychotherapists, and then consider what may be the psychopathology of such traits; their possible origins, advantages and disadvantages.

Persons and things

It is obvious that psychotherapists must be interested in people; that is, in the world of the personal rather than the impersonal. The majority of psychotherapists, whether medically qualified or not, are not primarily scientists. Research suggests that people who are attracted toward the exact sciences and those who are drawn toward the arts and humanities differ in temperament, and that this difference manifests itself early in life (Hudson 1973). Although it is unwise to generalize, and there are many outstanding exceptions, there are still 'two cultures' (Snow 1973). Potential scientists tend to show little interest in introspection; they make a sharp distinction between their private lives and their professional activities, and may be socially rather conventional. Those who are attracted by the arts, in contrast, show a greater capacity for introspection; react more emotionally toward others; make little separation between their work and their private lives; and take longer than scientists to settle down and achieve stability in life. The popular imagination associates ideas of pleasure with artists, ideas of value with scientists.

> 'Artist, poet and novelist are all seen in my studies as warm and exciting, but as of little worth. Mathematicians, physicists, and engineers are all seen as extremely valuable, but also as dull and cold.' (Hudson 1973)

Those who become scientists are temperamentally governed by the notion of self-control, while those who turn toward the arts are more influenced by the idea of self-expression.

Thus scientists are better able to exclude the emotional and the irrational from their experience; and that this partly determines their choice of an occupation that requires the greatest possible objectivity. It is clear that psychotherapists are likely to fall on the arts side of the line, and that this is appropriate. Although psychotherapists must be capable of a certain degree of detachment and objectivity, they must also seek to experience and enter into the emotional and irrational. Openness toward one's own emotions and the emotions of others go hand-in-hand; the psychotherapist is attracted toward work in which the expression of emotion is encouraged; and in which she has the opportunity of reaching a better understanding of her own emotions as well as those of her patients.

When psychotherapy becomes concerned with understanding people rather than with abolishing symptoms, it moves away from being a scientific enterprise, at least in the narrow sense. Psychotherapists who guiltily feel that they are not as 'scientific' as their colleagues in other medical and scientific specialities can comfort themselves with the reflection that, if they were so, they might not be as good at their job. Carl Rogers (1951) writes:

> 'There are also many whose concept of the individual is that of an object to be dissected, diagnosed, manipulated. Such professional workers may find it very difficult to learn or to practice a client-centerd form of psychotherapy.'

Against this might be set B. F. Skinner's (1971) vision of a Utopia (or is it a dystopia?) in which 'contingencies of reinforcement' will automatically produce socially desirable behaviour and general happiness:

> 'What is being abolished is autonomous man – the inner man ... the man defended by the literatures of freedom and dignity. His abolition has long been overdue ... A scientific analysis of behaviour dispossesses autonomous man and turns the control he has been said to exert over to the environment ... What is needed is more control, not less ... The problem is to design a world which ... is science or nothing ...'.

While Skinner's version of behaviourism has been overthrown, and the above perhaps is a deliberately ironized vision, traces of this attitude are to found alive and well in the 'evidence-based' culture which pervades modern social and medical policy. There really is a sense in which understanding another person is different from understanding a disease, an animal, or a tree. Isaiah Berlin (Berlin 1976) makes the point with his customary clarity:

> 'Understanding other men's motives or acts, however imperfect or corrigible, is a state of mind or activity in principle different from learning about, or knowledge of, the external world .... Just as we can say with assurance that we ourselves are not only bodies in space, acted upon by measurable natural forces, but that we think, choose, follow rules, make decisions, in other words, possess an inner life of which we are aware and which we can describe, so we take for granted – and, if questioned, say that we are certain – that others possess a similar inner life, without which the notion of communication, or language, or of human society, as opposed to an aggregate of human bodies, becomes unintelligible.'

This is an admirable statement of the mentalising perspective which is integral to psychotherapy. Understanding other human beings requires that the observer make use of his own understanding of himself, his own feelings, thoughts, intentions, and motives in order to understand others.

This kind of understanding is a refinement and deepening of the kind of understanding which we employ every day in our social lives, and without which social life would be impossible. Dennett (1973) refers to 'intentional explanations' which 'cite thoughts, desires, beliefs, intentions, rather than chemical reactions, explosions, electric impulses, in explaining the occurrences of human motions'. The impersonal, scientific stance (referred to by Dennett as 'mechanistic') can only inform us about another person's behaviour; and although, by adopting this attitude, we may be able to discern *causes* for this behaviour, our explanation cannot be in terms of intention, nor can we determine what this behaviour *means* to the individual concerned.

In our ordinary day-to-day encounters with individuals, we are bound to adopt the intentional stance. I cannot but assume that I myself have feelings, desires, thoughts, beliefs, and intentions, and, in the ordinary way, inevitably assume that others are similarly constituted. Rapoport (1960) points out that when we are playing a game, we are bound to make what he calls 'the assumption of similarity' about our opponent; that is, that he intends to win if he can, and that, in trying to do so, he has in mind the same kinds of strategy as we do ourselves. If we could not make the assumption of similarity, games would be impossible, as would social life.

The skills which the psychotherapist must develop, therefore, depend upon reciprocal understanding. The more she learns about herself, the more will she be able to understand her patients; the more she learns about her patients, the more will she be able to understand herself.

Empathy and other skills

Good psychotherapists must not only be interested in people, but also possess the capacity for empathy with a wide range of different types of personality. We all have our limitations; no one can empathize with every kind of person. But psychotherapists must have an interest in people who, at first sight, may not resemble themselves or share their interests. This capacity is also connected with a relative absence of repression. When one can recognize that embryonic features of the emotional problems with which the patient is struggling are present in oneself, one can begin to empathize with what the patient is feeling. To do this argues that one has not, too early in life, excluded from consciousness, and from what one conceives to be one's own character, possibilities that might have developed entirely differently. Perhaps one can fully understand only those aspects of personality in others of which one can find traces in oneself, including ironically, the very non-psychotherapeutic capacity for repression required in some scientific or military occupations. One of the reasons why personal therapy is so important for psychotherapists is that it extends the range of emotions – fantasies, fears, hatreds, psychotic fragments – that one encounters within oneself, and thereby enables one to put these to good use in one's work. But, as we shall see, the fact that psychotherapy demands a kind of flexibility toward oneself as well as toward one's patients, while essential, also has its disadvantages.

Psychotherapists need to be capable of genuine concern and warmth toward their patients. Warm acceptance facilitates personality change, just as criticism tends to arouse defensiveness and hostility, and therefore makes change more difficult. Psychotherapists must, of course, say challenging things from time to time; but, if the patient feels that the therapist is unequivocally on his side, it is astonishing how well he will be able to accept a critical assessment of his attitudes and relationships. Rogers' (1951) 'unconditional positive regard' is perhaps the most powerful of all therapeutic factors in psychotherapy. Psychotherapists should be especially able to extend positive regard toward those whom the world has rejected. As we have said, successful therapists generally possess an especial capacity for identifying with the insulted and injured.

Openness toward emotion should imply that psychotherapists display an unusual tolerance of emotional expression in others. If someone starts to shed tears, a common response is to become embarrassed, angry, feel at a loss, wish to escape, or compelled to 'do something' to alleviate the distress, even if this is no more than rushing in with tissues, rather than remaining in an 'actively passive' witnessing stance, confident that experiencing mental pain can be salutary and able to let feelings run their course. Psychotherapists by their very attitude need to be able to facilitate the expression of distress on the part of the patient, without themselves becoming intolerably distressed. It is important that patients be allowed to weep without the therapist immediately trying to stop them. A good deal of conventional comforting is as much aimed at relieving the distress of the comforter as that of the sufferer. Likewise, therapists must also be capable of facilitating the expression of anger, even when it may be directed toward themselves. A tolerant awareness of one's own angry potential is needed if this is to be accomplished.

Although the psychotherapist must be in touch with her own feelings if she is to understand those of the patient, the psychotherapeutic session is not a forum for displaying them. This is not to say that the therapist should try to be detached or cold. Psychotherapists need to be affected by their patients' emotions if they are to understand them; and the fact that they do understand will manifest itself in their manner and tone of voice, without competing with the patient in emotional display. This requires considerable restraint and self-abnegation on the part of the therapist. It is easy for intellectual, remote persons to tolerate the emotions of others; they do so by detachment and avoidance. It is easy for warm, sympathetic human beings to enter into another's distress; to proffer tea, sympathy, or love, and to share with the other person their own, not dissimilar experience. But the therapist has to be affected, without acting upon her own feelings: to feel, but to use these feelings in the service of the patient, as a guide to understanding, not as a means of demonstrating how kind, how loving and sympathetic she is. Only thus will she be able to help the patient better understand and master his own emotional problems.

The capacity for self-abnegation has obvious parallels with the degree of self-sacrifice entailed in bringing up children. Therapists' own personality are never fully expressed, but always orientated toward the needs of the other. More than any other professional, the psychotherapist needs to be less than normally self-assertive; if not an enigma, at least not a completely known quantity. Closely related with the capacity for self-abnegation is the reluctance on the part of the therapist to take over, give orders, or seek immediate practical solutions to problems. The successful therapist has to steer a subtle course. She has to be able to identify herself with the patient's experience while being able to distance herself sufficiently from it to subject it to critical scrutiny; there will be times when she guides and steers, but she needs always to be sensitive to the impact of that guidance, and the negative emotions such as impotence, envy or shame this may stir up.

The developmental experiences of psychotherapists

People drawn to psychotherapy as a profession prefer to exercise power in ways which do not require quick decision making, giving orders, or any other form of acting directly or assertively upon the world and people around them. Arguably Freud's greatest discovery was the technique of free association in which the didactic role of the doctor was abolished and the lead handed over to the patient.

Psychotherapists often have some personal knowledge of what it is like to feel insulted and injured, a kind of knowledge which they might rather not have, but which actually extends the range of their compassion. Freud himself experienced ridicule and hostility during the earlier part of his life, and, in old age, had to flee Vienna in order to escape from Nazi persecution. Many of his followers also became refugees. The experience of being rejected by one's fellows, whether for reasons of race, or because of personal difficulties in making peer relationships in childhood, may leave the individual with a curious mixture of hostility and suspicion towards ordinary people, combined with an especial compassion with those whom she feels have been rejected. Intrinsic in the role of the therapist therefore is to be something of an outsider. Paradoxically, the power of the therapist lies in being outwith the power structure of the society in which she works. Like the Shakespearean fool, the therapist can be confided in and speak truths that would be taboo to those trapped within the confines of normal society.

To summarize the discussion so far: ideally, psychotherapists should be, and often are, people of wide sympathies who are open both to their own emotions and to those of others: able to identify with a wide range of people; tolerant of the expression of both grief and rage; warm and sympathetic without being sentimental; predominantly non-assertive, but capable of quietly maintaining their own position: able to put themselves at the patient's service, and to accept that their reward for doing so may be both long-delayed and indirect. This picture may sound too good to be true; but if we look at possible developmental aspects of the therapist's childhood it will no longer appear so.

Sensitivity toward the feelings of others is an essential part of the psychotherapist's equipment; and such sensitivity can generally be traced to the circumstances of the therapist's childhood. Why should it be necessary for a child to develop a particular sensitivity to what others are feeling? Often because such sensitivity springs from an anxiety not to upset or anger or distress one or both parents. Suppose, for example, that a child has a particularly irritable, difficult father. She will surely learn to watch out for danger signals; to be more than usually alert to what might upset her father; to study the father's wishes, and comply with them, in order to avoid arousing wrath.

Or suppose that the child's mother is ailing or low-spirited. She will have to learn not to make demands upon her mother, and will also become sensitive to what factors seem to make her tired or ill or depressed. This anxious awareness of what may upset parents may inhibit natural, spontaneous behaviour, and sometimes has the result of making the child feel that her demands are selfish, illegitimate, or even potentially harmful. Instead of a freely expressed request which a parent might as freely either meet or refuse, such a child may come to feel that her own need for love is likely to be destructive. Moreover, if she comes to feel that her own needs and demands are bad, she will be left feeling anxious as to whether she is likeable or lovable, and an especial need to prove that she is so. This will reinforce her tendency to be over-anxious to please, or even be ingratiating. These 'weaknesses' may be put to good use for psychotherapists making an initial contact with patients who are hostile or suspicious.

If a child's behaviour is governed by anxiety over the effects which her demands may have upon her parents, she is giving precedence to her parents' needs. A child of this kind might, therefore, grow up to be an adult who is not only sensitively orientated towards what others are feeling, but one who also has a tendency toward self-abnegation and putting others first.

This attitude also has the effect of encouraging repression of the child's aggressive feelings; since self-assertion is felt to be dangerous, and self-assertion cannot be separated from aggression. One cannot be primarily orientated toward the feelings of others without repressing a degree of aggression. Psychotherapists, therefore, are not so 'nice' as they sometimes appear; a trait which did not escape the notice of Freud, who thought that therapeutic enthusiasm was a defence against sadism. During their training, many of those in the 'helping' professions have, reluctantly, to face and accept an aggressive aspect of their personalities which they might not have realized existed. If they succeed in doing so, it will be easier for them to tolerate any aggression which patients may display toward them, and easier for them to assert their own opinions and needs in social life, where this is appropriate.

Lack of self-assertion seems to go hand-in-hand with some uncertainty about identity. The necessary 'role responsiveness' (Sandler and Sandler 1984) of psychotherapists that enables them to make emotional contact with a wide range of people means that they are to an extent 'all things to all men', and perhaps lack firmness, consistency, and definiteness of personality. People who are excessively orientated toward understanding others rather than toward expressing their own views may never discover what they really think. It is desirable that therapists should be as free as possible of prejudice. But sometimes lack of prejudice may also reflect a lack of genuine conviction, of any formed or positive attitude toward the world.

There is one sphere in which a somewhat fluid sense of identity is a positive advantage. It is desirable that psychotherapists should not identify themselves too closely with the sexual stereotypes operating in whatever society they live in. They must be capable of receiving both the masculine and the feminine projections of their patients; to be both 'mother' and 'father'. If the therapist is too markedly feminine, or too obviously masculine, it is more difficult for the patient to project both kinds of image. Projections need hooks to which to attach themselves. It is also valuable for the therapist to be able to identify with either sex; to imagine what it would be like to be the opposite sex. This implies being aware of one's own contra-sexual traits. The greatest novelists, of whom Tolstoy is the supreme example, can identify with, and depict, the opposite sex with entire conviction. It is interesting that Tolstoy, who found difficulty in controlling his very powerful sexual drive, never achieved a consistent, firm identity. All his life, he alternated between sensuality and asceticism, arrogance and humility, idealism and cynicism. His lack of consistency may have contributed to his achievement as a novelist, but made him extremely difficult to live with.

People attracted to the practice of psychotherapy often seem to relate to others by identification rather than by mutual self-affirmation. While a large measure of identification with the patient may be necessary within the therapeutic setting, it is undesirable in relationships with friends, although an easy way of being initially accepted by them. It is tempting for psychotherapists to relate to people socially in ways which are more appropriate to the consulting room. Most people are only too willing to talk at length about themselves, and, since therapists are, or ought to be, experts at 'drawing people out', some of their social encounters may consist of a monologue on the part of the person with whom they are talking, with the therapist making no more contribution than she would when a patient was freely associating. Although such a conversation may leave the other participant with a conviction that he has been talking to someone particularly 'nice', he may, on reflection, recall that the therapist has said very little about herself, and that he therefore had had no real opportunity of judging whether she really was nice. There are a number of ruthlessly narcissistic people for whom the monologue is a substitute for conversation; but most of those who are less self-absorbed regard social encounters as an opportunity for interchange on more or less equal terms.

Although psychotherapists put their personalities and skills at the service of their patients, they are, in reality, in an exceptionally powerful position (Holmes and Lindley 1997). First, they are in a position to choose whether or not to 'take on' a patient. Since one of the objects of psychotherapy is to help those who are immature and uncertain of themselves feel more equal with others, this creates a built-in power imbalance which will need to be addressed as it arises in the transference. Second, therapists who are unaware of their own desire for power may, unconsciously reinforce it by failing to interpret the patient's dependency or to encourage him to overcome it. This hazard may be reinforced in private practice where the therapist is financially dependent on the patient.

Psychotherapy becomes an attractive profession if one has had the kinds of difficulties outlined, being a structured situation in which conventions and rules govern the interchange and in which intimacy is one-sided. It is certainly the case that one can be a better person in the consulting room than in everyday life, and that is not necessarily a sign of hypocrisy; just that one is playing a defined and circumscribed role. Provided that the therapist is aware of how her own psychopathology has contributed to her choice of profession, she can make use of it constructively, just as we aim to help our patients turn their weaknesses into strengths, their swords into ploughshares (and vice versa when necessary).

There are of course, as in any profession, a number of practitioners who are unsuited to the work. Some are highly intellectual types who dimly sense that there is a corporeal aspect to their life that is missing. Psychoanalysis appears to offer a way round this dilemma in that it is a complex intellectual system that purports to investigate, and indeed celebrates, the non-rational aspects of existence. Rycroft (1968) writes:

> 'Obsessional characters are often attracted to psychology, since it seems to hold out the possibility of knowing about and therefore being able to control precisely those aspects of themselves and others which are most elusive and unpredictable.

Psychoanalysts sometimes elevate their particular 'school' into a dogmatic faith, believing that only they, and a few other chosen spirits have any deep understanding of human nature. Such are those who believe in some mythical ideal of being 'completely analysed', and who denigrate those who do not subscribe to their beliefs as being insufficiently trained; who create splinter groups within analytic institutions, and who entirely fail to recognize that, in a relatively new discipline to which many and various types of mind may each have something to contribute, dogmatism is both out of place and a sign of insecurity. Is this not an example of being stuck in the paranoid-schizoid position, in the grip of covert contempt? For is not a characteristic of the paranoid personality to *know* that he is right and that others are wrong, while the person who has reached the depressive position is more easily able to doubt whether he himself or anyone else has the only key to understanding human beings? Inexperienced psychotherapists tend to be overawed by those with such strong convictions and need more time to work out where they stand on the continuum running from 'not-knowingness' to dogmatic rigidity. They must find ways both to celebrate and tolerate uncertainty, while standing firm by core beliefs.

The dangers of being a psychotherapist

What are the effects of practising psychotherapy upon the psychotherapist? At this stage in the book it goes without saying that both authors have found it an intensely interesting and rewarding profession. But there is also a negative side to being a psychotherapist, especially if it is one's exclusive and full-time occupation. When psychotherapy is practised every day and all day, there is a danger of the therapist becoming a non-person; a prostitute parent whose children are not only all illegitimate, but more imaginary than real (this, dear reader, the uncuttable sentence referred to in the prologue). Psychotherapists tend to forget, although they probably get to know their patients better than anyone else, that their contact is under special conditions for only a short time. They do not see them in action in the external world; and, naturally enough, hear more about their anxieties, failures, and hesitancies than they do about their successes. In imagination, therefore, they may have a distorted picture of them as less competent than in fact they are.

Living vicariously through one's patients is as much a danger for therapists as it is for some parents and their children. It is important for therapists to find areas in which she lives for herself alone, in which self-expression, rather than self-abnegation, is demanded.

Another danger for the therapist is that of being cut off from contact with ordinary people, unable to communicate with anyone other than patients and fellow analysts. These are those who spend eight or more hours per day seeing patients and then, when evening comes, dutifully attend an analytic seminar. Such a life reinforces the esoteric, dogmatic and faith-like aspect of some analytic groups. It is important that therapists have as normal a social life as possible, in which they meet as friends people in different walks of life who pursue entirely different vocations.

Another difficult aspect is the impact of their work on the families of psychotherapists. First, professional discretion means that therapists cannot freely discuss their patients with their family, who therefore may have only the vaguest idea of what the work entails. If the most important thing which has happened to one during the day is that a particular patient has shown a sudden improvement, or that another has broken off treatment, being unable to talk about this in any detail may increase a therapist's remoteness from her children or spouse, and make them feel excluded from a very important part of her life. Perhaps the families of spies, or even of politicians in possession of state secrets, who constantly have to watch what they are saying, suffer similarly. Of course psychotherapists can and do discuss some aspects of cases with their spouses, who are also required to be discreet: but generally it is a council of perfection not to go into any details, since to do so breaches confidentiality. Some therapists include their spouses within their 'ring of confidentiality'; others do not. Either course has its disadvantages. Perhaps this is one reason why many therapists end up marrying other therapists.

The second reason that the practice of psychotherapy may be deleterious to family life is that, after focussing all day on their patients, therapists may have little emotional energy to spare for their spouses and children. Although the reverse can also be the case, and the spontaneity, fun, and unguarded exuberance of family life can form a much-needed contrast to the reticence and measured intimacy of the consulting room.

A third danger is what Jung called 'unconscious infection'. However balanced the therapist, she is likely to encounter a few patients whose material is both particularly disturbing and fascinating, so that her own equilibrium is threatened. We have already discussed the dangers of falling in love or lust with one's patients; also this applies equally in other occupations such as teaching or the law. Specific to psychotherapy is the way in which contact with disturbed patients may activate unconscious areas within the therapist's own psyche which, in ordinary life, might never have been stirred up, or even seen the light of day in her own personal analysis. If one finds oneself preoccupied with a particular patient in one's spare time, or if they get into one's dreams, these are danger signs that need to be recognized. Bertrand Russell (1956) said of his friend the novelist, Joseph Conrad:

> 'He thought of civilized and morally tolerable human life as a dangerous walk on a thin crust of barely cooled lava which at any moment might break and let the unwary sink into fiery depths.'

Something of the same feeling can be evoked in working with patients with borderline personality disorder or psychosis. This can lead to inappropriate decisions or 'acting out' on the part of the therapist. Here the presence of a supervisor with whom one can discuss one's difficult cases and one's reactions to them is indispensable, whatever one's level of training and experience.

Supervision

Having access to regular supervision is as integral to the fabric of a therapist's working life as her consulting room and daily routine with her patients. Supervision is an important topic in its own right (Hawkins and Shohet 2006); here we shall touch only on a number of aspects.

Supervision is important and essential for a number of reasons. First, it provides necessary feedback and quality control for therapists. No one knows exactly what goes on in any psychotherapist's consulting room, whether they be a leading analyst or a beginner counsellor – nor which of these two professionals is likely to be more beneficial to the client (Lambert 2004). Second, supervision is essential as part of the self-monitoring which psychotherapy aims to instill in its patients, and which becomes a lifelong practice for the therapist as they develop their 'internal' (some might say 'infernal'!) supervisor' (Casement 1985). Third, to put it simplistically, no one can see the back of their own head; by borrowing the eyes and ears and mind of the supervisor, the therapist can begin to see herself from the outside. Fourth, if therapy is essentially a relationship between two people, albeit occupying different roles, then the presence of a third person, the supervisor, enables the lineaments of the relationship to be scrutinized in a way that is impossible from within the dyad. Fifth, there is a cascade, or mirroring, between the patient-therapist relationship, and that between therapist and supervisor; this 'parallel process' provides a template for understanding the themes of the consulting room.

In our view, supervision is essentially a collaborative relationship. A therapist's supervisor is unlike the 'supervisor' on the shop floor, or office – someone who controls and offers praise and criticism to a subordinate. Nor should a supervisor be viewed as a guru, 'one who knows' (Lacan 1977) at whose feet the therapist sits each week waiting for the oracle to pronounce. This is not to deny the genuine knowledge and authority that comes with experience. But just as the patient is the ultimate expert on himself, and the role of the therapist that of midwife or assistant, so in a supervisory relationship the therapist is the ultimate authority – only she knows what went on in the session and what she was feeling during it.

Of course transferential elements enter into the supervisory relationship: beginner therapists will inevitably sometimes be overawed by their supervisors, and find themselves feeling inadequate and clumsy compared with their mentor. Just as the aim of therapy is for the patient to install an 'internal therapist' in their psyche to tide them through life's vicissitudes, so supervision aims to create an 'internal supervisor' which the therapist can draw on in times of need (Casement 1985). But it is important to remember that it is easy to be wise after the event, and that the armchair sportsman seeing an action replay of a missed goal, easy putt that goes wide, or an unforced tennis error, forgets that in the heat of the moment they too might well have made such an egregious mistake (Tuber and Catflisch 2011). Getting things 'wrong' in therapy is inevitable and indeed desirable. Mistakes are almost always shaped by the patient's, and sometimes the therapist's, unconscious mind; one learns as much or more from them than therapies which appear to be running smoothly, often deceptively so.

The format and technique of supervision depends on context. For beginners, group supervision can be very helpful. It is illuminating, shame-reducing and reassuring to see one's colleagues struggling with the same sort of issues as oneself: how to maintain boundaries, learn to not give advice, when to stay silent, when to intervene, how to formulate an interpretation, how to handle a missed session, or a persistently late client, and so on. The supervisor encourages the group to think collectively about a client's material, and to use their free associations and reverie to tap into the client's unconscious. It is important to restrain group members from asking too many questions, or proffering intellectual formulations (often with the transferential purpose of impressing the supervisor), rather than expressing what they feel and fantasize. Often, when the therapist has voiced an authentic feeling-response to the patient and his material, all the supervisor has to say is: 'perhaps that's exactly what the patient needs to hear … '.

Such group reverie represents one pole of the two approaches to supervision. It might be called, after Ogden (1987), 'dreaming the patient', based on the idea that the therapist's counter-transference is the most important route into the patient's unconscious, and supervision can help extend and expand the process of reverie in ways that will enhance this understanding.

At the other pole lies the technique of 'the minute particulars' (Hobson 1985), in which, using the slowed-down 'action replay' method, one homes in on a moment or nodal point in a session; stops the action; and thinks collectively about what one might have thought, said or done; asking the therapist to hold back until the discussion has been allowed to develop. A group setting also allows the participants to role-play – trying out various interventions, and, assuming the role of the patient, to see what it feels like to be on the receiving end of different possible interpretations. Supervision depends on therapists keeping accurate and detailed 'process recording' of their sessions. This is a good discipline to get into early in one's training, although it means building into one's schedule sufficient time after sessions for 'writing up'.

Individual supervision is integral to psychotherapy training, and continues post-qualification. Mature therapists may opt for 'inter-vision' – i.e. peer group supervision, either in a co-supervision model with one colleague, or in a group format. Hawkins and Shohet (2004) have devised a useful grid for thinking about where, at any given moment, supervision is pitched: at the inner world of the client; client-therapist interface; the therapist's inner world as she responds to the client's material; the interface between therapist and supervisor, if 'parallel process' needs to be brought into the equation. In each case supervision fosters 'binocular vision' skills, in that one simultaneously considers the material, one's emotional reactions to it, and the scrutinizing process itself. Therapists need to be undaunted by this potential infinite regress, and learning to ride the twin horses of emotion and reflection comfortably around the circus ring of their work.

Being and becoming a psychotherapist: the four stages

To paraphrase *Twelfth Night*, some are born therapists, some achieve therapist-hood, and some, like those unfortunate biologically minded psychiatrists forced to do psychotherapy as part of their training, have therapy thrust upon them. There are those who are natural psychotherapists, gifted with intuition, empathy, and compassion combined with the necessary degree of detachment. They are the fortunate few. Nevertheless most who are attracted to our profession are interested in people (often starting with themselves!), are good listeners, and fascinated by the workings of the mind and its relationships. Many are pulled to psychotherapy as a natural extension of other professions such as social work, nursing or medicine, or pushed towards psychotherapy by their search for a discipline which captures the reality of the inner world, its miseries and malfunctions.

Stage 1: the natural therapist

Here, spontaneous empathy, optimism, and the wish to alleviate unhappiness rule. The would-be therapist then has to decide what kind of training she will undertake. The military adage 'time spent in reconnaissance is never time wasted' applies at this stage. Therapy training is expensive and time-consuming. It has a big impact on one's life and family. It is important to find the training organization that feels 'right'. Equally, once accepted, it is important to 'shop around' until one finds a therapist and supervisors that suit one.

Psychotherapy training traditionally relies on the triad of theoretical seminars, personal therapy and supervised practice. Rejected by the anti-semitic culture within the universities of his day, Freud created his own institutions for training and promulgation of psychoanalysis. While this fostered free-wheeling creativity, it also meant that psychoanalysis failed to keep step with many of the intellectual currents of the twentieth century: systems theory, observational child development, ethology, structuralist anthropology, neurobiology, linguistics and philosophy. In particular, psychoanalytic research was confined by Freud's conception of the individual case study, important though that is, rather than subjecting analytic therapies to the statistical and probabilistic methods of mainstream science. The twenty-first century has at last seen psychoanalysis with a significant presence in the universities. This has brought a more rigorous academic atmosphere into training, and it is now possible to study simultaneously for post-graduate academic degrees in psychoanalytic studies, and to acquire a professional qualification.

Stage 2: the eye of the needle

Undertaking a psychotherapy training brings therapists to 'Stage 2': the 'eye of the needle'. This is the painful process of unlearning one's habitual helping style, and acquiring the skills of a psychotherapist proper which we have attempted to lay out in this book. This can be an uncomfortable process. The natural musician who can pick out a tune will, if she is to progress, have to submit to the discipline of learning her scales and five finger exercises; the natural ball player will have to subject herself to the strangeness of the topspin grip on her tennis racquet. Similarly the would-be therapist has to learn to bite her tongue at times, and to balance spontaneity and warmth with the restraint and theoretically informed interventions which therapy training expect of their students as they gradually acquire a psychoanalytic stance.

Psychoanalytic competencies have been systematized by Lemma *et al* (2008) and include a) *generic competency* – engagement, maintaining the therapeutic alliance, assessment and formulation, dealing with endings; b) *dynamic competency* – sensitivity to unconscious communication, making interpretations, working with transference and counter-transference, recognizing defences; and c) *meta-competency* – being able to apply dynamic ideas flexibly and appropriately to the client's needs. This schema appears sensible and unexceptionable, but stands in marked contrast to the traditional cultish atmosphere of some psychotherapy training, now thankfully becoming obsolete. There was a time when students were kept in semi-darkness about the aims and objectives of the process of becoming a therapist, awaiting the machinations of mysterious training committees before they were finally admitted to the fold.

Stage 3: finding one's authentic voice

What about life post-qualification? This third stage might be thought of as that of 'finding one's voice'. In Piagetian terms one needs to move from accommodation to assimilation. (This is a useful alimentary metaphor which can be applied to many aspects of learning and development. 'We are what we eat' in the sense that we first 'accommodate' to our ingestions in the stomach; at this stage they are still external to our being. They then need to be broken down into their constituent parts and assimilated into the being and nature of the consumer.)

The identifications of training – with one's therapist, supervisors, chosen therapeutic 'school' – become absorbed into one's own authentic working style, so that a consistent therapeutic identity begins to emerge. Gabbard and Ogden (2009) describe this in Oedipal terms: one needs *both* to be able to 'kill the father', and to honour one's ancestors, (a process not irrelevant to preparing this edition of AOP). There will be a certain distancing from one's training; the parts that don't fit will be discarded; at the same time fealty to the profession, and the particular corner of it that one has chosen to occupy, increases. At this stage each new patient represents a challenge, and the therapist begins to build up a bank of experience forming part of their burgeoning professional identity.

A simple but not often mentioned point is that one has to work hard and long hours in order to make a reasonable living as a full-time psychotherapist. This may explain the number of part-timers, who spend the rest of their week doing something else. This may be looking after their family, occupying a more conventional role in the helping professions, or some form of 'applied psychodynamic therapy' such as running supervision groups for front-line mental health workers, convening Balint Groups, offering organizational consultancy etc. An advantage of these non face-to-face contact hours is that they provide an opportunity to interact with peers and an escape from the loneliness of the long-distance therapist.

Stage 4: the mature therapist

Stage 4 could be called that of the 'mature therapist'. Here the practitioner comes back, full cycle, to her 'natural therapist' self. Artists and musicians at the top of their game break the rules. Ashkenazi plays the piano with his nose; McEnroe hits tennis balls between his legs. The forms and format of therapy have become so ingrained that the therapist can allow herself to go a little off-piste – perhaps be more self-revealing than she would have been heretofore, more encouraging, more informal. This is a stage perhaps of greatest creativity as a therapist – but also of gravest danger. Mature therapists may dispense with supervision, begin to think of themselves as above the law, and at worst exploit their patients sexually or financially (Holmes and Lindley 1997). This must be resisted. As AS (Storr 1997) put it, 'even the Pope has a confessor'.

Unlike surgery or sport, psychotherapy is a profession where, assuming physical and mental health, one may actually improve with age. There are subtle changes, of course. Younger therapists tend to identify more easily with their patients' adolescent rebellious selves, and hold parents responsible for their offspring's hang-ups; the older therapist will be more likely to see the parents' point of view as well, and believe that most psychological difficulties need to be approached from at least a three-generation perspective, a point particularly emphasized by Lacan (1977). With age also comes a more balanced view of what and what cannot be achieved therapeutically. One is more prepared to help people towards acceptance and co-existence with their difficulties, rather than aiming for eradication.

There comes a point where therapists need to retire. This is one of those contingent endings described earlier. It is wise to set a date a good way ahead – perhaps two years – and to inform one's long-term patients of one's intentions. Colleagues to whom one can refer people need to be alerted. One also needs to have arrangements in place should one unexpectedly be unable to work, through illness, bereavement, or indeed one's own death. Here too, a trusted colleague is needed who will help the patients through what for them will also be a bereavement, albeit perhaps occasionally a welcome one!

Epilogue: Beyond Therapy

Freud rightly defined psychic health as the ability to love and work, but on the whole psychotherapy tends to value the former over the latter. This has two disadvantages. First, it flies in the face of the facts. Although a close confiding relationship protects against depression when faced with loss, so too does employment outside the home (Brown and Harris 1978). Second, unless the word 'love' is interpreted rather widely, as it should be, it contains an implicit over-valuation of relationships. This can make people who are single or bereaved, or who choose to live alone, feel that they are in some way psychologically lacking, even if they are quite capable of loving – a lost spouse, non-live-in partner, children, pets, God, or some social ideal.

The capacity to be alone

It is true that for many people intimate attachments are the mainspring of their lives and the most important determinants of happiness or unhappiness. But this is not true of everybody. Many of those fortunate enough to have satisfying intimate ties with their families and others, also spend a good deal of their time in occupations and pursuits which do not involve close relationships. Interests, whether formal employment or leisure pursuits, enrich a person's life. They may even be a main factor in preserving mental health. The assumption that intimate personal relationships constitute the only possible road to happiness is unjustified. Because psychotherapy itself is essentially a relationship, we pay less attention to those insights and changes of attitude which come about when people are alone and not distracted.

It is important for psychotherapists to recognize and value these internal processes alongside those provided by the therapeutic relationship. Oscillation between relationship and solitude is built into the fabric of everyone's life to a greater or lesser extent. We all withdraw into ourselves and our fantasy life when we are asleep, whether or not that sleep is 'shared' with others. We have seen how psychological health entails getting that balance right for any particular person; those with psychological difficulties are troubled either by being alone and therefore tend to cling to their object, or by intimacy, in which case they isolate themselves emotionally. Those who are highly disturbed often alternate between the two: wanting to be out when they are in, and in when they are out.

In the nineteenth century, the American neuro-psychiatrist Silas Weir Mitchell instituted the 'rest cure', which involved removal from relatives and partial isolation (Storr 1988). This technique afforded opportunity for quiet reflection; and allowed a natural scanning and sorting process to take place within the patient's mind, putting into perspective previously threatening emotional problems. In his famous paper 'the capacity to be alone' Winnicott (1971) sees the ability to tolerate being alone, even when in the company of others, including in states of post-coital bliss, as a mark of emotional maturity. One of the legacies of secure attachment is that it sets up a 'good internal object' which provides the internal relatedness which carries us through the rhythms of closeness and separation, attachment and loss, which are the warp and weft of the human condition.

Scanning and sorting takes place in the mind during sleep, and may be one reason why sleep is necessary (Hobson 2012). During the day, most of us are exposed to sensory input which might prove overwhelming if we could not retreat into the solitude and quiet of sleep. Depriving subjects of sleep is a rapid method of inducing mental stress and malfunction; acute outbreaks of mental illness are often heralded by a period of insomnia. While its neurobiology remains obscure, we do know that sleep is essential for the preservation of mental equilibrium.

Many people have had the experience of being unable to decide between two courses of action, and of going to bed with the problem still unresolved. On waking, the solution is often obvious. Conventional wisdom rightly recommends 'sleeping on it' when faced with a difficult dilemma. Here problem-solving taking place solely within the individual, without reference to relationships with others, and indeed there are many decisions which can only be taken on one's own, although the capacity to ask for help and guidance before doing so is also important.

Psychotherapists will frequently encounter patients who have been bereaved, and who find it difficult to come to terms with loss (Parkes 1986). Mourning can be a very long process; and although confiding in a psychotherapist can speed this to some extent, the hour or two per week which the psychotherapist can offer is not enough to encompass all the problems posed by the loss of someone who played an intimate role in every aspect of the bereaved person's life. In dealing with such patients, it is important that the psychotherapist should be aware of the ways in which people may prolong their grief by never really facing it. It is often necessary for bereaved people to spend some part of the day alone, in order that they may be able to allow their deepest feelings to manifest themselves. Those who, when alone, can bring themselves deliberately to recall the details of their relationship with the deceased, the good and bad times spent together, the ups-and-downs which are part of every intimate relationship, will find that they come to terms with loss more quickly than those who avoid such memories. If bereaved people feel inclined to write an account of, or even unposted letters to, the deceased person, so much the better. Many families have unpublished memoirs which, even if not of general interest, are enthralling to their descendants.

Work as an object

As we mentioned earlier it is often useful to encourage depressed, middle-aged patients to recall the daydreams of their adolescence, and if possible to revive interests which had been allowed to lapse during the busy years of raising a family and establishing a position in the world. A woman who has devoted herself to the care of children during most of her adult life may find herself depressed when they no longer need her. Perhaps, as a girl, she had some interest in art, in music, in gardening, or in dressmaking which the demands of her family stifled. People often believe that, when they reach middle age, it is too late to pursue interests which absorbed them when young, or feel that they will be unable to learn anything new. Such a conviction may be part of their depression, but it is also the case that people generally underestimate the capacities of older people. Grandma Moses did not have her first solo exhibition until she was 80, and went on painting until she was 100. Tolstoy did not have his first bicycle lesson until he was 67 (Baker 1982). Psychotherapists, because of their concentration upon object-relations, tend to underestimate the importance of such interests in promoting psychological vitality.

One aspect of this is that psychoanalysis has not conceptualized work and activity with the same depth that it has brought to the study of relationships. The concept of 'sublimation' (a chemical metaphor describing the transformation of a solid into a gas without passing through the liquid phase) is a delightful idea about how sexuality could underpin great works of science and art, but hardly constitutes a serious theory.

Eagle (1981) disputes the very notion of sublimation, i.e. that interests are the product of diverting sexual aims to 'higher' pursuits. He points out that research has demonstrated that even very young infants discriminate between various auditory and visual stimuli, and show preferences for particular colours and shapes, as if they were orientated toward an interest in non-personal objects from the beginning of life. Moreover, both infant monkeys and infant humans show attachment to objects which provide comforting contact, irrespective of whether such objects also relieve hunger and thirst. Eagle (1981) concludes:

> 'All the evidence taken together indicates that an interest in objects, as well as the development of affectional bonds, is not simply a derivative or outgrowth of libidinal energies and aims, or a consequence of gratification of other needs, but is a critical independent aspect of development which expresses an inborn propensity to establish cognitive and affective links to objects in the world.'

People who know nothing of psychoanalysis will think this conclusion banal. Ordinary observation demonstrates that the majority of people have interests of some kind, ranging from stamp-collecting to music; from fishing to playing the stock market. But Freud was so persuasive, and so certain that he was right, that he convinced generations of psychotherapists that sexuality was the basic motive force within the psyche, and that anything which mattered emotionally must be sexual in origin.

Since psychotherapists are predominantly concerned with interpersonal relations, it is all the more important for them to realize the importance of abiding interests and values and how they too can provide something to live for. Bettelheim and others have shown that, under the appalling conditions prevailing in concentration and prisoner-of-war camps, those who survived often had ideals and beliefs which transcended the life of the individual (Bettelheim 1961), whether these were religious or socialistic. We know that, when one partner in a long-term relationship dies, the survivor is more likely to become ill or to die than others belonging to a similar age group. But those who are fortunate enough or provident enough to have developed some passionate enthusiasm unconnected with their partner will have something to live for which will see them through their mourning.

The creatively gifted often use their work rather than their interpersonal relationships as their primary source of self-esteem and personal fulfilment (Storr 1972). But those who are not particularly gifted may also be orientated toward the impersonal as well as toward the personal. The English passion for gardening sustains and enriches the lives of many people who have no intellectual pretensions; and the same is true of the range of sporting, handicraft or other pursuits which enliven the weekends of those who are working, and alleviate the tedium which may afflict those who have retired.

Jung

As we have noted, psychotherapy tends to be more concerned with relationships than with the internal processes of integration which take place when the individual is alone. A notable exception is Jung (Storr 1973). Virtually the whole of Jung's later work is concerned with what he called 'the process of individuation'; that is, the quest for wholeness and integration conceived as an internal rather than primarily relational, process. It is no accident that Jung specialized in the treatment of older patients. The people who most interested him were mostly middle-aged and over, whereas Freud thought that patients near or above the age of fifty were unsuitable for psychoanalysis. It remains true that Freudian psychology is predominantly concerned with childhood and youth, whereas Jungian psychology is more orientated toward later life. Jung's patients were often people who had married, raised a family, and attained a position in the world. Then, perhaps after going through a mid-life crisis, so-called, as Jung himself had done, they sought therapy because their lives seemed meaningless and empty.

Jung maintained that the problems of the second half of life were of a different order from those of the first half. A young person's psychological task is to emancipate him or herself from Oedipal ties; to find sexual fulfilment; found a new family; and make a living. But, supposing one has achieved all this and yet, when reaching the threshold of middle age, finds nothing but dust and ashes?

Jung's approach was, that by encouraging such patients to focus on their dreams and fantasies, a process of internal development was set in motion, culminating in a new attitude to life based on acceptance and equanimity. Jung advised such patients to set aside a part of the day in which they could be quietly alone, and then to enter a state of reverie, in which consciousness is preserved, but judgement suspended. The patient was enjoined to note what fantasies occurred to him, and then to let them pursue their own path without conscious interference. Jung called this process 'active imagination'. Whether this needs to be so formalized is open to debate, but the essential point is that the patient's imaginative life is celebrated, however this may manifest itself – through poems, drawing, music, daydreams, dance, play, sport, or even some simple yet symbolically significant activity such as sorting through one's cupboards or undertaking a thorough spring cleaning.

Jung's attitude to fantasy is the opposite of Freud's. Freud linked together play, fantasy, and dreaming as essentially escapist manoeuvres designed to avoid reality. He considered that these activities were an expression of 'primary process'; that is, of mental functioning governed by wish-fulfilment and the pleasure principle. Freud thought that these childish or primitive mental activities should be outgrown and replaced by 'secondary process'; that is, by rational thought governed by conscious planning and the reality principle. Jung, on the other hand, encouraged his patients to make use of 'primary process', because in his view fantasy could be creative rather than merely escapist. Jung found that, by getting in touch with the irrational, imaginative aspects of his psyche, the patient not only rediscovered aspects of himself which had been neglected, but came to realize that his own ego could never be paramount, but was always dependent upon integrating factors which could not be consciously contrived.

The reverie which Jung encouraged is comparable to the state of mind in which most creative discoveries occur. Although there are few instances of new ideas stemming directly from dreams, the majority of creative people describe solutions to problems or new inspirations occurring when they are in a relaxed state of mind in which they are not deliberately directing their thoughts, but passively allowing them to arise. Jung discouraged his patients from thinking that the fantasy material which they produced was in any way related to art in the formal sense; he wanted them to retain spontaneity by not attempting to order or shape the material:

> 'My aim is to bring about a psychic state in which my [sic] patient begins to experiment with his own nature – a state of fluidity, change, and growth where nothing is eternally fixed and hopelessly petrified' (Jung 1954).

Therapy outside the consulting room

The average psychotherapist may find she encounters few patients of the esoteric kind described by Jung. Most people presenting for therapy suffer from symptoms more specific and definable than a general sense of emptiness and futility. But Jung's approach directs our attention to the fact that healing processes go on outside the psychotherapist's consulting room. Patients can be encouraged to speed the processes of self-discovery and self-healing by doing the sorts of thing that Jung advocated. In contemporary urban life, it may be difficult for people to find a space in which they can be alone or time for reflection. Encouraging this can be a useful part of some therapies. Even if a man or woman works all day in a busy office, and then comes home to a house full of children, it is usually possible to arrange to go for a brief walk, or to insist upon being undisturbed for a limited period. The current interest in mindfulness and meditation (Bien 2006) bear witness to the therapeutic value of periods of solitude in which the frenetic business of life is brought to a temporary standstill.

Because the process of psychotherapy is often a compelling journey of exploration, both patients and their therapists are inclined to believe that what goes on during the hours of therapy is overridingly important, and that anything which takes place outside them is of lesser significance. But psychotherapists should realize how much can be accomplished by patients working at their problems on their own. There is a sense in which psychotherapy is never completed; the aim is to set in motion a process of development which may continue throughout the subject's life. Jung thought of neurosis as an impasse in life, in which change and development was halted. His aim was not to reach some chimerical nirvana of complete cure, but to bring about a state of fluidity, change, and growth. If psychotherapy enables the individual who was stuck to travel hopefully, the psychotherapist can rest content. We must accept that we never achieve complete integration or perfect adaptation. There is always another step to be taken, a new problem demanding solution.

However, we do not want to end by leaving an impression that psychotherapy is so beset with uncertainties and ambiguous outcomes as to deter anyone who is likely to be good at it from taking it up. Psychotherapy, like other professional activities, has its disadvantages; but its interest far outweighs them. Human beings are endlessly fascinating; complex amalgams of all kinds of qualities, good and bad. There is no trait of personality, no human characteristic, which does not have two sides to it. Living with and trying to unravel this ambivalent complexity is the essence of our work. Our lives have been greatly enriched by our profession. We are grateful for having had the opportunity of penetrating deeply into the lives of so many interesting, lovable, and unforgettable people, and for the reciprocal influence and confidence that becoming and being therapists has given us in return.

References

Recommended introductory texts are marked with *

Alanen, Y., González de Chávez, M., Silver, A-L. et al. (2009) *Psychotherapeutic Approaches to Schizophrenic Psychoses, Past, Present and Future.* Hove: Routledge.

Alexander, F. and French, T. (1946) *Psychoanalytic Psychotherapy.* Lincoln: University of Nebraska Press.

Allen, J. and Fonagy, P. (2006) *Mentalising in Clinical Practice.* Chichester: Wiley.

APA (1994) *Diagnostic and Statistical Manual of Mental Disorders (DSM-IV)* 4th Edition. Washington DC: American Psychiatric Association.

Bacal, H. (2006) Specificity Theory: Conceptualising a personal and professional quest for therapeutic possibility. *International Journal of Self Psychology*, **1**, 133–155.

Baker, J. (1982) *Tolstoy's Bicycle.* New York: St Martin's Press.

Balint, M. (1968) *The Basic Fault.* London: Tavistock.

Baron-Cohen, S. (2003) *The Essential Difference.* London: Penguin.

Bateman, A. and Fonagy, P. (2008) Randomised controlled trial of outpatient mentalisation-based treatment versus structured clinical management for borderline personality disorder. *American Journal of Psychiatry* **166** 1355–1364.

Bateman, A. and Fonagy, P. (2003) Health utilisation costs for borderline personality disorder patients treated with psychoanalytically oriented partial hospitalisation versus general psychiatric care. *Am. J. Psychiat* **160** 169–171.

Bateman, A. and Fonagy, P. (2004) *Psychotherapy for Borderline Personality Disorder: Mentalisation based treatment.* Oxford: OUP.

Bateman, A. and Fonagy, P. (2008) 8-Year Follow-Up of Patients Treated for Borderline Personality Disorder: Mentalization-Based Treatment Versus Treatment as Usual. *Am J Psychiatry* **165**: 631–638.

*Bateman, A. and Holmes, J. (1995) *Introduction to psychoanalysis: contemporary theory and practice.* London: Routledge.

*Bateman, A., Pedder, J. and Brown, D. (2010) *Introduction to Psychotherapy: an outline of psychodynamic principles and practice.* London: Routledge

Bateson, G. (1972) *Steps towards an ecology of Mind.* Chicago; University of Chicago Press.

Belsky, J., Jonassiant, C., Pluess, M., Stanton, M., Brummett, B., and Williams, R. (2009) Vulnerability genes or plasticity genes? *Mol. Psychiatry* **14**: 746–754.

Benthal, R. (2010) *Doctoring the Mind: why psychiatric treatments fail.* London: Penguin.

Berlin, I. (1976) *Vico and Herder.* London: Hogarth.

Bersani, L. and Phillips, A. (2008) *Intimacies.* Chicago: University of Chicago Press.

Bettelheim, B. (1961) *The Informed Heart.* London; Thames and Hudson.

Bien, T. (2006) *Mindful Therapy.* Somerville MA: Wisdom.

Bion, W. (1970) *Learning from Experience.* London: Hogarth.

Bion, W. (1967) Notes on Memory and Desire. *Psychoanalytic Forum*, **2**, 1–21.

Blatt, S. (2008) *Polarities of experience: Relatedness and self-definition in personality development, psychopathology and the therapeutic process.* Washington DC: American Psychological Asssociation.

Bollas, C. (1987). *The Shadow of the Object, psychoanalysis of the unthought known.* New York: Columbia University Press.

Bowell, J. (1799) *The Life of Samuel Johnson.* Oxford: Clarendon Press.

Bowlby, J. (1975) *Separation, Anxiety and Anger.* London: Penguin.

Bowlby, J. (1973) *Anxiety.* London: Penguin.

Brod, M. (1948) *Franz Kafka: A Biography.* London: Secker and Warburg.

Brown, G. and Harris, T. (1978) *The Social Origins of Depression.* London: Tavistock.

Busch, F., Milrod, B., and Sandberg, L. (2009) A study demonstrating the efficacy of a psychoanalytic psychotherapy for panic disorder: implications for psychoanalytic research and practice. *J. Am. Psychoanal. Assoc.* **57** 131–148.

Busch, F., Oquendo, A. Sullivan, G., and Sandberg, L. (2010) An integrated model of panic disorder. *Neuropsychoanalysis* **12** 67–79.

*Casement, P. (1985) *On learning from the Patient.* London: Tavistock.

Clarkin, J. F., Levy, K. N., Lenzenweger, M. F., and Kernberg, O. F. (2007) A multiwave RCT evaluating three treatments for borderline personality disorder. *American Journal of Psychiatry*, 164, 922–928.

Dalal, F. (2012) *Thought Paralysis.* London: Karnac.

Dalsimer, K. (2004) Virginia Woolf (1882–1941) *Am J Psychiat* **161** 809–809.

Dennett, D. (1973) Mechanism and responsibility. In *Essays on Freedom of Action.* (Ed. T. Honderich). London: Routledge.

Diamond, D., Blatt, S. and Lichtenberg, J. (Eds.) (2007) *Attachment and Sexuality.* New York: Analytic Press.

Dimen, M. (2011). Lapsus Linguae, or a Slip of the Tongue?: A Sexual Violation in an Analytic Treatment and Its Personal and Theoretical Aftermath. *Contemp. Psychoanal.*, **47**:35–79.

Dozier, M., Stovall, K. and Albus, K. (2008) Attachment and psychopathology in adulthood. In *Handbook of Attachment* Eds J Cassidy and P. Shaver 2nd Edn. New York: Guilford.

Driessen, E., Cuijpers, P., de Maat, S., Abbass, A., de Jonghe, F., and Dekker, J. (2010) The efficacy of short-term psychodynamic psychotherapy for depression: a meta-analysis. *Clinical Psychology Review* **30**:25–36.

Eagle, M. (1981) Interests as Object Relations. *Psychoanalysis and Contemporary Thought*, **4**, 527–565.

Eissler, K. (1962) *Leonardo da Vinci: psychoanalytic notes on the enigma.* London: Hogarth.

Elliot, T. (1953) *Four Quartets.* London: Faber and Faber.

Fairbairn, R. (1958) On the nature and aims of psychoanalytical treatment. *International Journal of Psychoanalysis*, **39**, 16–34.

Fairbairn, R. (1976) *Psychoanalytic Studies of the Personality.* London; Routledge.

Fairbairn, W. (1954) *An object relations theory of the personality.* London: Hogarth.

Fanon, F. (1961) *The Wretched of the Earth.* London: Penguin.

References

Ferenczi, S. (1980) *Final contributions to the problems and methods of psychoanalysis.* (Eds. M. Balint and E. Mosbacher) London: Karnac.

Fonagy, P. and Lemma, A. (2012) Psychoanalysis: does it have a place in modern mental health services? *bmj* **433**; e1211.

Fonagy, P. and P. Luyten (2009). A developmental, mentalization-based approach to the understanding and treatment of borderline personality disorder. *Dev Psychopathol.,* **21**(4): 1355–1381.

Freud, A. (1936) *The Ego and the mechanisms of defence.* New York: International Universities Press.

Freud, S. (1895) Obsessions and Phobias. *SE 3* 69–82. London: Hogarth.

Freud, (1905b) Three Essays on the Theory of Sexuality. *SE 7* pp135–243. London: Hogarth.

Freud, S. (1900) The Interpretation of Dreams. *SE 4 and 5.* London: Hogarth.

Freud, S. (1905) Fragment of analysis of a case of hysteria. *SE7* pp 3–132. London: Hogarth.

*Freud, S. (1911–1915) Papers on Technique. *S.E. 12.* London: Hogarth.

Freud, S. (1914) On Narcissism: An Introduction. *SE 14* pp 67–102. London: Hogarth.

Freud, S. (1917) Mourning and Melancholia. *SE 14* pp 237–258 London: Hogarth.

Freud, S. (1918) From the history of an infantile neurosis. *SE 17* pp 1–122 London: Hogarth.

Freud, S. (1919) Lines of advance in psycho-analytic therapy. *SE 17* pp 157–168. London: Hogarth.

Freud, S. (1920) Beyond the Pleasure Principle. *SE 18* pp 7–64 London: Hogarth.

Freud, S. (1923) The Ego and the Id. *SE 19* pp 1–59 London: Hogarth.

Freud, S. (1926) Inhibitions, Symptoms and Anxiety. *SE 20* pp 87–172 London: Hogarth.

Freud, S. (1929) Civilisation and its Discontents. *S.E. 21* pp 57–145 London: Hogarth.

Freud, S. (1933) New Introductory Lectures on Psycho-analysis. *SE 22* pp 1–182 London: Hogarth.

Freud, S. (1937) Analysis terminable and interminable. *SE 23* pp 209–253. London: Hogarth.

Freud, S. (1940) Splitting of the ego in the service of defence. *SE 23.* pp 271–278. London Hogarth.

Freud, S. and Breuer, J. (1893) *Studies on Hysteria. SE 2* pp 1–309 London: Hogarth.

*Gabbard, G. (2010) *Long-term psychodynamic psychotherapy.* Arlington VA: American Psychiatric Publishing.

Gabbard, G. and Hobney, G. (2012) A Psychoanalytic Perspective on Ethics, Self-deception and the Corrupt Physician. *British Journal of Psychotherapy,* **28**, 235–248.

Gabbard, G. and Ogden, T. (2009) On becoming a psychoanalyst. *International Journal of Psychoanalysis* **90**, 311–327.

*Gabbard, G., Beck, J. and Holmes, J. (2005) (Eds.) *Oxford Textbook of Psychotherapy.* Oxford: OUP.

Gabbard, G., Gunderson, J. and Fonagy, P. (2002) The place of psychoanalytic treatments within psychiatry. *Arch Gen Psychiat* **59** 505–510.

Goldfried, Marvin, R., Raue, Patrick J., Castonguay, Louis G. (1998) The therapeutic focus in significant sessions of master therapists: A comparison of cognitive-behavioral and psychodynamic-interpersonal interventions. *Journal of Consulting and Clinical Psychology,* **66(5)**, 803–810.

Grunbaum, A. (1984) *The Foundations of Psychoanalysis: A Philosophical Critique*. Berkley: University of California Press.

Guardian newspaper (2001) Anthony Storr Obituary.

Hawkins, P. and Shohet, R. (2006) *Supervision in the Helping Professions* (3rd Edn). Buckingham: Open University Press.

Heimann, P. (1950) On countertransference. *International Journal of Psychoanalysis*, **31** 81–84.

Hesse, E. (2008) The Adult Attachment Interview. In *Handbook of Attachment* (2nd Edn) Eds. P. Shaver and J. Cassidy. New York: Guildford.

Hinshelwood, R. (2011) *A Dictionary of Kleinian thought: New edition*. London; Free Association Books.

Hobson, A. (2011) *Dreaming: A Very Short Introduction*. Oxford: OUP.

Hobson, R. (1985) *Forms of Feeling: the Heart of Psychotherapy*. London: Tavistock.

Holmes, J. (2010) *Exploring In Security: Towards an Attachment-informed Psychoanalytic Psychotherapy*. London: Routledge.

Holmes, J. (2012a) Psychodynamic psychiatry's green shoots. *British Journal of Psychiatry* **200** 439–441.

Holmes, J. (2012b) Seeing, sitting and lying down: reflections on the role of visual communication in analytic therapy. *Psychoanalytic Psychotherapy* **26** 2–12.

Holmes, J. (2012c) Donnel Stern and Relational Psychoanalysis. *British Journal of Psychotherapy* **27** 305–315.

Holmes, J. (2012d) From Freud to fMRI: The psychodynamic clinician in the mood disorder laboratory – what can we learn and (what) can we contribute? *Psychiatry* (in press).

Holmes, J. (2012e) Superego: an attachment perspective. *International Journal of Psychoanalysis* **92** 1221–1240.

Holmes, J. and Bateman, A. (2002) (Eds.) *Integration in Psychotherapy*. Oxford: Oxford University Press.

Holmes, J. and Elder, A. (2001) (Eds.) *Psychotherapy in Primary Care*. Oxford: OUP.

Holmes, J. and Lindley, R. (1997) *The Values of Psychotherapy*. 2nd Edition. London: Karnac.

*Howard, S. (2010) *Skills in Dynamic Counselling*. London: Sage.

Hudson, L. (1973) *The Cult of the Fact*. London: Cape.

Jacobs, M. (2004) *Psychodynamic Counselling in Action*. (3rd Edn). London: Sage.

Jones, E. (1957) *Sigmund Freud: Life and Work*. London: Hogarth.

Jung, C. (1931) *The Practice of Psychotherapy. Collected Works Vol 16*. London: Routledge.

Jung, C. (1932) Psychology and Religion. *Collected Works, 11*. London: Routledge.

Jung, C. (1954) The Practice of Psychotherapy. *Collected Works, Vol 16*. London: Routledge.

Kandel, ER: (1999) Biology and the future of psychoanalysis: a new intellectual framework for psychiatry revisited. *Am J Psychiatry* **156**:505–524.

Karlsson, H. (2011) How psychotherapy changes the brain. *Psychiatric Times* 20–28.

Klein (1935) A Contribution to the psychogenesis of manic-depressive states. In *Contributions to Psychoanalysis*. pp 282–311. London: Hogarth.

Klein, M. (1975). *Envy and Gratitude and Other Works 1946–1963*: Edited By: M. Masud R. Khan. The International Psycho-Analytical Library, **104**:1–346. London: The Hogarth Press and the Institute of Psycho-Analysis.

Kohut, H. (1977) *The Restoration of the Self*. New York: International Universities Press.

Lacan, J. (1977) *Ecrits: a Selection*. Trans. A. Sheridan. London: Tavistock.

Laing, R. (1960) *The Divided Self*. London: Penguin.

Laing, R. (1977) *Conversations with Adam and Natasha*. New York: Pantheon.

Lakoff, G. and Johnson, J. (1980) *The metaphors we live by*. Chicago: Chicago University Press.

Lambert, M. (Ed.) (2004) *Handbook of psychotherapy and behaviour change* (5th Edn.). New York: Wiley.

Lambert, M., Whipple, J., Smart, D., Vermeersch, and Stevan, L. (2010) The effects of providing therapists with feedback on patient progress in therapy: are outcomes enhanced? *Psychotherapy Research* **11** 49–68.

Lear, J. (2003) *Therapeutic Action: an earnest plea for irony*. London: Karnac.

LeDoux, J.E. (2000). Emotion circuits in the brain. *Annu Rev Neurosci.*, **23**, 155–184.

Leischenrigg, F. and Rabung, S. (2011) Long-term psychodynamic psychotherapy in complex mental disorders: update of meta-analysis. *British Journal of Psychiatry* **199** 15–22.

*Lemma, A. (2003) *Introduction to the Practice of Psychoanalytic Psychotherapy*. Chichester: Wiley.

Lemma, A. (2009) Commentary on Christie (2009) In *Good Feelings: psychoanalytic reflections on positive emotions and attitudes* (Ed. S. Akhtar). London: Karnac.

Lemma, A., Roth, A. and Pilling, S. (2008) *The Competencies Required to Deliver Effective Psychoanalytic/psychodynamic Therapy*. www.ucl.ac..uk/clinical-psychology/CORE/psychodynamic_framework.htm

Lemma, A., Target, M. and Fonagy (2012) *Brief dynamic interpersonal therapy: a clinican's guide*. Oxford: OUP.

Makari, G. (2008) *Revolution in Mind: the creation of psychoanalysis*. London: HarperCollins.

Malan, D. and Della Selva, P. (2006) *Lives Transformed: a revolutionary method of dynamic psychotherapy*. London: Karnac.

*Malan, D. (1979) *Individual psychotherapy and the Science of Psychodynamics*. London: Butterworth.

Mallinckrodt, B., Daly, K. and Wang, C. (2008) An attachment approach to adult psychotherapy. In *Clinical Applications of Adult Psychotherapy and Research*. Eds. J. Obegi and E. Berant. New York: Guilford.

Mann, J. (1973) *Time-limited therapy*. Cambridge MA: Harvard University Press.

Matte-Blanco, I. (1975) *The Unconscious as Infinite Sets*. London: Routledge.

McCullough, L., Kuhn, N., Andrews, S., Kaplan, A., Wolf, J. and Hurley, C.L. (2003) *Treating affect phobia: a manual for short-term dynamic psychotherapy*. New York: Guildford Press.

McGilchrist, I. (2010) *The Master and his Emissary*. London: HarperCollins.

McGlashan, T. (1988) A selective review of North American long-term follow-up studies of schizophrenia. *Schizophrenia Bulletin* **14** pp 515–542.

*McWilliams, N. (2004) *Psychoanalytic Psychotherapy: A Practitioner's Guide*. New York: Guilford.

Michel, K., and Jobes, D. (2010) Eds. *Building a Therapeutic Alliance With the Suicidal Patient*. New York: American Psychological Association.

Mikulincer, M. and Shaver, P. (2010) *Attachment in Adulthood: structure, dynamics and change*. New York: Guilford.

Mill, J.S. (1873) *Autobiography*. London: Longman.

Milner, M. (1969) *The Hands of the Living God*. London: Hogarth.

Moffitt, T., Caspi, A., Rutter, M. and Silva, P. (2001) *Sex differences in antisocial behaviour, conduct disorder, delinquency and violence in Dunedin*. Cambridge: Cambridge University Press.

Nicholi, A. (1978) Ed. *The Harvard Guide to Modern Psychiatry*. Cambridge Mass: Harvard University Press.

Nolte, T., Guiney, J., Fonagy, P., Mayes, L. and Luyten, P. (2011) Interpersonal stress regulation and the development of anxiety disorders: an attachment-based framework. *Front. Behav. Neurosci.* **5**:55. doi: 10.3389/fnbeh.2011.

Novick, J. (1988) The timing of termination. *International Journal of Psychoanalysis* **15** 307–318.

Ogden, T. (1987) *The Matrix of the Mind*. Hillsdale NJ: Jason Aronson.

Ogden, T. (1996) Reconsidering Three aspects of Psychoanalytic Technique. *International Journal of Psychoanalysis* **77** 883–899.

Panksepp, J. (2004) *Affective Neuroscience: the foundations of human and animal emotions*. Oxford: OUP.

Parkes, C. (1986) *Bereavement*. London: Penguin.

Proust, M. (1970) *Time Regained*. Trans A. Mayer. London: Chatto.

Racker, H. (1968) *Transference and Counter-transference*. London: Hogarth.

Rapoport, A. (1960) *Fights, games and debates*. Ann Arbour: University of Michigan Press.

Reich (1950) On the termination of analysis. *International Journal of Psychoanalysis* **31** 179–183.

Reik, T. (1948) *The inner experience of a psychoanalyst*. New York: Farrah Strauss.

Reik, T. (1968) Reik speaks of his psychoanalytic technique. *American Imago* 25 16–20.

Renn, P. (2012) *The silent past and the invisible present*. London: Routledge.

Rey, H. (1994) *The universals of psychoanalysis in the treatment of psychotic and borderline states*. London: Free Association Books.

Rizzolatti, G., Fogassi, L. and Galesi V. (2006) Mirrors in the mind. *Scientific American* Jan 2006 54–69.

Rogers, C. (1951) *Client-Centered Therapy*. London: Constable.

Rogers, C. (1967) *On becoming a person*. London: Constable.

Rudden, M., Milrod, B., Aronson, A. and Target, M. (2008) Reflective functioning in panic disorder patients: clinical observations and research design. In *Mentalisation: Theoretical Considerations, Research Findings, and Clinical Implications*. Ed. F. Busch. New York: Analytic Press. Pp 185–205.

Russell, B. (1955) *History of Western Philosophy*. London: Allen and Unwin.

Russell, B. (1956) *Portraits from Memory*. London: Allen and Unwin.

Rutter, M. (1981) *Maternal Deprivation Reassessed*. London: Penguin.

*Rycroft, C. (1979) *The Innocence of Dreams*. London: Hogarth.
Rycroft, C. (1985) *Psychoanalysis and Beyond*. London: Chatto and Windus.
Rycroft, C. (1968) *Anxiety and Neurosis*. London: Penguin.
Ryle, A. (1990) *Cognitive Analytic Therapy*. Chichester: Wiley.
*Safran, J. (2012) *Psychoanalysis and Psychoanalytic Therapies*. Washington: American Psychological Association.
Salberg, J. (2010) (Ed.) *Good enough endings*. London: Routledge.
Sandler, J. and Sandler, A-M. (1984) The past unconscious, the present unconscious, and interpretation of the transference. *Psychoanalytic Inquiry*, **4**, 367–399.
Schore, A. (1991) *Affect regulation and the origin of the self: the neurobiology of emotional development*. Hillsdale: Lawrence Erlbaum.
Schore, A. (2011) The right brain implicit self lies at the heart of psychoanalysis. *Psychoanalytic Dialogues* **21** 75–100.
Sharpe, E. (1930) The technique of Psycho-analysis. *International Journal of Psycho-analysis*. **11** 361–386.
Shaver, P., and J . Cassidy, J. (2008) Eds. *Handbook of Attachment* (2nd Edn) New York: Guildford.
Shedler, J. (2010) The efficacy of psychodynamic psychotherapy. *American Psychologist*. **65** 98–109.
Skinner, B. (1971) *Beyond freedom and dignity*. New York: Knopf.
Smit, Y., Hibers, M., Ioannidis, J., van Dyck, R., van Tilburg, W. and Arntz, A. (2012) The effectiveness of long-term psychoanalytic psychotherapy – a meta-analysis of randomised controlled trials. *Clinical Psychology Review* **32** 81–92.
Snow, C. (1973) *The Two Cultures*. Cambridge: Cambridge University Press.
Solms, M., and Turnbull, O. (2002) *The brain and the inner world*. New York: Other Press.
Stepansky, P. (2009) *Psychoanalysis at the Margins*. New York: Other Press.
Stern, D. (2010) *Partners in Thought*. London: Routledge.
Storr, A. (1960) *The Integrity of the Personality*. London: Pelican.
Storr, A. (1968) *Sexual Deviation*. London: Penguin.
Storr, A. 1968) *Human Aggression*. London: Penguin.
Storr, A. (1972) *The Dynamics of Creation*. London: Secker and Warburg.
Storr, A. (1973) *Jung*. London: Fontana.
Storr, A. (1988) *Solitude*. New York: Free Press.
Storr, A. (1989) *Churchill's Black Dog, Kafka's Mice and other phenomena of the human mind*. London: Collins.
Storr, A. (1989) *Freud*. Oxford: Oxford University Press.
Storr, A. (1992) *Music and the mind*. New York: Ballantine.
Storr, A. (1997) *Feet of Clay*. London: HarperCollins.
Strachey, J. (1934) The nature of the therapeutic action of psychoanalysis. *Int. J. Psycho-Anal*, 50: 275–292.
Sulloway, F. (1979) *Freud: biologist of the Mind*. Cambridge, Mass: Harvard University Press.
Suomi, S. (2008) Attachment in Rhesus Monkeys. In *Handbook of Attachment* Eds J Cassidy and P. Shaver 2nd Edn. New York: Guilford.

Swinburn, A. (1992) *The Garden of Proserpine*, In Selected Poems. London: Everyman.

Szasz, T. (1965) *The Ethics of Psychoanalysis*. New York: Basic Books.

Tolstoy, L. (1964) *Childhood, Boyhood, Youth*. London: Penguin.

Trevarthen, C. (2005) First things first: infants make good use of the sympathetic rhythm of imitation, without reason or language. *Journal of Child Psychotherapy*, **31(1)**: 91–113.

*Tuber, S. and Catflisch, J. (2011) *Starting treatment with children and adolescents*. London: Routledge.

Tudor Hart, J. (1971) The inverse care law. *Lancet*, **1**, 4–5–12.

Twemlow, S.W., Gabbard, G.O. (1989) The lovesick therapist. In: Gabbard G.O. *Sexual exploitation in professional relationships*. Washington (DC): American Psychiatric.

Tyrer, P. (2007). Personality diatheses: a superior description than disorder. *Psychological Medicine*, **37**, pp1521–1525.

Vaillant, G. (1992) *The Ego mechanisms of defence: a guide for clinicians and researchers*. Washington DC: American Psychiatric Association.

Vaughn, B., Bost, K. and van Ijzendoorn, M. (2008) Attachment and temperament: additive and interactive influences on behaviour, affect and cognition during infancy and childhood. In *Handbook of Attachment* (2nd Edn) Eds. P. Shaver and J. Cassidy. pp 192–216. New York: Guildford.

*Waddell, M. (1998) *Inside Lives*. London: Karnac.

Wallerstein, R (1990) Psychoanalysis: the common ground. *International Journal of Psychoanalysis*, **71**, 3–20.

Weber, N. (2009) *The Bauhaus Group*. New York: Knopf.

Weinfield, N., Sroufe, A., Egeland, B. and Carlson, E. (2008) Individual differences in infant-caregiver attachment: conceptual and empirical aspects of security. In *Handbook of Attachment* (2nd Edn) Eds. P. Shaver and J. Cassidy. pp 78–101. New York: Guildford.

Westen., D., Shedler, J., Bradley, B. and DeFife, J. (2012) An empirically derived taxonomy for personality diagnosis: bridging science and practice in conceptualising personality. *American Journal of Psychiatry* **169** 273–284.

Winnicott, D. (1971) *Playing and Reality*. London: Penguin.

Winnicott, D.W. (1965) *The Maturational Processes and the Facilitating Environment: Studies in the Theory of Emotional Development*. London: The Hogarth Press and the Institute of Psycho-Analysis.

Wood, H. (2011) The internet and its role in the escalation of sexually compulsive behaviour. *Psychoanal. Psychother.*, **25**:127–142.

Yalom, I. (2002) *The Gift of Therapy*. New York: Harperperennial.

Yeats, W. (1968) He Wishes For The Cloths Of Heaven. *In Collected Poems*. London: Faber and Faber.

Zur, O. (2007) *Boundaries in Psychotherapy: Ethical and Clinical Explorations*. Washington, DC: APA Books.

Index

12-session take-it-or-leave-it approach 107

AAI *see* Adult Attachment Interview
abandonment 69–70, 73, 76, 89
absence, patient 9
abuse, sexual 55
acting out 119
action replay method 120
active imagination 127
active listening 22
active passivity 22–3
active therapists 41
adjunctive therapy 59
adolescent therapy 13–14
Adult Attachment Interview (AAI) 99
adversity, strength in 98
advice giving, hazards of 19–20
affect phobia 65, 72, 88
aggression 74
    anxiety–aggression cycle 74–5, 76
    healthy 68, 69
    and obsessionality 78–9
    unexpressed/repressed 18–19, 68, 74–6, 116
agoraphobia 23, 24, 75, 95
'agreeing to differ' 69
allele polymorphism 98
alone, capacity to be 124–5, 128
ambiguity, tolerance 75, 128
ambivalence 74, 77, 128
amnesia 83
amygdala 99
analyst-analysand 12
'analytic attitude' 4, 11, 41–9
'analytic third' 11–12
anger 24, 75, 100
anxiety 73–80, 82, 100
    and attachment theory 73–4
    and Borderline Personality Disorder 97
    and control 75–7, 78–9
    defences against 75–7
    depressive 74, 76–7
    Freud on 73
    Klein on 74–5
    and obsessionality 77–80
    persecutory 74, 76–7
    separation anxieties 73–5
    sources of 73
anxiety–aggression cycle 74–5, 76
archetypes 28
arousal, hair-trigger 97
art of psychotherapy 57, 98
Asperger's syndrome 88
assertiveness, lack of 67, 68
attachment
    disorganized 74, 83, 95
    insecure 82–3
    secure 12, 124
attachment theory 51, 54–5, 73–4
attention
    bi-hemispheric 58
    evenly suspended 29
attention-seeking behaviours 84–5
authentic voice 122
autistic spectrum 88–94
autonomy 106, 107
    see also independence
avoidant personalities 36, 61–2, 74, 88–94, 107–8
awe 40–1
Axis II Disorders 82

Balint, M. 107
Balzac 65
Baron-Cohen, S. 92
Bateman, A. 95
behaviourism 112
being-in-the-world 59
'bending the rules' 42–3
benzene ring structure 34
bereavement 125, 126
Berlin, Isaiah x, 112–13
Bettelheim, Bruno 90, 126
binocular vision 58, 120
Bion, Wilfred 59, 74
bipolar disorder 38, 56, 64
    subclinical 65
Blatt, S. 64
body 27, 92–3
Bollas, C. 17
Borderline Personality Disorder 28, 94–7, 99–100, 119

borderline-dysregulated grouping 83
Boswell, James 80
boundary crossing/violation 47–8, 97
Bowlby, John 51, 54, 73
brain, plasticity 99
breast 90, 108
Brendel, Alfred x
Breuer 11, 50, 102–3
brief therapy 106–7, 108
British Psychoanalytic Society (BPS) viii
Busch, F. 100

'can't talk/won't talk' attitude 14–15
caregivers
    emotionally absent 95
    inconsistent 74
    see also mother; parents
case-notes, patient access to 9–10
CAT therapists 107
chairs 1–2
challenging patients 81–97
character analysis 103–5
childhood, and dreams 32–3
childhood experience, traumatic 103
    and fear of intimacy 61–2
    and hyperactivating strategies 83–5
    meaning making from 23–5
    and memory 99
    persistence into adulthood 24–5
    of the therapist 111, 115–18
    and transference 50–3
children's needs, parental failure to consider 84–5, 90, 115–16
Churchill, Winston 65, 71, 72
classification of psychodynamic therapies xiii–xiv
claustro-agoraphobia 95
closed systems 106
Cognitive Behavioural Therapy (CBT) viii, ix, 62, 82, 100–1
Coleridge 72
Colombo stance 40–1
compartments 24, 97
competency 122
concordance 12
confidentiality 9–10
Connor, Jimmy 107

Conrad, Joseph 119
conscious mind 33, 34
containment 75, 114
contracts 8–9
control freaks 78–9
conversation xii, 16–17, 116–17
cortical regulation 18
couches 1–2
counter-transference 42, 57–8, 108, 120
    and defence mechanisms 60
    and hysteria 86
    and sexual fantasies 44
'creative block' 38
creativity 31, 37–8, 93–4, 125–7
critical appraisal 18
criticism 18, 37–8, 67, 93–4
cure, notion of 102–3, 104, 128

damaged, the, championing of 48–9
daydreams 31, 35–7, 125
deactivating personalities 83, 95, 107–8
defence mechanisms 18, 60, 64–5, 71–2, 75–7, 80
deferation 67
defining psychotherapy xii–xiii
delusions 91–2, 94
Dennett, D. 113
dependence 19, 44–5, 53–5, 66, 69, 110
depression 18, 61–73, 79, 82, 100, 125
    anaclitic 64–5
    and avoidant personalities 88–9
    and Borderline Personality Disorder 96
    buffers from 104
    context of 64
    and creative activities 37–8
    and daydreams 37
    and the depressive position 71–2
    developmental 64–5
    and ending therapy 106
    flight into health from 69
    and insight 65–6
    introjective 64–5
    major depressive disorder 64
    manic defences against 71–2
    middle-aged 37
    obsessional defences against 80

origins of 64–5
and self-esteem 65–8
and suicide 70–1
therapeutic strategies 68–70
depressive anxiety 74, 76–7
depressive position 53, 71–2, 108
Descartes, René 92
destructiveness, imagined 76–7, 90–1, 115–16
detachment, scientific 103
developmental psychopathology 98–9
diagnosis 59–63
Diagnostic and Statistical Manual of Mental Disorders (DSM) 94
    Fourth Edition (DSM-IV) 82
diary keeping 37
diathesis-adversity model 98
disempowerment 19–20
disillusionment, with the therapist 108
disorganized strategies 74, 83, 95
dissociation 95
distress, containment 114
dogmatism, therapeutic 117–18, 118
domination 24–5, 89–90
Dora (patient of Freud) 51, 106
double meanings 29
dream-self 57
'dreaming the patient' 120
dreams 31–5, 127
    as day's residue 31
    failure to remember 32
    latent/manifest content 33
    as polysemic communications 33–4
    recurrent 32
drug metaphor 102
dumping 28–9
duration of therapy 8

Eagle, M. 125–6
Eagleton 24
efficacy, therapeutic, evidence for 99–100
ego 53, 92, 104
    auxiliary 105
Einstein, Albert 36
Eissler, K. R. 27
emotional expression, tolerance of 114
emotional maturity 105, 124

emotional object constancy 54
empathy 48, 113–15
end of therapy 54, 56, 102–10
engagement 95
engulfment 90
envy 2
epistolotherapy 10
equilibrium 33
erotic transference 54–5
explanation 21
exploitation, sexual 39, 43–4, 97
exploration 74
externalizing grouping 83

Fairbairn, R. 88, 106
Fairbairn, W. 54
family life, effect of being a therapist on 118
family therapy viii, 101
fantasies 43–4, 46, 91–2, 94, 127
fantasy realms 91
fear
    of dependence 19
    of domination 89–90
    of intimacy 28–9, 61–2, 89–91
    of taking things through 14
    of upsetting others 25
feelings
    over-sensitivity to those of others 115–16
    unexpressed 25–6, 28, 68, 74–6, 116
Ferenczi, S. 58
fetishism 92
fMRI *see* functional magnetic resonance imaging
Fonagy, P. 95
free association 11–12, 22, 51, 75, 103, 115
Freedom of Information Act 9–10
frequency of sessions xiii–xiv, 8–9
Freud, Anna 60
Freud, Sigmund ix, xiii, 11, 55, 84, 98, 116, 126
    on anxiety 73
    on character disorders 103
    on the counter-transference 57
    on 'cures' 102–3
    on dreams 31, 32–5
    on the ego 53
    on evenly suspended attention 29

on fantasy 127
on fetishism 92
on free association 115
on infantile sexuality 54
on interpretation 21, 26, 27–30
on Neurosis 106
on obsessionality 77
on patient selection for psychotherapy 62–3
on psychic health 124
on psychoanalytic training 121
on quasi-erotic love 44
on schizophrenia 100
on self-analysis 16
on sexuality 126
on switch words 29
on therapeutic dependency 45
on transference 50, 51, 57
fugue states 83
functional magnetic resonance imaging (fMRI) 99
funding, third-party 106–7
'fusion of horizons' 17
futility 88–9

Gabbard, G. 97, 122
Gelder, Michael x
generalization 52
genetics 98–9
genitality, full 105
genograms (family trees) 7
Gergeley 85
gifts 55–6
God 26–7
'good enoughness' 77, 106, 108
good object 53, 68, 74, 124
greetings 5
guilt 14

hatred 108
Hawkins, P. 120
Heimann, P. 58
helplessness 32, 65, 66, 67, 68
history-taking 6–7
histrionic patients 84
honesty 84, 87, 97
hopelessness 65, 67, 68

hostility 68, 69–70, 88
Hudson, Liam 41
humour 41–2
hyper-reactivity 77
hyperactivating strategies 83–8, 95, 108
hypnosis 11
hypothalamic-pituitary-adrenal (HPA) axis 99
hysteria 11, 21, 27–8, 82–8, 103

id-impulses 73
idealization 52–4, 69–70, 86–8
identification 43, 58, 99, 116
identity 116, 122
ideology, implicit, of the therapist 28
imagination, active 127
Improving Access to Psychological Therapies (IAPT) ix
incomprehensible, making comprehensible 23–4, 28
inconsistency 74
indecisiveness 25
independence 19, 110
    see also autonomy
individuation ix, 126–7
infantile dependence 66
infantile needs, of the patient 108
infantile sexuality 33, 54
ingratiating behaviour 116
initial interviews 4–10
inner world 36, 58, 106
innuendo 29
insight 65–6, 104
integration 105
intellectualization 79
internal object 28, 68, 124
internal supervisor 120
internalization 53–4
internalizing grouping 83
International Psychoanalytic Association (IPA) viii
interpersonal psychotherapy (IPT) 101
interpretation 21–30, 31–5
intimacy 28–9, 61–2, 89–91, 98–9
introspection 112
IPA *see* International Psychoanalytic Association
IPT *see* interpersonal psychotherapy
isolation 36, 89–90, 94–5

140

jargon 23
Jesus 27
Johnson, Samuel 80
Jones, Ernest 11, 27
Joyce, James, *Ulysses* 17
Jung, Carl Gustav 19, 28, 126–8
    on dreams 32–5
    on individuation 126–7
    on objectivity 48
    on self-free nirvana 59
    on stuckness 105
    on transference 51
    on unconscious infection 118–19
Jungian therapists ix, x, 28

Kafka 90
Kandel, Eric 99
Kant, Immanuel 78
Kekule 34
Kierkegaard 105
King's Speech, The (film) 42–3
Klein, Melanie 28, 71, 74–5
Kleinian theory 53, 58, 71, 90–1
Kohut, H. 52

Lacan, Jacques 123
Laing, R. D. 26–7, 90
latent content 33
lawless nature 78
Leischenring, F. 100
Lemma, A. 122
Leonardo da Vinci 27
Lewis, Sir Aubrey x
liking for patients 42
listening
    active 22
    with the third ear 58
long-term psychodynamic psychotherapies (LTPP) 100
loss 68–9, 89, 107, 109, 125–6
lost object 109
lovableness, doubts regarding 51–2, 69, 97, 116
love 43–4, 66, 124

Magic Flute, The 44
Mahler, Gustav 102

Malan's triangles 25, 57
Mallinckrodt, B. 12
mania 64
manic defences 64, 71–2
manifest content 33
manipulative patients 84
Mann, J. 107
manualization of psychotherapy 102
marginalization of psychotherapy 98
Marvell, Andrew 110
masturbation 36
Matte-Blanco, I. xiii
mature object relationships 105
mature therapist 122–3
maturity, emotional 105, 124
Maudsley Hospital x
McGlashan, T. 100
McHeigh 83
meaning making 23–6
medical model 59
meditation 128
memory, declarative/implicit 99
mentalisation 18
mentalisation based therapy (MBT) 100
mentalising 18, 58, 74, 81, 95–7, 100, 104, 113
meta-analysis 99–100
Mill, John Stuart 71–2
Milner, Marion 45
Milrod, B. 100
mindfulness 128
minute particulars (technique) 120
mirror neurones 99
mirroring 85, 105, 119
mistakes, therapeutic 120
Mitchell, Silas Weir 124
modules 24
monologue 17–18, 116–17
Moses, Grandma 125
mother
    abandonment by the 89
    ailing/low-spirited 115–16
    anxious 23
    'face as mirror' concept 85
    'good enough' 108
    narcissistic 61–2
    neglectful 61–2
    overbearing/controlling 24

separation from 54, 66
  suicidal merger with an idealized 70
mother-child dyad, giving up 108
mother-child relationship 25, 55, 66, 108
mother-infant relationship 17, 28–9, 53
mourning 109, 125, 126

narcissism 85, 100, 108, 117
  healthy 48
needs adapted approach 101
neo-cortical control 18
neurobiology 18
neuroplasticity 98, 99
neuropsychoanalysis 99–101
neurosis 60, 90, 102, 106
neutrality, of the therapist 50
Newton, Isaac 89, 94
nightmares, childhood 32
nirvana, self-free 59
noise 2–3
not-knowing 75
note-taking 3
Novick, J. 108

object
  good 53, 68, 74, 124
  internal 28, 68, 124
  lost 54, 109
object constancy, emotional 54
object relationships, mature 105
objectivity 43, 48
oblivion, seeking 70–1
obsessional personalities 24, 77–80, 82, 88, 110, 117
obsessive-compulsive disorder (OCD) 62, 75, 77, 80
'oedipal' issues 46, 59, 74, 122, 127
Ogden, T. 11–12, 120, 122
omnipotence 108
openness to experience 106, 112, 114
opinions
  lack of personal 67
  over-concern with those of others 67, 69
other people
  over-concern with the opinions of 67, 69
  over-sensitivity to the feelings of 115–16

outcome measures 102
outcomes, positive 105–9
ownership of therapy 13–14, 19

paintings 37
parallel processes 119, 120
paranoid psychosis 15
paranoid-schizoid position 71, 117
parent-child relationship 51
  see also mother-child relationship
parent-figure 51–5
parents
  disregard for their children's needs 84–5, 90, 115–16
  exhausted 90–1
  over-dominating 24, 25
  unconditional love of 66
  see also mother
Parker, Dorothy 77
part-time therapists 122
passivity 41
  active 22–3
  depressive 67, 68, 69
patient selection 62–3
pattern detection 24–5, 28
Paul, St 91
persecutory anxiety 74, 76–7
persona 91, 92–3
personality
  classification 60, 81–97, 83
  of the therapist 111
personality disorder 28, 82, 94–7, 99–100, 119
personalized medicine 98
Phillips, Adam 39
phobias 91–2
  affect 65, 72, 88
  agoraphobia 23, 24, 75
photographs, personal 2
plasticity 98, 99
play-acting 84
pleasing others 67, 69, 83, 91, 116
pleasure principle 127
pornography 36
positive suggestion 11
post-analytic improvement 110
power, of the therapist 117

powerlessness 90
pre-Oedipal client 59
prejudices, of the therapist 40–2
preliminaries 5–6
primary process 127
primate studies 66, 126
'problems in living' xiii, 103
progress making 16–20
projection 50, 52, 81
projective identification 58, 99
promiscuity 85
proto-conversations 17
Proust, Marcel 92
psyche, as self-regulating 33
psychic growth 128
psychic health 124
psychic space 1–3
psychodynamic formulations 59–63, 81
psychosis 15, 94, 100–1, 119
    see also schizophrenia
psychotic breakdowns 38
puns 29

questions, framed as statements 13

Rabung, S. 100
Rapoport, A. 113
reaction formation 18
reality, re-connection to 106
reality principle 127
referring patients 42
Reich 109
relational psychoanalysis 45
relationships
    professional xii
    protective 73
    see also therapeutic relationship
repetition 22
repression 18–19, 68, 74–6, 100, 116
resentment, unexpressed 25
resistance 11–15, 74, 106, 108
response-prevention 75
rest cure 124
reverie 127
Rey, H. 95, 97
rituals 75, 77
Rogerian devices 22

Rogers, Carl 48, 105, 112, 114
role responsiveness 12, 116
rooms, therapy 1–3
ruminations 75
Russell, Bertrand 92, 119
Rycroft, Charles viii, 117
Ryle, A. 107

sadism 116
sadomasochism 92
Sandler, A.-M. 12
Sandler, J. 12
schizoid personalities 82, 88–94
schizophrenia 63, 82, 94, 100–1
science of psychotherapy 98–101
secondary process 127
security 9, 12, 74, 81, 124
Self 53, 59
    True/False 93
self 18–19, 57
self-abnegation 114–16
self-analysis 16–17
self-assertion, as dangerous 116
self-defeating patterns 24–5, 28
self-esteem 20, 48, 65–8, 94
self-free nirvana 59
self-harm 71
self-knowledge 105
self-mentalising 81
self-monitoring 119
self-psychology 52
self-realization 105
self-reflection 81, 128
self-revelation 45–9
self-soothing, pathological 95
separation anxieties 73–5
settings, therapeutic 1–3, 9
sexual abuse 55
sexual difficulties 36
sexual exploitation 39, 43–4, 97
sexual fantasies 43, 44, 46, 92
sexual stereotypes 116
sexuality 33, 54–5, 85, 125–6
shaping sessions 12–13
Sharpe, Ella 5
Shedler, J. 104
Shohet, R. 120

sibling rivalry 19
Siegfried 44
silence 11, 19, 22, 51
similarity, assumption of 113
sincerity, lack of 84, 86, 97
Skinner, B. F. 112
Slavney 83
sleep 124–5
Sleeping Beauty 44
Snow, C.P. x
social context 108
Socrates 78
space
    psychic 1–3
    quasi-dream 11–12
'special' patients 42–3
splitting 24, 53, 92
stereotypes, sexual 116
Stern, Donnel 17
Strachey, J. 29
stuckness 22, 128
sublimation 125–6
submissiveness 24, 25, 79
suffering, alleviation xii
suicide 70–1
super-therapists 101
superego 66, 104
superiority, pose of 91–2, 94
supervision 119–20
Swinburne, A. 70
switch words 29
sympathy 45
symptom reappearance 108
Szasz, T. xiii, 105–6

teleological perspective 74
TFT *see* transference focused therapy
theatre 85–6
therapeutic alliance 12
therapeutic continuum 117–18
therapeutic relationship 17, 39–49,
    51, 104
therapeutic space 1–3, 9
therapist
    absences 56–7, 69–70, 96
    active 41

analytic attitude 41–9
and anxiety disorders 75–6
childhood experiences of 115–18
in control 19
dangers of being 118–19
dependence on the 44–5, 53–5, 110
division of labour 96
erotic feelings regarding 54–5
fallibility of the 46–7, 86–7
four stages of becoming 121–3
gifts to 55–6
global denigration 86
gradual disillusionment with the 108
idealization of the 52–4, 86–8
implicit ideology 28
life and work of the 2, 46, 111–23
marital status 46
natural 121, 122
neutrality of the 50
and obsessionality 79–80
part-time 122
patient envy towards 2
as patient's auxiliary ego 105
personality of the 111
power of the 117
and preconceptions 40–1
prejudices of the 40–2
and role responsiveness 12
secure attachment to 12
self-esteem 44–5
self-revelation 45–9
silence of the 19, 22, 51
skills 113–15
super-therapists 101
and supervision 119–20
tasks of the 21–8, 81
threat 73–4, 75
time and timing
    duration of therapy 8
    frequency of sessions xiii–xiv, 8–9
    initial interviews 7–8
time-limited therapies 106–7, 108
Tolstoy, Leo 35–6, 116, 125
touch 5, 92
training 121–2
transference 42, 50–8, 109
    and defence mechanisms 60

    erotic 54–5
    and gifts 55–6
    negative 51, 52–3
    positive 52–3, 69, 86
    in supervision 119–20
    and time-limited therapy 107
    universality of 56–7
transference enactments 55
transference focused therapy (TFT) 100
tyranny 79

uncertainty, tolerance of 75, 118, 128
unconditional positive regard 48, 114
unconscious
    and the counter-transference 120
    and dreams 31, 32, 33
    in reciprocal relationship to the
        conscious 33, 34
    of the therapist 57–8
    and transference 50
'unconscious infection' 118–19
'unformulated experience' 17

'unthought known' 17
Utopia 112

Valliant, G. 60

Wallerstein, R. 28
warmth 114
Warneford Hospital x
Westen, D. 83, 104
wild beast nature 78
Winnicott, D.W. 7, 27, 53, 75, 85, 93,
    108, 124
wish-fulfilment 127
Wolf Man (Freud case) 106
Woolf, Virginia 38
work 93–4, 124, 125–6
working through 57
writing 37–8

Yeats, John 52